MW01079726

The Lessons of Nonviolence

Also by Tom H. Hastings

Nonviolent Response to Terrorism
(McFarland, 2004)

The Lessons of Nonviolence

*Theory and Practice
in a World of Conflict*

TOM H. HASTINGS

Foreword by Kathy Kelly

McFarland & Company, Inc., Publishers
Jefferson, North Carolina, and London

LIBRARY OF CONGRESS CATALOGUING-IN-PUBLICATION DATA

Hastings, Tom H.
    The lessons of nonviolence : theory and practice in a world of
conflict / Tom H. Hastings ; foreword by Kathy Kelly.
        p.   cm.
    Includes bibliographical references and index.

    ISBN-13: 978-0-7864-2773-4
    ISBN-10: 0-7864-2773-6
    (softcover : 50# alkaline paper) ∞

    1. Nonviolence.   2. Passive resitance.   3. Peace movements.
    I. Title.
    HM1281.H36   2006
    303.6'1—dc22   2006029037

British Library cataloguing data are available

©2006 Tom H. Hastings. All rights reserved

*No part of this book may be reproduced or transmitted in any form
or by any means, electronic or mechanical, including photocopying
or recording, or by any information storage and retrieval system,
without permission in writing from the publisher.*

Cover photograph ©2006 Artville

Manufactured in the United States of America

McFarland & Company, Inc., Publishers
    Box 611, Jefferson, North Carolina 28640
    www.mcfarlandpub.com

To the women and men who fight for all they're worth,
using the most powerful, risky forms of nonviolent struggle they can —
to Christian Peacemaker Teams, to all Plowshares resisters
and to all who place their bodies in the path of the death culture
and ask for transformation. Their stories will remake the world.

*Let me indicate here how men and women can prove
that their words are their own:
let them put their preaching into practice.*
— Seneca

It is from our stories that we will remake the world.
— Alice Walker

Table of Contents

Foreword

by Kathy Kelly

In the 1980s, living in a blighted neighborhood on Chicago's North Side, I was part of a loose network affectionately dubbed "the do-gooders' ghetto." An array of good works, operating on shoestring budgets, was in full swing throughout the decade. One hub for much of this activity was St. Thomas Canterbury parish.

On Sunday mornings, after attending mass, parishioners would head downstairs to mingle in the church basement. Over weak coffee and day-old doughnuts, seated on brown metal folding chairs, we'd catch up on neighborhood news and often plan the week ahead.

The basement was in constant use. While senior citizens wrapped up afternoon bingo, volunteers were chopping up vegetables for the evening soup kitchen meal. Often immigrant Vietnamese community members would wait patiently for the last dishes to be washed so that they could begin social center activities.

Over the years, in the church basement, I watched humanity come together. Recent college graduates built friendships with people living on the streets. New immigrants needing low-rent apartments rubbed shoulders with elderly people who found, in the church basement socials, a welcome weekly escape from lonely apartments; residents of various shelter care facilities chatted with people looking for a place to find more meaning in their faith. And activists for all manner of projects met potential recruits.

Muralists had covered the basement walls with harsh scenes from the neighborhood's stark history. One section showed people fleeing a building consumed by flames after a landlord had paid an arsonist to burn the place. Another depicted an eviction, and next to that, huddled teenagers under arrest. Many parishioners could easily embellish the stories told on these walls from personal experience, and still others could narrate newer stories of ordeals caused by poverty, humiliation, dispossession, and shame.

Stories surrounded us, and transformed us.

I think we were a community of need, all yearning for immediate responses to pressing demands.

For me, a certain satisfaction came in being able to place a hot meal in front of a hungry person at the soup kitchen, or open the door to a hundred people filing into an overnight shelter. Something was better than nothing, but over time and through many conversations, "the do-gooders," myself included, began to pay more attention to what caused the ordeals our impoverished neighbors were undergoing, day in, day out.

At the height of the Cold War, we certainly saw one cause as the U.S. government's insistence on pouring U.S. wealth and productivity into weapons. Those resources were needed, desperately, for health, education and welfare programs.

We started to listen for stories about how to stop this waste of resources — and lives. Bob Bossie, a priest who lived in our neighborhood and often celebrated the Sunday morning liturgy, would regularly tell us about nonviolent direct actions aimed at confronting U.S. militarism. I remember feeling intensely curious about a series of disarmament actions at a nuclear missile-guidance facility called Project ELF, located in the northern woods of Wisconsin. The risks Tom Hastings and his colleagues had been taking still seemed impossible to me. But actions like theirs grew to seem more "possible," more like something I could do, particularly after Joe and Jean Gump, grandparents from a Chicago suburb, went to federal prison for disarming nuclear weapons buried among Missouri farmers' fields.

By the summer of 1988, in the church above our basement, liturgies were being offered for me and other parishioners in jail for having taken part in the "Missouri Peace Planting." We climbed fences into missile silo areas and planted corn in the soil above the instruments of death. Serving a year in federal prison, I had plenty of time to finally learn more about Tom Hastings, whose journey had greatly influenced my own.

That was many years and many stories ago. Many of the stories I have since told have been about the horror of the economic sanctions inflicted on the people of Iraq from 1991 to 2003, which is what many people (I think incorrectly) regard as a period of peace "in between the two gulf wars." The families of perhaps well over a million sanction casualties, mostly infant casualties, have different stories to tell. So does the U.N. Charter, which makes very clear that achieving political ends through economic warfare — through starvation warfare and through the type of "germ warfare" which aggressors wage not by introducing germs but instead by blockading medicines and water purification resources so disease proliferates and kills — is illegal under the laws of humanity.

In this book, Tom Hastings explores the impact of economic sanctions on civilian populations and raises questions about whether sanctions can be an effective nonviolent alternative to war.

He challenges the notion that the only criterion of success or failure, in imposing sanctions in Iraq, would be the impact of the sanctions on Iraq's ability to develop weapons of mass destruction (WMD). Hastings points out that the sanctions caused massive destruction.

I've also told stories, stories I've heard told and stories I've seen happening, from the beleaguered territories of Palestine. Tom calls for people opposing the Iraq occupation to speak mainly about the Iraq occupation and to develop a secondary focus on Palestine and on Israel's ongoing 38-year occupation of that tortured land. Readers will do well to persist with dialogue on this critical issue. Can these two stories, that of Iraq and that of Palestine, be disentangled from each other? How can we effectively challenge the official story which our "leaders" tell about the Middle East, a story about "Arab terrorism" and "our restrained response," without telling the simple paired truths that it is the U.S. nation that commits the worst terrorism in Iraq, and our allies the Israelis who are perpetrating the worst of the terror in the conflict over Palestine?

And if we never build our movement beyond the sole demand to retreat from Iraq, if all stories are not heard in our movement, then what pressure are we really applying to challenge the war makers into actually retreating? American elites pulled us out of Vietnam in fear of a movement that was building to transform America not only for our endangered troops abroad but for everyone affected by policies of death: the people of Vietnam, all people in the region, and indeed all Americans seeking security and meaning, like those in our church basement back in the do-gooders' ghetto.

Asked to foreword this book, I felt grateful for a chance to join Tom Hastings in advocating that we build our campaigns through face-to-face conversations and encounters, in meetings, on the street, in bars and offices, and in our homes. Telling our own stories helps build common ground and trust. Tom Hastings urges us to engage in earnest dialogue, to avoid becoming ideologues. We will all have plenty of opportunities for dialogue as we move forward in our different ways to end all illegal warfare and occupation, to call off our war against nature, and to build a world where all stories are heard.

Kathy Kelly, a co-founder of Voices for Creative Violence based in Chicago, is a lifelong nonviolent resister to militarism. A former Catholic worker and former high school teacher, Kathy has served time in several U.S. prisons for her nonviolent resistance to nuclear weaponry and to U.S. military interventions.

Preface and Acknowledgments

Nanapush: The coughball of an owl is a packed lump of everything the bird can't digest— bones, fur, teeth, claws, and nails. An owl tears apart its catch, gulps it down whole, and nourishes itself on blood and flesh. The residue, the undissolvable, fuses. In the small, light, solid pellet, the frail skull of a finch, femur of a mouse, cleft necklace of vertebrae, seed-fine teeth, gray gopher and rabbit fur. A perfect compression of being. What is the essence, the soul? my Jesuit teachers used to ask of their students. What is the irreducible? I answer, what the owl pukes. That is also the story—what is left after the events in all their juices and chaos are reduced to the essence. The story—all that time does not digest.
— Louise Erdrich, *Four Souls* [Erdrich 2004, 71]

This is not a book defending the use of nonviolence; for brilliant, though not uncontroversial arguments that make these kinds of cases, look elsewhere. Peter Ackerman, Elise Boulding, Robert Burrowes, Patrick Coy, Barbara Deming, Jack DuVall, Barry Gan, Mohandas Gandhi, Robert Holmes, Jessie Hughan, Kathy Kelly, Martin Luther King, Chris Kruegler, Les Kurtz, Aung San Suu Kyi, George Lakey, John Lewis, Alice and Staughton Lynd, Brian Martin, David McReynolds, Michael Nagler, Arundhati Roy, Chaiwat Satha-Anand, Jonathan Schell, Kurt Schock, Gene Sharp, Michael True, Stephen Zunes and many others have made such arguments. I accept them and try to live them, even though I recognize the failure of absolute moral proof and certainly the failure to establish efficacy under all circumstances (Vorobej 1994, 172).

This *is* a book that looks at some personal experience, a few others' personal experiences, and some of the literature and that tries to examine theory in the light of practice and develop practice in the light of theory.

5

While I don't claim that those of us who practice nonviolent resistance to militarism and violence are necessarily skilled at proper adaptive management (all too frequently just the opposite), that proper adaptive management is generally the goal and is the reason this book is in your hands. If we as a species are ever to leave violence in the dustbin of history, we had better learn to study and try, experiment and fail, tweak our thinking and try again. We need humility and boldness, sensitivity and bulldog determination.

One more try is the driving notion, but not just another try at the same tired tactic that has failed before — or even succeeded under other circumstances. We hope to learn enough about this form of conflict management so that it can offer more and more security to a fearful species in parlous times. We are called to continue this nonviolent action for our lives; we live in a war system and it is simply a lifetime process to oppose it and offer alternatives if we wish to create a peace system in its place (McElwee 2003, 148). We elect belligerent types and we elect rhetorically peaceful types, but the war system goes on and the main party politicians only quibble over the details in their modern Kulturkampf; as Hillary Clinton so succinctly said when asked about pulling out of Iraq, "We've been in Korea for 50 years. We are still in Okinawa" (Massen 2005, 233). Both parties are war parties; one is just more virulent and bellicose than the other. The challenge to nonviolence is permanent. The reflection on the lessons we can gain from stories is also permanent and that is our purpose in this book.

And we hope the stories are mildly amusing to you. Some are at the transnational level, most are at the transpersonal stratum, and most are completely unimportant, except insofar as they illustrate a principle of nonviolence. Some of them may be a bit boring — one must pupate before launching into beautiful butterflyhood — but they all have points and, we hope, lessons large and small for the student of nonviolence.

Staying up late with the best raconteurs in the nonviolent world is a great way to absorb the lessons of nonviolence; I will never forget one memorable evening in Albany, New York, listening to Kathy Kelly and Patrick Coy regale our table with stories from the Balkans and the Gulf as they laughed about how funny we humans can be, even as we seriously propose to substitute nonviolence for violence. I hope even one of the following stories can leave you with a memorable impression of the efficacy of nonviolence — or of a mistake you don't wish to emulate.

Thank you to Rhoda Moore for her many considerations, her peace and nonviolence inquiry and her love; she asks the right questions and offers the right spirit. Thanks to those who have read chapters and commented so helpfully and with great challenging insight — Nicole Anderson, Rhonda Baseler, Peter Bergel, Amanda Byron, Gordon Clark, Kathy Kelly, Sue McGregor, and Emi Noma. Thanks to Portland State University, Portland Community College and Oregon PeaceWorks for supporting me financially as we try to teach peace together. Thanks so much to Kathy Kelly for her gracious foreword and detailed corrections to several chapters; she is a nonviolent practitioner of great power who is known around the world and humbles me with her dedication. And thank you to fellow Catholic Workers — from Portland Catholic Workers including Gail Skenandore, Joy Ellison and Lisa Hughes to all the rest around the table, around the country and around the world — for your faithful persistence in the teeth of one of the worst regimes since Theodore Roosevelt promoted U.S. imperialism and racial superiority. Many of you have gone to jail and prison in this time and many more will as we resist this violence and injustice. We are each other's powdermilk biscuits; we give each other the love, support and strength to get up and do what needs to be done.

Sources

Erdrich, Louise, *Four Souls*. NYC: HarperCollins Publishers, 2004.

McElwee, Timothy A., "Instead of war: The urgency and promise of a global peace system," *Cross Currents*, Summer2003, Vol. 53 Issue 2, p148–170, 23p.

Massen, John B., "The Democratic Party, like the Republican Party and the media, covered up the deep complicity in the 9/11/01 attack by Bush-Cheney-Rumsfeld-Myers," in: Phillips, Peter, and Projected Censored, *Censored 2006: The Top 25 Censored Stories*. NYC: Seven Stories Press, 2005.

Vorobej, Mark, "Pacifism and wartime innocence," *Social Theory & Practice*, Summer94, Vol. 20 Issue 2, p171–191, 21p.

Acronyms, Initialisms, Abbreviations

AFSC . . . . American Friends Service Committee
ALC . . . . Atlantic Life Community
ANC . . . . African National Congress
CPT . . . . Christian Peacemaker Teams
CTBT . . . . Comprehensive Test Ban Treaty
CW . . . . Catholic Worker
DoD . . . . Department of Defense
DV . . . . Dignity Village
ELF . . . . Extremely Low Frequency (U.S. nuclear navy command facility)
FAIR . . . . Fairness and Accuracy in Reporting
FMNL . . . . Farabundo Marti National Liberation
GLIFWC . . . . . Great Lakes Indian Fish and Wildlife Commission
IDF . . . . Israeli Defense Force
IEN . . . . Indigenous Environmental Network
INGO . . . . international nongovernmental organization
IRA . . . . Irish Republican Army
IRS . . . . Internal Revenue Service
ISM . . . . International Solidarity Movement
KLA . . . . Kosovo Liberation Army
LUB . . . . League of Universal Brotherhood
MPT . . . . Muslim Peacemaker Teams
NAACP . . . . . . National Association for the Advancement of Colored People
NGO . . . . nongovernmental organization

NPT . . . . Nonproliferation Treaty (nuclear, 1968)
NRA . . . . National Rifle Association
ODOT . . . . Oregon Department of Transportation
PLO . . . . Palestine Liberation Organization
PM . . . . Prime Minister
PPRC . . . . Portland Peaceful Response Coalition
PSU . . . . Portland State University
PTBT . . . . Partial Test Ban Treaty
RNC . . . . Republican national convention
SNCC . . . . Student Nonviolent Coordinating Committee
SoA . . . . School of the Americas (now **WHINSEC**)
SSCC . . . . South Side Christian Center
SSOD . . . . Special Session on Disarmament
SUV . . . . sport utility vehicle
TNC . . . . transnational corporation
UNICEF . . . . . UN Children's Fund
UP . . . . upper peninsula (of Michigan)
UPI . . . . United Press International
VitW . . . . Voices in the Wilderness
WHINSEC . . . Western Hemisphere Institute for Security Coopera-
              tion (SoA renamed)
WILPF . . . . . . Women's International League for Peace and Freedom
WMD . . . . weapons of mass destruction
WRL . . . . War Resisters League
WTC . . . . World Trade Center
WTO . . . . World Trade Organization
WTR . . . . war tax resistance

Part One

Introduction; or,
The Value of Stories

It is a time nonviolence researchers need to tell nonviolence stories to the world.
— Chaiwat Satha-Anand, Thammasat University, Bangkok [Satha-Anand 1997, 12]

Knowledge supplies the mind with facts; stories give sensation to the heart.
— Alice Walker [Walker 2005, 223]

In the winter of 1987, nonviolent soldier of misfortune, I hitchhiked to Washington, DC, in order to resist the nuclear weapons of the Soviet Union. I had been doing nonviolent resistance of the U.S. weapons of mass destruction and I had a gnawing sense that it would make my own message more clear if I demonstrated my willingness to take risks in opposition to the nuclear weapons that targeted the land I love, my homeland.

It was a trip of special interactions, a time of little stories:

•As I hitched in the winter weather, most of my rides came from poor people or people who understood the harsh weather. Indeed, as I entered the post-blizzard country in Indiana, the temperature plunged, as it usually does after a large snowfall. Driving was tough. I was picked up by a van full of a poor family. The door of the old van was so rusted it barely worked. I piled into the back where little children shivered in the cold. The father asked where I was going and I said, well, I guess I'm going to Fort Wayne for the night and I'll find somewhere to stay. They went out of their way to get me to the place they knew would at least afford me a place to be indoors as temperatures headed below zero. I looked at their gas gauge. Almost empty. I insisted they take some cash. They were so sweet, so poor, so helpful in a time of threatening weather. Most often, poor people are the most compassionate even when it means sharing and sacrifice of the little they have.

•That night, as it got bone-chillingly below-zero frigid, I sat in the front lobby of the mission, where a few of us were forced to sit up all night in metal chairs under blazing fluorescent lights, since there were no more beds. It was a lesson in homelessness and lack of empathy. It was exhausting and was the kind of scene that built resentment toward patronizing religious charitable institutions.

•Hitching through the rust belt of Ohio, I was picked up by a fabulously gnarly truck driver dressed like the motorcycle gang member that, it turns out, he was. Leather vest with metal studs, smacked-up face with missing teeth, he drove his own flatbed rig and roared along over snowy roads, telling the usual stories of fighting and other dramatic, macho events. He asked why I was heading to DC. This was about two weeks after King Day, which was a new and still controversial national holiday. I said that I was inspired by Dr. King and was heading to do some nonviolent resistance to the Russian nukes. He laughed and said, "Hell, if we get a holiday for killing one of 'em, I say kill more!" I was quiet and looked at him for a few moments and finally said, "You don't mean that." He looked at me as if to say, "I *don't?*" It was a turning point, as though I had accessed the better side of him, the side that picked up lone hippies hitching on back highways in the freezing winter. He thought about it and smiled at me and said nothing more that one might interpret as racist, and took me a total of more than 400 miles along my way, even buying me a meal. I had challenged him to human-ize himself, so that he could stop objectifying others, and, even with his rough ways and his hardscrabble history, he was a naturally good man who wanted an excuse to be better. We ask for blackguard behav-ior and we get it. We expect the best and it just might happen.

•Hitching through the Allegheny mountains, I was picked up by a man who, once I told him the nature of my trip, unburdened himself, telling me that he worked at a nuclear power plant and he thought they were very risky, highly and dangerously complex, and that, in his estima-tion, there would likely be worse accidents than Harrisburg, where the Three Mile Island plant almost melted down. Since he was unknown to me, I believe it was his opportunity to get that off his chest. The doubts and concerns of those who work with potentially dangerous technologies may never see the light of day, but they are out there. He felt he had a sympathetic listener and one who wouldn't raise problems for him, almost as though he had a rare opportunity he couldn't pass up. I would expect he was representative of an invisible constituency of very concerned scientists, engineers and technical people who have private worries about many of the very projects they are paid to create and manage.

•Finally coming to DC, I sought out Thomas, a man who had been vigiling full time in Lafayette Park ever since Ronald Reagan was elected. His vigil was 24–7, except when incarcerated. I liked Thomas and visited him every time I visited Washington. So we chatted and I told him my plan, which was, essentially, to do a one-person symbolic occupation of the Soviet embassy until they promised in good faith to immediately dismantle at least one of their nuclear weapons and challenge the U.S. to do the same. He liked the idea and walked me to the embassy, telling me of a similar action that he had done a few years earlier. "Here we are," he said, and I hugged him goodbye. I went in — the iron gate was unlocked, as was the front door, even though it was the outpost of the evil empire in the center of our land of the free — and the first question I got, in a thick Russian accent, was, "Do you vant asylum?" Evidently, that happened often enough to make it the default question, or else I just looked particularly in need of such. I tried to explain, she called in a very pleasant man who utterly failed to get what I was up to, who called in another very pleasant fellow, who made every effort to negotiate with me. "How about if I arrange an interview with Tass?" he asked. "Well, that would be fine, but I'm still going to continue to symbolically occupy until you give me your official word," I said, knowing he couldn't do that.

•Eventually we struck a deal, in which he handed me over to the U.S. Secret Service at the gate. Interestingly, a classically attractive blond woman had come into the embassy while I was talking with him. I momentarily mused that she was the beautiful Soviet spy who would seduce our Secretary of Defense and extract information and promises from him, but as I stood handcuffed in the snow, flanked by two Secret Service agents, the same woman walked out of the embassy and walked directly up to me and asked very sincerely, "Were you arrested for peace?" I looked into her face and thought, "Do I know you?" but simply responded, "Yes, do what you can, friend." At that moment, a van came fishtailing around the corner and Billy Joel, the musician, popped out and yelled and waved. The woman turned and walked through the snow, got in the van, and away they went. One of the Secret Service agents turned to the other and said, "John's gonna be pissed he missed Christie Brinkley." "Oh," I thought, "now I remember; she's the one on Lee's bedroom poster." My son had her picture on his wall, which is where I knew the face, though she looked different all bundled up for winter weather than she had in her postergirl bathing suit.

•In my interview with the Secret Service, all alone in a cell, the agent looked at me long and intently. Then, suddenly, he asked, "Did you come to Washington to attempt to assassinate president Reagan?" *Huh? I'm here to offer nonviolent resistance to Soviet weapons, I'm arrested at the Soviet embassy for that and you ask me this? Isn't that a non-sequitur?* He looked at me for a few more moments and then I saw the faintest sign of a smile. "I have to ask," he said. It's my job." *No, for the record, I did not come to assassinate anybody. I disapprove of assassinations, period.* He sighed a little, as though heading into a dumb moment into which he was bound by duty to enter. "Did you come to Washington to attempt to assassinate Vice-President George Bush?" *Whoa! You broke the code!* He went on to more fruitful questions.

•In the precinct jail that night, I shared a cell with a middle-aged African-American man who was an unemployed bricklayer with six children. He was going to serve two years for shoplifting $5 worth of groceries from Safeway, as this wasn't his first arrest for trying to feed his family. He had been out of work for several weeks. A drunk just two cells away and across the hall was yelling imprecations about the jailer and the jailer's mother and, at regular intervals, picking up the steel cot and letting it slam down with a terrific blam! It kept me, and I expect most everyone, awake. Some guys were warning him that he was going to get roughed up if he didn't shut up. He paid them no mind. At about 2 a.m. I awoke to a terrible ruckus and heard the jailer's keys. I immediately assumed the jailer had heard enough insults and was coming to beat the drunk. I began shouting, "Please, for Godssakes, don't hurt him!" In seconds a man from the next cell pirouetted into the hall, on fire, and collapsed to the floor, where the jailer put out the fire and then the paramedics came to take the victim away. This was back in the day when jails allowed smoking and the man had apparently fallen asleep with a lit cigarette. I apologized to the jailer for yelling at him and he said no problem. Within an hour the paramedics returned to bring out a junkie who was withdrawing, hallucinating, bleeding and shaking, just two cells down the other direction.

•Later, as I was sitting in the main Washington, DC, central jail transfer room, I was talking to an earnest young African American man (I was usually the only white man in the room, or perhaps one of two or three, even amongst 200 or more inmates) and he told me his life plan: *I'm going to get a job, save up $1,500, and live off the interest.* I was so sad at the level of education that would produce a vision that underinformed, that innocently ignorant in the midst of the center of power on Earth, Washington, DC.

•After some four days I finally made it into general population in the DC jail. I was the only white guy on my cell block floor, though there was one poor white guy two floors down who came up to meet me the first afternoon. *Hi. My name's Pat.* I shook his hand and told him to have a nice evening. I had no intention of forming a white guy's affinity group.

•I fasted and gave away my food, which made a little friendly gesture. After dinner I left my cell, went to the TV room and watched in horror as some news report, lasting 10 minutes or more, showed the history of some super–Aryan white supremacist group, wearing Nazi uniforms and giving the nazi salute. Muttering amongst the other men — all African Americans — and glances at me combined with my own revulsion at the imagery, made me wish I could go invisible. Suddenly, one of the more relaxed looking men came to sit next to me, looked at me and asked, *Do you know Ladon Sheats?* You could have knocked me over with a clichéd feather. Ladon was a mentor to my close friend and former Jonah House member Mike Miles. I had spent some hours now and then in fascinating conversation with Ladon and had driven many miles through northern Wisconsin snowstormed highways to pick him up as he was let out of jail for his nonviolent resistance to Project ELF. Ladon was known to the entire nonviolent movement as a sincere, brilliant, fearless nonviolent resister to militarism and injustice. His life routine had become nonviolent resistance and prison witness, then time in some monastery, followed by time spent giving volunteer hospice care, and then back to resistance. He and I had several correspondences when he or I were incarcerated. As it turns out, Ladon had made quite an impression on this man during one DC jail stint and this man had somehow intuited that I might know Ladon (are we that obvious or was he that intuitive?) and that I would be redeemed a bit by a conversation with him. He was correct on all counts; his initiative was placative to all in the TV room and I was safe. Ladon, who crossed over in 2000, may well have saved me from some serious trouble in the DC jail, though he was probably 4,000 miles away, caring for some dying person in California.

•Finally in court after the few days knocking around the DC jail system, I immediately renounced my U.S. citizenship to the magistrate, who just looked bored and took zero notice of my long-rehearsed speech, which was predicated upon a rejection of nationalism and nuclear weaponry. *Four days, credit for time served,* was his pronouncement. I looked around and there were Marcia Timmel and Paul Magno, who had managed to track me down and were there to collect me. I was shaken and so grateful to see them. I told them, *I'd rather go back and spend four months in a nice friendly northern Wisconsin jail than four days in the DC jail. I don't know how you all do it here on the East Coast.* They laughed. They were both Catholic Workers and part of the Atlantic Life Community, hardest of the hard core resisters. Years later, in his funny and poignant book *Bomber Grounded,* Ciaron O'Reilly referred to Jonah House — the epicenter of the ALC — as The Barracks. And years after that Larry Cloud Morgan told me that he had seen an old friend back in Minneapolis for the first time in months and had told him, *Hey, you're looking fit. Where've you been training?* The fellow told him, well, no, he had been staying at Jonah House and all they ever had in the refrigerator was blood (the ALC folk frequently throw their own blood on targets representing militarism, from the pillars of the White House to the halls of the Pentagon). I was just a rookie compared to these nonviolent warriors and was grateful indeed for their tender care.

CHAPTER 1

Stories and Conflict Management

There is the story of the brothers who were fighting so long and hopelessly over a piece of land that they finally called in their spiritual advisor to at least listen to their positions. She asked them to bring her to the place in question, which they did. The old woman listened carefully to both. They looked at her expectantly. She thanked them for their stories and knelt and said, "Now I need to hear from the third party."

For Nova Southeastern Conflict Resolution professor Jessica Senehi, this story "questions assumptions about ownership and control" (Senehi 2000, 96). She goes on to describe the storytelling role in conflict resolution in peacebuilding in Guatemala in particular, and asserts that "Understanding the role of storytelling in peace-building is significant for facilitating cultural spaces where people can participate in defining their communities, voicing their experiences, healing from past conflict, and shaping their future."

Similarly, Conflict Resolution professor Jay Rothman found during years of work with deep identity conflict in Israel Palestine, the stories of Israelis and Palestinians, while hard to hear, were crucial in helping to make the transition to being able to properly discuss options for mutual gain. Unless the stories were told and heard neither side could view the other as anything other than perpetrator and neither side could see themselves as anything other than victim. It was painful for all and absolutely crucial to progress (Rothman 1997, 25).

There is a limit to the good dialog and listening to stories can do if no action is forthcoming and no structural change occurs (Lederach 1997; Spence and McLeod 2002, 61). Parties in Northern Ireland and Palestine

Israel alike report that, first is the pain, then the relief and beginnings of camaraderie, and then frustration and ultimately anger and abandonment of dialog *if the party with power does little or nothing to alleviate the suffering of the other.* Thus, when Catholics remain the poorest sector in northern Ireland, or when Israel arrogates unto itself some four times the water per capita as Palestinians are allowed, when Palestinians are kept out of their homeland or kept out of areas with a viable economy, when their homes are bulldozed or when their olive trees are crushed and ripped away — if all this can continue even as the privileged Israelis go home after the dialog to relative prosperity then frustration grows and festers. Benefic personalism is necessary but not sufficient. The metaphorical bridge to trust takes much longer to repair than does a stone or steel bridge. Nonviolent process works best when fastened somehow to practical progress toward justice.

The theory of stories as it relates to scholarship is one of gathering stories, reconstructing them, connecting them to the literature, naming the challenge or problem, describing the plot, moving toward resolution, and gathering additional stories (Smith and Piers 2005, 272). Along the way, we use stories, then, to help us determine which stories are ungathered and how those stories might help us move closer to problem-solving. The value of stories depends upon evaluation, synthesis, and, ultimately, application. An individual story is most useful when it is considered in that context with those steps, and as a piece in the larger puzzle.

In a sense, almost all books and films are simply story telling platforms; this is how we learn. Watching *Bush's Brain,* a film about Karl Rove, I can get a picture of who this person is and how he tends to act, according to the storytellers who produce and direct the film. In this 2004 film, we are shown the stories of those he has emnified and how he has destroyed many of their lives. The point of that film is to tell a story that warns the citizenry to act to stop someone whose deeds are plaguing our society and abusing power. The storytellers do a good job, beginning with a look at how Karl Rove started in school using dirty tricks to intimidate his debate opponents by bringing in ever-increasing amounts of debate notecards, many of them blank but not visibly so. Then the film told of how Rove pretended to discover a recording bug in his office when he was managing a campaign of a republican candidate for governor of Texas, creating just enough change in the polls to steal the victory for his man. Rove also put two Texas Department of Agriculture officials in prison for doing what thousands of Texas politicians do on a routine basis, and went on from there to be Bush's hit man and his Machiavelli all the way to creating the

Iraq War, a war he helped conceive and invent rationale to justify (Mealey 2004). At the end, the story is powerfully cogent because it adds up to a serious pattern of such abuse of position and miswielding of power. Stories are crucial in everyday life and in the decisions made by an entire people.

Watching, reading, listening and observing real life, we integrate stories by a combination of the synoptic — this story is in this genre, offering this basic narrative — with the particular. The specifics are what matter to the critical consumer of each story. Thus, watching the 2005 film *Paradise Now,* directed by Hany Abu-Assad, a story of two young Palestinians who have been selected by the resistance to commit a double suicide bombing, we have layers of lessons available to the student of nonviolence. Perhaps the arguments on both sides — we *should* do this because the occupation defines the resistance, because life in the Territories is already worse than death, because we must honor the sacrifices of those in resistance before us, because nothing else works against the Israelis, because the international community doesn't care, because this sacrifice is more noble than humiliation of occupation; you *shouldn't* do this because it only gives Israel another excuse to keep us penned up and without sovereignty, because there are alternatives (though never explored or explained, leaving a gross lacuna in the argument against), because you die and leave behind the rest of us who will just be punished more — all those arguments are old to serious students of this struggle, of this conflict.

But the particulars of how Nablus looks, the expressions on the unique faces of Palestinians and Jewish settlers, IDF troops and the resistance leadership, and the subcomponents of the complex of decisionmaking — these specifics make the value of the film. Considering the lives of the two young men, Said (Kais Nashef) and Khaled (Ali Suliman), as they struggle with these weighty issues in the context of their lives of comparative misery and poverty in Nablus, is to think on their stories as both quite individual and as exemplars of a generation of refugees and noncitizens. For me, the most illuminating element was not the arguments of the young woman who tried to dissuade them — though that was powerful and extremely evocative — but rather the lesson of the effectiveness of the persecution within the resistance movement on the willingness to commit further atrocities. Turns out that videos of the confessions and subsequent executions of collaborators were more popular, even, than videos of the statements of suicide bombers as they prepared to die. Turns out that Said's father was an executed collaborator. Turns out that Said spent time laying on his father's grave as he wrestled with his decision, that he heard all the excellent arguments against his combination murder-suicide and ultimately was the one who decided to go forth with his grisly, tragic, fruitless mission. As a viewer trying to understand in the context of my field — Nonviolence, Conflict Resolution — it was suddenly, painfully obvious how much the brutality of the resistance upon its own people kept them in line, even down through the generations. First the father executed — which only serves to draw the son in rather than alienate him from the resistance, and then the son is channeled successfully into his "martyr" role and the violence is given more power on all sides. Paradoxically, Suha (Lubna Azabal) — the young woman attracted to Said, is the daughter of a martyr and has powerful arguments against the bombing (Abu-Assad 2005). Thus, the stories of each help us understand the value of the overall story. Gather the story, process it, and gather more stories, as we move toward some kind of resolution.

It may be that stories and human development are so linked that we overlook the obvious. Read about the peace heroes, says Louise Diamond, and you become more like them (Diamond 2001, 123). This wisdom-by-osmosis is related to the value of stories to our most rapidly developing humans, children, whose heroes will at times shape their lives, if not directly then indirectly. When my father — certainly my hero for many years in my childhood — told me about his fight with the neighborhood bully, and when he made it clear that you stand up to bullies in some fashion, he told me to live like that. I continue to try, even as I enter my own elderhood. The story changed my life. Its impact survived my transition from violent youth to nonviolent adult. Had I been taught from an early age that standing up to bullies might best be done with nonviolence, had I been trained in the skills needed to do that, and had I been given that model by my father, I would have been light years ahead in my development.

Reading comics about World War II was a weekly dose of raw story, muscular men fighting evil supermen, and that development probably hurt me. Those stories were unhelpful in my development as a peace person, certainly, with the rage on the faces of the good guys and evil ones alike, with the objectification of the other so saturated in the story. Rather than say, *Well, it couldn't have hurt too much because see what a peaceseeker I've become in my life?* I would say rather that, without that mental trash perhaps I could have avoided all the mistakes of hubris, impatience, domination, controlling, interruption, unilateralism and other typically adversarial, testosterone-poisoned behavior I've had to work through over the decades. Indeed, when I'm impatient, it may be that those formative stories are still contaminating me.

Three elementary schoolteachers — Sandy Rizzo, Doris Berkell and Karen Kotzen — prepared a peacemaking skills manual for teachers, parents and group leaders of kindergarten, first graders and second graders. It offers more than 20 group activities for that age group, including the proactive and reactive competencies needed to resolve their conflicts using nonviolent communication and conflict skills. In one activity, Peace Table, they teach the ground rules for conflict resolution amongst little children who role play these activities under the supervision of teachers. The ground rules — "Tell the truth; listen without interrupting; no name-calling or blaming; list ideas to solve the problem; choose the best solution" — are simple (Rizzo, Berkell, Kotzen 1997, S43). Still, I think about them in the context of my childhood — and that of most children around me as I grew up, and most children today — and I realize that I was in my thirties before I was taught that there is this method for resolving conflict. It is one thing to tell children, "Don't fight," and there is a vastly different and much more effective method that gives them the tools to fight using nonviolence. When this training saturates our culture, our culture will undergo sea change toward peace.

CHAPTER 2

Master Narrative Versus Justice in the Margins

When I was a young girl, I would lie on my stomach on sun-warmed grass covering the hills of Southern Wisconsin and absorb stories. I was shy and preferred to run away from the ordinary chaos of our family's old farmhouse into the ancient rolling fields. The books I tucked under my arm opened worlds that were not always fairy tales or the forests of Narnia. I was also drawn to read stories telling of Native American genocide and the long Trail of Tears, Anne Frank's diaries in besieged Amsterdam, and Bridge to Terabithia, *about a young boy whose best friend dies.*
— Jensine Larsen, editor, *World Pulse: Women & Children Transforming Our World*

On 30 August 1991 the Soviet Union ended. The long experiment with using any and all means to achieve liberation for those who had been oppressed by colonialism and monarchy was over, at least from the standpoint of a superpower sponsor state. The idea that a guerrilla movement might be supported by a home base of revolutionary rhetoric, theory, training and arms was finally finished. But what was the story of the dominant culture in the U.S.?

The *New York Times* trumpeted *"The Soviet Union, born of the 1917 Revolution, was pronounced dead this week after a lingering illness. The cause of death was diagnosed as a congenital defect called Communism"* (Yost 1999, 96).

This assumed defect was thus determined to be received wisdom, as surely unassailable as the sun rising in the east, and yet it was a non sequitur. That an economic system based on sharing much more with working people than does capitalism, for example, was defective, is utterly unproven. It might be argued that the system broke down because the sponsor state, the Soviet Union, not only didn't exploit colonies but didn't have nearly the native resource abundance that the U.S. did. Further, the SU was giving massive aid to places like Cuba and Mozambique, whereas the U.S. was extracting much more from so-called developing lands and peoples than it was offering in aid. Of course the U.S. fared better; it was robbing people that the Soviet state was trying to help. The Soviet system was bleeding resources that it didn't have and the U.S. was gaining resources at gunpoint from all over the world, plus it was more blessed with a temperate climate and all the other rich agricultural ecological benefits that kept it well fed and outproducing most of the rest of the world, especially the cold and famine-vulnerable Soviet Union.

The difference between the master narrative in the U.S. and that understood by the rest of the world on this question and others is stark and accounts for much of our conflict. The master narrative in the Wahabi region of Saudi Arabia, for example, tells babies and youth and adults that Jews are subhuman and that the U.S. government is under control of the Zionist master monsters in Israel. This is basic knowledge, unquestioned and conventional to them, just as the image of Palestinians as suicidal, fanatical hatemongers is well taught to Israeli children.

The power of this master narrative in any culture is how we learn to accept falsehood, oppression, injustice and foul means to what we are assured are fair ends. *It's the only language they understand* is the mantra about the necessity of violence. The stories are the foundation for this incorrect, destructive rationale. It is the story written from the point of view of whomever is the dominator in the society, victors' history, victors' narrative, victors' stories, much as the trials of losing leadership following military victory have rightly been called victors' justice.

Other stories, less known, studiously ignored and even actively suppressed at times, teach us that "Nonviolent action, or nonviolent struggle, is a technique of action by which the population can restrict and sever the sources of power of their rulers or other oppressors and mobilize their own power potential into effective power" (Sharp 2005, 39). Some of the stories of nonviolence teach that without commentary; they are immediately and patently obvious in their lessons. Others need interpretation and exegesis. All need maintenance, as the tendency of those who construct and maintain the master narrative is to diminish and marginalize stories of nonviolent power (Wink 1992, 243). At times, it seems, the master narrative is so successful in the face of the facts, that violence is in fact the only language the masses and the elite understand and nonviolence is a sort of solecism, an incorrect use of language, spoken by a group who just can't seem to let go of misuse of language. I've been before a harsh, retributive judge who burst out in exasperation during a pretrial motion hearing, when I referred to an act that I had committed as nonviolent: "Stop telling me it was nonviolent! I *know* it was nonviolent." I was referring to cutting down massive 60-foot wooden poles, three of them, which came crashing to the Earth attached to a 14-mile, 3-inch thick cable. Thank you, judge, for affirming that such an act could be nonviolent, and thank you for doing so for the record, as it reads forever in the transcript.

Nonviolence falls into the master narrative cracks, honored in absentia even when present in force, e.g., the Martin Luther King Jr. holiday celebrating brotherhood, not nonviolent resistance. Or the emnification of the Basque culture and thus the Basque people by Spanish mainstream culture — and the reverse. "Every tradition," says researcher Maria del Mar Llera, "is mediated in a hermeneutic way. It is fed by interpretation, through which it is connected with the present, providing it with a meaning which is aiming at the future" (Llera 2003, 242). Stories are crucial and are seen with special meaning, using a filtered interpretation. Spaniards are cowardly bullies; Basques are irrational madmen.

In Europe, immediately following the rapid success of the nonviolent Velvet Revolution that brought down the Berlin Wall, ended two generations of Soviet Union–dominated puppet governments and swept away the Warsaw Pact, the story was that nonviolence not only works but *really* works, as these victories were achieved without bloodshed. The master narrative changed and, in Italy, the nation began to look for nonviolent alternatives to use of armed military under some circumstances. During that period, peace scientist Antonio Drago from the University of Naples noted that "people are concerned about contributing to the process rather than to ideals only" (Drago 1998, 120). In other words, they had been convinced that nonviolence could work on a mass scale to defeat an oppressive, armed and dangerous power. They were now ready to discuss whether, to what degree, and how they might prepare to do that with their own national defense.

Thus, the stories of success of nonviolence are incalculably important. When those stories happen in front of a witnessing world, they are most convincing. When those stories are drawn from history, they have some power and instruction to counter the master narrative.

Sadly for the prospects of humanity, the old brains — those that Ornstein and Ehrlich said evolved to learn to react to sabertooth tigers — remember violence and forget nonviolence. Cognitive psychology researchers Adrian Furnham and Barrie Gunter learned in one experiment on types of news, times of day and accuracy of recall, that people remember violence more accurately than they do nonviolent news stories. Interestingly, they also recall print best, even though they've seen audiovisual depictions, and they generally do better if they hear or read the story in the morning rather than afternoon or evening (Furnham and Gunter 1987, 255). Read about nonviolence in the morning and it may stick, at least if factual accuracy is the intent behind telling and consuming the story. A word is worth a thousand pictures.

The stories of nonviolent success introduce some element of balance into the unbalanced and oppressive master narrative of all cultures, especially the dominant culture within the hegemonic nation-state. Resisting the master narrative is the first step toward resisting the militaristic dominance of the last remaining superpower.

> *As I raced for that Wall, with the bomb in my hand,*
> *I noticed that every last Yook in the land*
> *was obeying our Chief Yookeroo's grim command.*
> *They were all bravely marching,*
> *with banners aflutter,*
> *down a hole! For their country!*
> *And Right-Side-Up Butter!*
> — *The Butter Battle Book,* Dr. Seuss

In Dr. Seuss's case, of course, he used his children's story platform to offer lessons, just as almost all storytellers do. In *The Butter Battle Book,* his 1984 classic, he mocked the silly notion that two militaries ought to be threatening to blow up each other and all the people in order to show disapproval for some superficially different practice. I've read that book, which I keep at the ready in my library, to many children and adults. While Theodor Seuss Geisel ("Dr." Seuss's actual full name) meant to poke fun at the U.S.–S.U. nuclear arms race in the most dangerous period of the Cold War — both sides had, by the mid–1980s, tens of thousands of nukes and the growing destabilizing first-strike accuracy and command structures to make that war more likely than ever — his point in that children's book remains valid. Or, as my old woodsman friend Eric used to say, "They have fixed up real permanent solutions to real temporary problems." Seuss used stories to teach children that such means were really inane. He did something similar with his book *The Lorax.* That book taught children with a great story that it was a good idea to protect the forests. Indeed, one might wonder how many young forest defenders who are sitting in trees or sitting in jail for doing so might have been read to with that story when they were little. The power of stories should not be underestimated; fables and myths are enduring and affect the posture of entire peoples. Few activities are more important than resisting the master narrative by better and more consistent storytelling.

Master narrative of war and peace

War, says media scholar Jean Seaton, is defined by mainstream media. In the U.S., most citizens might answer that war is happening in Iraq, that it is over in Afghanistan, and that maybe there's one other war on Earth right now, somewhere in Africa probably. That would be the information they generally work with, a product of the master narrative in the U.S.

The definition of war, by most conflict researchers, is 1,000 or more battlefield deaths in any year (Worldwatch 2005, 124). There are approximately 25 of these conflicts raging around the world, approximately one-third of them in Africa. This is not a part of the master narrative, if by that we mean what is commonly understood. If the wars aren't understood — or even known about — by most citizens in the U.S., they are not going to be addressed seriously. The U.S. has the most military clout of any nation, ever, in human history. The U.S. has the largest economy in history. What the U.S. citizens don't know, they don't care about, and what they don't care about remains largely unaddressed.

As I teach, students are constantly surprised by information about what is going on in the rest of the world. Frequently, they believe the UN's budget is huge and that it is a threat to the sovereignty of the U.S., even physically. They believe, often, that the UN is corrupt and doing "nothing." They believe the UN is in need of massive reform or abolition and that the U.S. is the best agent to accomplish that. Of course, the students have a range of opinions about the UN, but the notion of the huge budget and military is simply a fictive product of rightwing propagandists that, sadly, finds its way into the master narrative and is a blatant lie.

Some lies are misunderstandings. Some are exaggerations that are obviously the work of extremists who are marginal. Some, however, are a part of how the extremists have seized control of the master narrative. The battle for control of that narrative is important; to the extent it devolves to grassroots eyewitness control, it is controllable. A master narrative is much like the Taoists say of tools: Good servants, bad masters. A master narrative in service to all of humankind and our beautiful Earth is a master narrative that employs and enjoys power-with everyone and all of life.

Currently, however, the master narrative is a power-over story. This power over situation needs to be *turned* over, and wresting control of the master narrative from the elite is a sincere first step. Telling the stories from the standpoints of the vulnerable ones is a part of that seizure of power-with.

Of course, this tension has existed in the field of journalism since before it was so termed, from the days of the first emergence in Europe of a popular press and literacy that began with Martin Luther's insistence that the people deserve religious literacy, not merely a set of incomprehensible Latin dicta imposed by priests and higher Church authorities. Following immediately on the heels of religious literacy in the 16th century came political literacy, which spread to England and elsewhere, perceived immediately and correctly as a threat to state power. The Tudor monarchs moved swiftly to impose penalties for written opposition to their rule or policies and the printers immediately responded with self-serving self-censorship by the Stationers' Company, proving right away that a bit of occasional brutality to serve as example was effective in producing a severely circumspect media.

Story repositories

In the world of nonviolent resistance to empire in the U.S., there is no more pertinent or complete journal of stories than *The Nuclear Resister*, published sporadically by Felice and Jack Cohen-Joppa from their home in Tucson, AZ. They began their work in Madison, WI, in the early 1980s and, with remarkable faith and endurance, continue as the chronicle for antiwar actions and the prisoner support that follows nonviolent resistance.

In the current issue, number 137, 29 July 2005, there are stories of military personnel learning about the very existence of conscientious objection and following their hearts into trouble seeking such a status, Puerto Ricans who chased the U.S. navy out of their island, Vieques, and are in prison for property damage, an Iraqi-American convicted of providing unofficial humanitarian aid to his countrypeople in dire need, two women serving time for resisting the school that trained the assassins of Peace Village leader and village members in Colombia, the recent punitive move of Leonard Peltier to Terre Haute, IN, anti-military recruitment actions, many other stories of nonviolent resistance and the writings from military prison of CO Camilo Mejia when he was locked up for refusing to return to kill in Iraq. Also, in every issue, is the first place I turn, the current addresses where I can write to prisoners of conscience. When I was in prison, or in jail, my days revolved around mail call, when letters and cards came in from the outside, mostly from people who read my address in the pages of *The Nuclear Resister*. They were my lifeline to reality, to a worldwide group of people who valued the resistance to militarism that I and all the others felt was crucial, and for which we were imprisoned. Each day I received more mail than anyone in prison, which set me apart from those who were there because they hurt someone. I was there for trying to help without hurting and the messages inspired by *The Nuclear Resister* in turn inspired me daily.

In their pages, I can rely on reading about friends each issue in this story collection, published for 25 years. These kind of special publications are the heart and soul of a movement, making the vital connections that keep us netted in nonviolence and wedded to community. The power of stories to give strength is on display nowhere so convincingly as in the pages of *The Nuclear Resister*. Begun to chronicle a specific movement and now having outgrown its name, it is the place to read of all antiwar actions that involve potential incarceration all around the world.

Oral fixations: indigenous stories

Peace and calm, gentleness and serenity, is much more common in indigenous oral tradition than is understood in the popular media or urban legend. Peace chiefs and groups of women leading the voices of nurturance are the norm, not the exception.

In Hawaii, Lono is the god of peace and the people maintain conflict management methods that stress reconciliation, as well as hospitality, mercy and healing. Peace with each other and peace with the Earth are stressed in that tradition (Guanson 1991, 3). This is what we find in various versions of indigenous spiritual tradition, illustrated by stories, around the world.

At age 82, author of more than 20 successful novels, Kurt Vonnegut writes about the story in his acerbically funny *Man Without a Country*. Vonnegut wryly claims that indigenous stories aren't the Hollywood success stories, but rather follow a more steady line that isn't always a mass marketing blockbuster formula. He's kidding in some ways, but does note that the most successful stories involve a kind of opening that finds the protagonist just living, possibly with some aspirations, and that there is a great downturn and a struggle, followed by a victory and triumph that elevates the position of the protagonist above the beginning point (Vonnegut 2005, 27). The sociologist might note here that raised expectations give hope, which fosters more action, more participation. Part of what Vonnegut offers us, then, is to appreciate the value of each story of nonviolent success. It was on that theory that I offered to write the 2002 War Resisters League calendar, just focusing on stories of nonviolent success. Geov Parrish volunteered to edit my scrivening and Francene Hart volunteered the cover. Rick Bickhart volunteered to design the layout and Ruth Benn produced it. It sold out and was apparently quite popular. Some two years later, after it was dated and out of print, I read a little story in the Philadelphia paper about a little old lady who was in a wheelchair and blocked the Federal building to offer nonviolent resistance to the war on Iraq. She held up our little WRL calendar book and said something to the effect that *Everyone should read this!* Imagine how we felt. I was almost in tears; why does a 90-year-old woman in a wheelchair have more courage and initiative than 99.9 percent of college students these days? What a great woman...

CHAPTER 3

Theories of
Nonviolent Power

On February 13, 1960, just 12 days after protests in Greensboro, North Carolina, ignited a sit-in movement across the South, Nashville students launched their own campaign against segregation. Within three months they had desegregated the city's lunch counters, scoring one of the first sit-in movement victories in the South [Mack 2003, 110].

What are the theories? How did Gandhi get anything done in the face of the mightiest empire the world had ever known? What enabled the Sit-In Kids — not a single one of whom could have called a single powerful person in Nashville or the world as they began to confront the powerful owner/political/law enforcement clique in town — what was it that allowed them to completely win in just a few months? How on Earth did the little nonviolent nuns bring down the mighty U.S.–supported Marcos dictatorship in the Philippines in 1986? Why would a hyperarmed Polish government collapse in the face of the nonviolent and apparently powerless Solidarity union? How could powerless kids in Serbia in a small group called Otpur engineer the collapse of the regime of the Butcher of the Balkans, Slobodan Milošević? That these events happened is history, not theory, but our initial theoretical supposition is basic, offered by Kenneth Boulding: *Can we agree that if something exists, it is? Can we agree that if something has been achieved by humans in the past, there is a chance they can do so in the future?*

Some elements of the theories of nonviolent power:

- When faced with mortal threat, people are hard-wired to react with infinite ways, not merely fight or flight.

•Nonviolence doesn't add to the level of violence in the world.

•Conflict is inevitable, even if injustice isn't occurring.

•Injustice will continue to occur, even without bad motives.

•Greed will cause unjust human behavior at times.

•The cycle of violence is so robust that nonviolence often requires unilateralism.

Bitterness, says Rubin Carter, is what society gives us, though we are born fully conscious and innocent. Since we are born to those who inherited acculturated hatred, we, in turn, practice it and pass it on (Klonsky 2003, 6). Forgiveness, wrote Berrigan, isn't optional. If we wish to remain involved and nonviolent, we are going to have to learn to practice it outwardly and, to stay healthy, inwardly (Berrigan 2001, 146). Just guerdons — the punishments so seemingly deserved by the greedy or brutal — are the province of God, karma or some greater schema, not ours. Vengeance and nonviolence are mutually exclusive. Or, achieving liberation is the best revenge, and that liberation includes all oppressors and those who have served them.

•Fear can cause violence.

•Violence causes fear.

•The threat of violence causes fear.

•People can confront other people without engendering fear.

•If people become ungovernable, they can cause a government to collapse.

•Most people who participate in a nonviolent movement do not subscribe to a moral or religious nonviolent ethic. This is simply because, in most cases, the masses who participate don't understand their religion as requiring nonviolence, nor do they particularly share the absolute moral value of nonviolence. They simply find themselves caught up in a social movement that seems to be working and is calling for nonviolence for tactical reasons. The Velvet Revolution was certainly like this; the masses of erstwhile communists had no particular grounding in either religion or nonviolence. But even the mass of those acting with Gandhi in India were following his lead in tactical terms, not necessarily religious terms (Hindus, Muslims and Sikhs have no religious absolute proscription on violence). Leadership — e.g., Gandhi, King, Chavez — may usually have those commitments, but *not* usually the mass of those participating. They are simply following the requests of their leadership, in general.

•A disciplined, trained nonviolent movement can withstand provocation, intimidation and violence.

•Leaders understand that they must have the coöperation of citizens and make attempts to keep that by manipulation of public opinion.

•Oppressors use fear and terror to ensure coöperation.

•Oppressors use apathy to ensure coöperation.

•Oppressors use assurances of protection from outside threats to generate coöperation.

•Oppressors use real or false benevolence to engender coöperation.

•Nonviolent campaigns do best when they disrupt and delegitimate oppressors' public relations.

•Nonviolence can debunk the terror of the oppressor when it reveals the true power of the citizenry.

•Nonviolence can invalidate and expose the ersatz benevolence of an oppressor.

•Nonviolent campaigns recruit most effectively when they are constructed of winnable battles.

•Nonviolent sacrifice can challenge opponent and ally alike to change.

When Clare Hanrahan — a warm, caring woman from South Carolina — finally put her life affairs in order so that she could be free to be incarcerated, her friends held a send-off when she went to prison. For many, it was their coming out as activists (Hanrahan 2000, 117). People silently sympathetic can be moved by the risk-taking behavior of those they regard as good, innocent people.

•Showing fear and anger indicates acceptance of oppressor's value system and legitimates further oppression.

•Retreat often invokes the predator/prey reaction and is not advisable.

•While nonviolent struggle is laudable on an individual basis, it is vastly more effective when undertaken on a mass scale.

•A precondition for mass nonviolent noncoöperation is mass hostile opinion toward the target regime (Bleiker 1993, 33).

This means that, in some fashion, public opinion has to reach actionable levels. Nonviolent civil resistance may prod that public opinion, if done in a fashion that dramatizes grievances and concomitantly invites sympathy, making a kind of successful appeal to the conscience of a majority. Recruitment to support and even participation can find fecund fields under those conditions.

•Taking more risks in collective action than one does on a day-to-day basis is appropriate and sensible.

This facet of nonviolent theory is generally true, with the proviso that individual or small group actions that are high risk can inspire larger numbers to take a lower risk action.

•Using the scientific method — hypothesis, experiment, evaluation and learning, new hypothesis, experiment, additional evaluation and learning, further experiment, and so forth — will produce ever-evolving and improving theories of nonviolent power.

This book, then, examines some of these theories in the light of stories. Some of those stories are from the literature, some from film, some from the author's memory and journals, some from interviews of others. Some effort will be made to offer critiques of other stories that show the theories of nonviolent power to be weak or inconsistent. This is not to claim that all the theories of nonviolent power are immutable laws of nature; everything we posit about human behavior can be shown false upon occasion; we are not batches of chemicals under controlled conditions that can be manipulated to replicable results every time. The human spirit is complex far beyond a few simple rules and thus the value of stories is that they establish not merely examples of when and how theories work but also some of the complexities and context unique to each situation. We use stories to establish a weight of examples, not a perfect predictive capability. A story of William Lloyd Garrison burning the American flag (Gowan 1976, 5) is from a context that is very different than a screaming young person with face metal and tattoos and a ski mask burning the flag. Stories offer context that separate technical similarities from underlying concepts, illustrating deeper meanings by offering details that provide clues to all who hear or read. We must examine the stories, great and small, of the actual failures of nonviolence, and look too, toward the case studies of nonviolence working almost despite itself. There are also stories of nonviolence as a work-in-progress, such as the liberation of Burma, or of Tibet (Hastings 2002, 81). This is not a cheerleading book of uncritical lessons from a master, but rather a close look at how a conflict management model has worked in many of its wrinkles, facets, elements and outcomes.

Sources for Part One

Abu-Assad, Hany, "Paradise Now," Warner Independent Pictures, 2005.

Berrigan, Philip, "The genius of forgiveness," in: Baggarly, Steven, et alia, *Disciples & Dissidents: Prison Writings of the Prince of Peace Plowshares.* Athol MA: Haley's, 2001.

Bleiker, Roland, *Nonviolent Struggle and the Revolution in East Germany.* Cambridge MA: Albert Einstein Institutions, 1993.

Conboy, Martin, *Journalism: A Critical History.* Thousand Oaks CA: Sage Publications, 2004.

Furnham, Adrian, and Barrie Gunter, "Effects of Time of Day and Medium of Presentation on Immediate Recall of Violent and Non-violent News," Applied Cognitive Psychology, Oct/Dec87, Vol. 1 Issue 4, p255–262, 8p.

Gowan, Susanne, et al., *Moving Toward A New Society.* Philadelphia PA: New Society Press, 1976.

Guanson, Lou An Ha'aheo, "Hawaiian," in: Paige, Glenn D., and Sarah Gilliatt, eds., *Nonviolence in Hawaii's Spiritual Traditions.* Honolulu: Center for Global Nonviolence Planning Project, 1991.

Hanrahan, Clare, *Jailed for Justice: A Woman's Guide to Federal Prison Camp.* Asheville NC: Brave Ulysses Books, 2002.

Hastings, Tom H., *Meek Ain't Weak: Nonviolent Power and People of Color.* Lanham MD: University Press of America, 2002.

Klonsky, Ken, "Going the distance: Rubin Carter's long journey from convict to crusader," *The Sun* 332, August 2003 (6).

Larsen, Jensine, "See healing," *World Pulse: Women & Children Transforming Our World* 1:2, Spring 2005 p2.

Llera, Maria del Mar, "Pragmatic approaches to intercultural ethics: The basis for fostering communication among nationalist groups," *Sign Systems Studies;* Mar2003, Vol. 31 Issue 1, p239, 22p.

Mack, Adam, "'No illusion of separation': James L. Bevel, the Civil Rights movement, and the Vietnam War," *Peace & Change* 28:1, January 2003 (108–133) (p110).

Mealy, Joseph, and Michael Shoob, *Bush's Brain*, film, 2004, based on book by James C. Moore and Wayne Slater.

Rizzo, Sandy Tavlin, Doris Berkell, Karen Kotzen, *Peacemaking Skills for Little Kids.* Miami: Grace Contino Abrams Peace Education Foundation, 1997.

Rothman, Jay, *Resolving Identity-Based Conflict in Nations, Organizations, and Communities.* San Francisco: Jossey-Bass Inc., 1997.

Satha-Anand, Chaiwat, "Two plots of nonviolence stories: From the streets of Bangkok to the forests of Thailand," Social Alternatives, Apr97, Vol. 16 Issue 2, p12, 4p, 1bw; (AN 9704154806), p12, 4p, 1bw.

Satha-Anand, Chaiwat, and Michael True, eds., *The Frontiers of Nonviolence*. Honolulu: International Peace Research Association, 1998.

Senehi, Jessica, "Constructive storytelling in intercommunal conflicts: building community, building peace," in: Byrne, Sean and Cynthia L. Irvin, *Reconcilable Differences: Turning Points in Ethnopolitical Conflict*. West Hartford CT: Kumarian Press, 2000.

Seuss, Dr., *The Butter Battle Book*. NYC: Random House, 1984.

Smith, Mary Jane, Patricia Liehr, "Story Theory," Holistic Nursing Practice; Nov/Dec2005, Vol. 19 Issue 6, p272–276, 5p, 1 chart.

Spence, Rebecca, Jason McLeod, "Building the road as we walk it: Peacebuilding as principled and revolutionary nonviolent praxis," *Social Alternatives*, Autumn 2002, Vol. 21 Issue 2, p61–64, 4p.

Vonnegut, Kurt, *A Man Without a Country*. NYC: Seven Stories Press, 2005.

Walker, Alice, *The Way Forward Is with a Broken Heart*. NYC: Random House, 2000.

_____, *Now Is the Time to Open Your Heart*. NYC: Ballantine Books, 2005 (original 2004).

Wink, Walter, *Engaging the Powers: Discernment and Resistance in a World of Domination*. Minneapolis: Fortress Press, 1992.

Worldwatch Institute, *Vital Signs 2005: The Trends That Are Shaping Our Future*. New York: W.W. Norton & Company Ltd., 2005.

Yost, Jack, *Planet Champions: Adventures in Saving the World*. Portland OR: BridgeCity Books, 1999.

Part Two

Civil Rights
and Sequelae; or,
An Expanded Movement

Satyagraha — Gandhi's word for nonviolence — means holding fast to truth whatever the cost may be. King(sought not only to discover these truths and to hold fast to them but to attempt in his life to live and give full manifestation to the truths he said he believed.(He knew that truth unlived is not truth, that truth proclaimed in words alone cannot sustain us in our hunger.
—Vincent Harding (Harding 1996, 117)

When I was 17 years old, a senior in high school in a suburb of Minneapolis, Minnesota, I took Sociology. Our teacher brought in a guest speaker, Susan Sponsel, who captivated us with her description of what she had done since graduating from our high school — Edina — just a few years before. She had gone on to college and then she moved in with the South Side Christian Center in Chicago. She and our teacher set up a field trip to visit the South Side Christian Center, which several of us did. It completely changed my life.

I met African American kids my age who were not only very cool but very authentic and ready to help me understand what it was that I was seeing in front of me in the most segregated of the northern urban areas in the U.S. Chicago, home of the urban blues and other powerful cultural expressions of blacks in the northern U.S., was overwhelming to a Minnesota boy. It was scary. "Don't go out alone," I was told. "Gangbangers, Black P. Stone Rangers." But I made friends.

I decided to return for a longer visit, which I did, and I really began to see another world, another universe inside my own nation. I saw families living in metal-sided shacks, in garage attics, in squalid projects hemmed in by freeways and train lines, and I roomed with kids who had been living in those circumstances. I saw millions of black people crammed into neighborhoods, crowded streets with no white people except for me, and I rode the public transport with my new friends, who protected me even though I didn't know they were doing so. My ignorance was stunning and the more I learned, the more I saw it.

The Civil Rights movement had gone through several stages by then. Until 1955 it was slowly gathering momentum as African Americans watched the rest of the world — especially Africa — decolonize. As European empires were evicted from the direct rule of African nations, the pressure built on African Americans to decolonize their oppressive situations, especially beginning in the segregated South. From 1955 to 1965 this movement was essentially and identifiably nonviolent and great gains were made, especially in social norms of announced policy and racial stereotyping. The dignity of the nonviolent struggle for freedom won hearts and minds of otherwise uninvolved Americans — certainly including young ones like me. This is basic utilization of an external power — the northern white majority of the U.S. in this case — to leverage change where the challenger has a shortage of leverage (Schock 2005, 54). That only failed when the external leverage was sacrificed so that northern blacks could exert their own leverage in the form of street battle.

Beginning with the Watts uprising, the Los Angeles riot of 1965, northern urban blacks began to express rejection of integration and nonviolence so central to the previous decade of activism (Katz 1989, 53). This new message of militancy and rejection of white culture and even white participation in the struggle for freedom and equality of black Americans presented young whites like me with a confusing array of possible allegiances. I vacillated from week to week as I took in the cultural choices and political initiatives. Indeed, the country vacillated and even some particular black communities were flipping back and forth. "I knew that if the city [Chicago] was being hit by nonviolent demonstrations, there was less chance of rioting in the streets. The nonviolent demonstration gives the ghetto dweller a ray of hope that perhaps the power structure will hear his just demands and so something to alleviate the problems" (Gregory, 1971, 196).

I met Steve, a young African American my age who was raising himself up by his bootstraps and who was exceeding bright; he was hoping to go to college even though no one in his family had ever graduated from high school. He was one of eight children living in a lean-to sided with galvanized metal, and he had moved into the South Side Christian Center. He was small, skinny and lovable.

Vince was the brilliant light-skinned kid who looked a great deal like a younger Julian Bond. Everyone called him Baby Einstein and his wide smile and wild curly black hair were fascinating to a boy like me, so used to a school full of Scandinavian kids.

"Pigeon" was the reformed gangbanger, the 18-year-old who walked with the pimplimp that marked him as too cool for me to even understand. He brought me to places like "Jewtown" on the West Side, where he intervened when he saw me getting threatened even though I had no idea I was being threatened. He interpositioned himself between me and a very large black man who had approached me in the street market and who was trying to sell me a watch from amongst all those on his forearm. Since I was incompetently trying to tell him no and he was getting more frustrated and enraged with me by the moment, Pigeon had to jump in between us. He looked up directly into the face of the looming fellow and said about me, "He's cool, he's cool; he's with us." Probably saved me from getting mugged, smacked, beaten or worse.

Eric was older — a very mature 19 — short cropped hair and bass voice, the mature leader of this group of young men. He was quiet and sensible, bringing us all back to ground if we were too "rambiscotious." Very occasionally, he would smile and initiate communication. Usually, he quietly led and let the rest scramble for the quick word or laugh.

We held no real church services at this Christian Center, run by "the Rev," but when the choir performed, it was a rocking, moving time of high spirit. Rev was white, about which I felt increasingly weird, but he had known and admired both King and Malcolm X, so I felt he was legitimate, even though I was uncomfortable with him leading an organization in the ghetto. His moral focus affected the music, and there was no dancing at the performances I attended, but the undercurrent was there. During some of the songs, I certainly wanted to dance, something then–LeRoi Jones (now Amiri Baraka) wrote about in his then-current 1963 classic, *Blues People* (Jones 1963, 43). John Lewis, Civil Rights hero and U.S. congressman from Georgia's 5th district, wrote about his childhood backwoods Georgia church services:

> There were no hymnbooks in either church I attended as a child. Neither were there musical instruments. No piano. No organ. But there was music, music richer and fuller and sweeter than any I've ever heard since. I'm talking about pure singing, the sound of voices fueled by the spirit, people keeping

rhythm with a beat they heard in their hearts, singing songs that came straight from their soul, with words they felt in every bone of their body. These people sang with no self-consciousness and no restraint. Young and old alike, all of whom lived the same hard life, toiling in the fields, struggling with poverty and doing their best to make the best of it, found joy and meaning in the midst of hardship and pain [Lewis 1998, 22].

That music coming out of *that* community at *that* time was hard-wired all the way back to Reconstruction hopes dashed, the Civil War and the Emancipation Proclamation and slavery, and back to Africa. Even a Minnesota white boy could get that and get it to the core of my person, permanently. I can still hear and feel *Glory, glory, hallelujah, no more sickness, no more sorrow, since I laid that heavy burden down.* I can still see, hear and feel the choir and the very young African American kid out in front with the "shakers." The suits and formal dresses couldn't hide the canorous joy and inner dance of those kids and they gave that to me and to all who were there. African Christian churches simply *moved* and it wasn't like the church I grew up in whatsoever. Christianity became more connected to my entire spirit in the South Side Christian Center, partly through the music, partly through the relationships to black kids my age. That was the Civil Rights era, and those songs were living libretto of resistance (Carawan 1990, 92).

It was the beginning of what would become my version of what came to be known as liberation theology, a term vastly misunderstood to mean the justification of guerrilla warfare on behalf of the poor in Latin America and, by extension, anywhere else. The three elements of the actual doctrine, which originated from religious workers in Latin America, have nothing to do with violence and are:

- God does not want anyone to be poor, which mandates confrontation with institutions that create and maintain poverty, often referred to as structural violence or institutional violence.

- There is a preferential option for the poor, viz., it is proper and in fact required to stand on the side of the poor in their struggles.

- It is imperative to gain and maintain the dignity and self-activity of poor and working people (Lynd 1995, 45).

These were the elements of the South Side Christian Center as I observed them while I was affiliated with that community. I learned those guidelines without ever hearing the term liberation theology, and they were being put into practice insofar as I could tell. This personalist theology was also at the core of Martin Luther King's beliefs and his web of persuasive ideas, writings and rhetoric (Chernus 2004, 163). When I went out with the South Side Christian Center to southwestern Michigan to look over a piece of property, they told me more of their vision, which was to buy a farm and become much more financially independent and have, then, two ministries, one in the country and one still on the South Side of Chicago. It was a vision of lightening the poverty all around them and achieving that by the dignity and self-generated wholesome activity of farming. They bought that land and I was one of their workers for a time, harvesting cherries, peaches, pears and, mostly, apples. I interested my father in their project and he came to help for a bit, and also sponsored a canoe trip for two of the boys and me, with him, to the Boundary Waters in northern Minnesota. I helped with many other projects as well in my short stint of just a few months at the SSCC and fell in love with the kids. I was always just a little uneasy with the Rev, as he was a powerful man and I was just a youth, but I learned from him, though I also rejected some of his methods. I felt he modeled a patriarchy and power that made me uncomfortable because it wasn't as fostering of dignity and self-respect as a more egalitarian model might be. He crossed the line from authoritative to authoritarian all too often, especially in his relationships with the young men, though, as a volunteer, I never felt that, which also made me feel odd. He was a liberator, but it was not a perfect model, and I wanted to keep searching.

Until then, I was on a track to attend college and was otherwise directionless, though increasingly disaffected, as were many in my alienated generation who had been slowly coming of age amidst the Civil Rights struggles and the growing awareness that the war in Vietnam was unjust and senseless. The trip to Chicago in the spring of 1968 in my senior year exposed me to poverty in a spectacular fashion and stripped away my illusions of an America of equal opportunity in one weekend. It was both devastating and challenging. I knew that college kids had gone south to help in the Civil Rights movement, beginning mostly in the summer of 1964, and I vaguely understood that some colleges might be interested in teaching from a justice perspective, but mostly I was powerfully influenced by Malcolm X as he seemed to feel universities were centers of American imperialist education. Indeed, at many colleges the kids were involved in the Civil Rights movement in the South despite the administrations, such as Juniata College in Pennsylvania, from where young students flocked south to help with the Selma campaign in the summer of 1965 over the opposition of the Juniata administration (Durham 1991, 175). I finally rejected college for this complex of reasons. Years later I would reject my personal learning style of one part nescience, one part experience, and one part randomized information gathering and seek that college I had scorned from my idealistic youth, but at the time it seemed logical.

It was during that spring of my 17-year-old awakening that, on April 4, Dr. King was shot and the question seemed called nationwide as riots broke out in what was ironically the worst memorial to him imaginable. His nonviolence was rejected by these outbreaks in scores of U.S. cities and it served to further polarize a nation already divided. Many blacks went deeper into an almost al-Qa'ida–like rejection of white society and whites became fearful. Still totally idealistic with no true basis of reality, I jumped back and forth without irony, without compunction. I followed integrationists and separatists. I read King and Malcolm X with equal fervor. Moving from sheltered suburb to gangbanger Chicago upon high school graduation and living with SSCC for some months, I absorbed it all without a functioning critical analysis. One week I was a proselyte to nonviolence, the next a raging white supporter of black nationalism and separatism, a devotee of the Black Panthers spouting reverse racism and retributive rhetoric — *For every pork chop, there is a frying pan! Signetur!* That is why I am so tolerant of my students and other young people now (I'm fast to argue, slow to judge); they are still formulating their basic philosophies and are open to thinking and changing on a massive scale, still experimenting, as they should. I just try to let them know about all the mistakes I made personally and all those I believe my generation made and invite them to learn from those mistakes and take the best, eclectically, from what we boomers can offer, discard the errors, and build from there. That is how we progress, at least in theory, though I do see the same old mistakes made again and again, on a constant basis.

At age 17, then, even before graduation from high school, I was urging my family to read *The Autobiography of Malcolm X* and could not relate to their failure to experience some kind of ultimate epiphany over its message. My mother read it, handed it back and said something like, "Well, that was interesting." Interesting? It was cataclysmic! My bewilderment over her tepid reaction, and my tepid reaction now when students demand I read the latest work that has them in thrall, all combine in my heart to make me so grateful for young people's passion. I get it when they just don't get why I don't lay down my life and join whatever campaign in which they are involved this week.

My sister Holly became interested, at least enough to give my father a paperback copy of King's 1963 classic, *Strength to Love*, a worn copy of which stands in my library now, given, in turn, to me during my undergraduate study years by my father. Holly gave him this on Father's Day, 1968, as we were all coming out of our suburban bubble. King's work is timeless: *Our hope for creative living lies in our ability to re-establish the spiritual ends of our lives in personal character and social justice* (King 1963, 70). Nothing could be more relevant in our battle to end the so-called War on Terrorism and usher in an era of global justice and nonviolent conflict management.

To at least a small degree, the entire family was drawn into this effort, my father much more than anyone else. The lone and sharp exception was my grandmother Mabel Hastings, my father's mother, who remained racist and intolerant, judgmental and imperious. My other grandmother, Elsie Zacher, my mother's mother, was sweet and gracious as I ranted and always received me and whatever company I brought with a loving generosity. When my Young Men for Peace — a group of African American junior high boys — invaded her apartment, she puttered around giving out treats and cold drinks, always wanting everyone to feel cared for.

I slowly began to integrate my young adulthood into the various issues of the day, sometimes intertwining them, sometimes keeping them separate. It was on one of the trips from Minneapolis to Chicago, in fact, that the issues of Civil Rights and the war in Vietnam became linked for me.

I was back and forth from Chicago, involved with groups in both towns, and trying to figure out my life. Near the middle of the summer, heading back to Chicago to pick up two of the SSCC kids for our canoe trip, I gave a ride to a young Jewish guy, very bright, who had been volunteering at the Phyllis Wheatley House in Near Northside. He talked to me about the war and my role in resisting it.

"Well," I told him in my old 1953 Chevy as we motored toward Chicago, "I think I'll probably join the navy. Everyone's getting drafted and I think the war kind of sucks, so I shouldn't get drafted and go in the army. I've taken all the tests and they said I could work on a nuclear sub."

He was animated. "The navy is highly involved in the war. If you don't like the war, don't go into any branch of the armed forces because they all contribute to it. Check out the Twin Cities Draft Information Center." He gave me their address.

I checked it out, talked to several great counselors, and decided to register as a Conscientious Objector. First, though, I went through some months of thinking it over, even after I turned 18 in October 1968. I wasn't sure that I could even agree with registering for the draft, since that implied coöperation with a system of war and involuntary servitude. In any event,

I met some incredibly influential people, went to lots of draft resistance events, watched cards being burned, and met people who later went to prison for their convictions. As I looked back on that time and how I felt about Dave Gutknecht and George Crocker heading to prison while I stayed free, I know that worked into my decisions later, decisions that would finally land me in jails and prisons for multiple nonviolent felonies. Dave and George were two of my counselors and were just a few years older than I. Indeed, I think those in their early 20s can probably affect the 17 and 18 year olds more readily than can anyone else, if my own experience is any guide.

By this time, by the fall when I was just graduated from high school at 17 the late spring before, I was volunteering at The Way, a black organization on Plymouth Avenue, where there had been "baby riots" in 1967. It involved a few windows broken and some relatively polite Minnesota disruption in the poorest black neighborhood. I moved right in after my summer in Chicago, and got an apartment on "Death Row," on Morgan Avenue North, just two blocks south of Plymouth Avenue. I brought my dog with me, a very high-strung miniature schnauzer, who barked and paced, eliciting complaints from downstairs neighbors. Big numerous cockroaches vied for my leftovers and my stereo was doomed as soon as I brought the dog back to my parents' home. It was a neighborhood that featured routine break-ins, and, as an innocent white boy who was working predictable hours, my gear was forfeit.

CHAPTER 4

Expanding the Movement

The Civil Rights movement not only resulted in sequelae around the planet, from the nonviolent campaigns of the IRA in the late 1960s in Northern Ireland to the American Indian Movement in the U.S., but in a greater recognition that human rights expands even beyond the Universal Declaration of Human Rights.

Thus, in the Black Hills in 2004, where hundreds of us met at the Indigenous Environmental Network gathering, the common theme of several speakers was that environmental rights are human rights, because the indigenous lifeways are impossible to live in an environment colonized and gridded out, impacted and drastically altered. A tribal economy dependent on wild rice cannot long survive a water authority that raises or lowers river and lake levels beyond the range wild rice can tolerate, which is exactly what has happened in Canada and the U.S. to satisfy power company demands and other constituent pressures. A village reliant on salmon cannot sustain its economy or its lifeways if logging, damming (for both electrical power and irrigation), pollution and overfishing both upstream and in the ocean have decimated the salmon. A band whose corrupt tribal government has made a deal with a corporation to install a medical waste incinerator on its reservation cannot properly carry on its spiritual practices with the stories of dogs running around with amputated limbs or of loose HIV/AIDS waste paraphernalia or the airborne products of extraordinary contagions incompletely combusted. Indigenous speakers from around the continent told of exactly these problems. *This is where environmental issues become human rights issues*, said one speaker, and that theme echoed for the duration of the conference.

This is a universal truth, and 2005 Nobel Peace Laureate Dr. Wangari Maathai says that about the Congo River basin, home to almost 20 percent of the world's rainforests and home to indigenous populations who, if that forest is harmed, will suffer directly and immediately. She relates security and stability to the health of native lifeways just as much as she equates it to the presence of security forces. She notes particularly strongly that the basin is experiencing hot conflict that is only made infinitely worse and more enduring when the environment is abused and overexploited (Environment, online). This is precisely what Native Americans insist upon. The IEN gathering helped bring those strands together.

I worked security at the gathering for three night shifts, 8 p.m.–midnight, which was easy duty at this alcohol-and-drug-free event. While we were more or less prepared for the surprise appearance of a random drunken truckful of rednecks, no one seriously regarded that as likely. Mostly, I stood or sat around the campfire at the entranceway, talking with my fellow security volunteers.

Billie is a young Cree woman who is working to build a network of Native youth. There are 36 affiliates in that network, from northern Canada and Alaska to Jamaica, from California to Connecticut. The issue she is focusing on currently is the potential damage to Native lands and lifeways of the upcoming Winter Olympics in British Columbia. She exchanged news with Sebastian, a young grad student from Berkeley whose people are Peruvian indigenous, and who is a student leader on the Berkeley campus. While they had not known each other prior to that night at the campfire, they discovered many mutual friends and made plans to collaborate on several campaigns. Late at night, the talk turned to violence and nonviolence and we had an interesting discussion. Billie is a self-described "big girl" who usually intimidates potential attackers. Sebastian is a martial arts trainer who found himself staring at one of his students in a surprising setting one day. Sebastian was protesting the beginning of the war in Iraq and, in full riot gear with mask down and truncheon at the ready was one of his students, a San Francisco policeman. "I am reassessing my teaching," said Sebastian.

Amit Srivastava, native to India, is Coördinator for Global Resistance, a Global Justice organization based in El Cerrito, California. We sat at the campfire one night and he talked of Cancun, where the WTO met in the winter of 2004 and where a Korean farmer committed suicide during the demonstrations opposing WTO policies that are anathema to farmers worldwide and that operate for the benefit of agribusiness and its corporate affiliates: seed companies, petrochemical companies, distributors, processors and machinery manufacturers. When policies of any one nation can be construed as negatively affecting the profits of any of these huge transnational corporate groups, WTO has been there to "correct" the problem. When these individual situations result in lowered incomes for farmers on the ground in a particular nation-state, that is just life. They cannot buck the global economic masters. But when the smaller struggles unite in a network, they can become much more powerful and address at least some of the asymmetry in the conflict.

Amit said he was still trying to wrestle with the Korean farmer's suicide. "It was so shocking, such a surprise, and it hurt so intensely," he said. "Immediately, we set up a vigil at the place where this poor man did it. There were rumors that the Korean farmers rehearsed this, which were even more shocking, and I choose not to believe those rumors. These were not the poorest subsistence farmers; they paid their own way and were a large delegation of about 150 of them, which must have been expensive, flying from Korea to Cancun."

I said it was reminiscent to me of the relatively well off Buddhist monks and nuns who self-immolated during the war in Vietnam; they were not the peasants most immediately affected by the U.S. war, but they chose this sacrifice with the notion that, as Thich Nhat Hanh told us, was felt to be not the end of them, but just a transition along their reincarnation karmic life. Still, it rarely communicates properly. Amit said if he had known, if he had been able to, if he had been standing near the man, he would have intervened physically to stop him. I absolutely understood and agreed, even while understanding that I do not understand or properly contextualize such a drastic act.

And so, through all the plenary speeches, the breakout workshops and other sessions, I found myself looking forward mostly to the security shifts, talking with others one-on-one or in small groups in the chill evening under the ceiling of stars over the Black Hills, warming ourselves by the flaming, crackling cottonwood.

CHAPTER 5

Nonviolence and Long Term Success

Like Muslims and Hindus in India after Gandhi's nonviolent victory, the U.S. hardly enjoys a perfectly equable, democratic, nonviolent relationship between African Americans and whites after the Civil Rights movement. Why is this and why can't we seem to see progress toward a more robust democracy?

Perhaps more nonviolence would help us get to a better democracy. Indeed, the best nonviolence works within a democracy, not to overthrow or subvert it (Kelly 1984, 27). It is not unlike any peace process. The signing of the peace accord is but one early step, though it may contain a sketchy blueprint for a better world. If one views a peace process as a continuum from chaotic warfare (or deep oppression) to the democratic equality and harmony we envision, the signing of the agreement is but an early point, far closer to chaos than equanimity. Peace, said Telliard de Chardin, is more than bovine placidity, and indeed it requires more work and a great deal more sacrifice after the agreement than even the tremendous sacrifice that led to the signing (e.g., Indian independence, or the Civil Rights and Voting Rights Acts of 1964–1965). It requires, among many other things, deeper dialog between and among groups (Nagle 2000, 37). Group-to-group conflict resolution necessitates ongoing work at the community level for success, something that has happened on occasion and been missed mostly in the U.S. in the aftermath of Civil Rights.

Indeed, the problems that beset a nation or nation-state following a nonviolent liberation struggle can often be traced to the elements of violence that contaminated that struggle. When the riots broke out in the U.S. after Blacks lost patience with slow progress toward full equality—

especially economic equality, which they believed would never be granted but would need to be seized — the Civil Rights era ended and racial fear reasserted itself, making future problems more likely and more intense.

Similarly, in India, Gandhi's legacy was the power of nonviolence but was ended by the ascension of leadership in the Indian National Congress — especially Nehru — who only subscribed to nonviolence as a tactic, not a philosophy. Nehru went on to build up the Indian army and rushed to defend Indian sovereignty by force of arms. Had the Indian leadership been not merely Gandhi's tactical allies but his philosophically nonviolent allies, it is possible that we might have seen the robustness and stability of nonviolence work its way throughout the huge multicultural nation. As it is, India has largely slid back into ethnic, religious and racial hatreds and pushed forward to such a focus on arms that it joined the nuclear club in 1974 and renewed that membership in 1998 with a bang as it tested its nukes pennacontemporaneously with Pakistan.

Rather, as former U.S. Senator Paul Simon has pointed out, nonviolence seems to get its endurance and utility so far by transference from one struggle to another; he linked the nonviolence of NAACP — founded in 1909 — to Gandhi's South African struggles (1906–1914) and the founding of the ANC (1912) to Gandhi's Indian campaigns (1915–1948) and back to the modern U.S. Civil Rights movement. The stability of nonviolence as a workable model for social liberation comes full circle (Simon 2001, 15).

When nonviolence stressed and fractured

Umoja (2003) and others have long identified the 1964 campaign in Mississippi as the beginning of the end of nonviolence as the primary method of struggle in the Civil Rights movement. When nonviolence is not the perceived method, violence is attributed to virtually all who engage in the struggle; when nonviolence is the perceived method of struggle, violence is seen as aberrant and not ascribed to anyone but the few who use it. Controlling the perception is paramount; the same amount of random violence in any particular movement may be perceived in either of those ways and the consequences for individuals and the movement in general are enormous.

Certainly the Civil Rights movement had every single right under all mainstream codes of conduct to employ violence. The Just War doctrine would have exculpated them entirely, since the injustices and unprovoked attacks on them were legion, documentable and pervasive. They were not the state but they were an identity group clearly aggrieved from the time they were stolen from their homelands to serve as slaves. Unequal rights for humans is one issue; the level of oppression inflicted by violence is related but clearly a separate issue and the bloody means by which African Americans had been subjugated even after their emancipation by Lincoln during the Civil War entitled them to use any means at their disposal, as Malcolm X eventually preached.

This is still not the best method of waging combat, however, if the goal is maximal change and minimal casualties. That may be seen by looking at virtually any nonviolent campaign with very few, if any, exceptions, and the Civil Rights movement was precisely that way.

When the 1964 campaign yielded the 1965 Voting Rights Act, it also began to yield to calls for violent defense, prompted by the attacks on marchers and other Civil Rights workers in the Deep South. Three African American Civil Rights workers had been murdered with impunity during the previous two years. The fresh murders of the three young Civil Rights workers outside Philadelphia, Mississippi — James Chaney, Andrew Goodman and Michael "Mickey" Schwerner — and, ironically, the national attention it received because two of the victims were northern whites, seemed to be the straw that broke the camel's back for some of the fiery, impatient young leaders. Stokely Carmichael and James Forman were probably the most notable as they began using the new slogan, "Black Power," which frightened whites, and as they began to first question and then eschew nonviolence. All this was done in an atmosphere of high tension, imminent and palpable danger and absolute justification. It was, perhaps, nearly inevitable, given the strain of maintaining nonviolence under such intense provocation. As with any conflict, the more prolonged the string of atrocities committed by one side, the more easily justified atrocities by the other. This was true of U.S. bombing civilians in WW II, regarded as shocking and barbarous when done early by the Germans and regarded as realistic and appropriate when done later by the Allies. This dynamic is predictable and a great challenge to the ability of nonviolence to persist in the face of such provocation.

The message of immediate, violent defense coming from within the Civil Rights movement eroded that movement almost immediately and justified the burgeoning mood of "by any means necessary" that was coming to a boil in northern ghettos of African Americans from Newark to Los Angeles. Many began to riot and the results were predictable; casualties increased and the population of whites across the land moved from the sympathy that had produced legislation and funding, to fear of blacks and gratitude for the thin blue line of police or the more blunt instrument of the National Guard that quelled riots. This dynamic unraveled the movement and halted the gains. The agenda of the Civil Rights movement thus remains unfinished and economic gains are nonexistent for most African Americans, even though rights to drink from the same water fountain remain enshrined. Like the liberation of Burma with Aung San Suu Kyi, the liberation of African Americans remains only partially completed. Nonviolence is not emotionally satisfying to anyone seeking revenge and yet is demonstrably the wisest path if enlightened self-interest is dispassionately pursued (Hastings 2004, 117).

And so, what we see now, is racial tension. The Nation of Islam and the Aryan supremacy groups are growing, no longer fading into nonexistence. The Nation of Islam — Black Muslims — preach separateness. They are a very understandable and logical expression of the disappointment felt by African Americans at perduring poverty and essentialism. Unlike the white supremacists, the Nation seeks no material or legal superiority over any other race or ethnic group; they seek a separate nation, a distinct nation-state, in which they can control their own destiny, make their own success or failure, and be sovereign. The rumors have been hinting lately at a possible nascent effort, a stepping stone toward that, by a lease agreement with a Southeastern U.S. tribe for a large tract of land on which the Nation would conduct an experiment in separate society, asking nothing from the U.S., developing its own national base and, presumably, setting the stage for ultimate legal separation, a real, sovereign nation-state.

This, I believe, would be a healthy development. It would afford African Americans someplace to point to, to say, this is where I can go if I decide to. It would be a safe zone, so to speak, and thus offer a sense of security to those African Americans still trying to attain a place of equality and democratic harmony in the U.S.

Rather than remain a rumor, I'd like to see this be a national discussion. I'd love to see no lease with a tribe, but a cession of land as due to African Americans, based on a sign-up, a percent of land of the landmass of the U.S., and an outright offer of land, not for peace, but for reparations and justice. Slaves were significant in the growth of the base of wealth in the U.S. and received no 40 acres and a mule reparations as promised; this land would be an overdue, one-time settlement. If, say, a sign-up end-date were fixed and, for example, nine percent of all Americans signed up to join this experiment (half of all African Americans), deed nine percent of the U.S. landmass to African Americans, with a grandfather clause that would allow a generation for everyone else to move out (or whatever fair arrangements might be negotiated). The best option I can imagine is if African Americans and Native Americans were given 100 percent of the military lands and asked to work it out between them — along with several $ billion to bioremediate the pollution on any of that land.

And in the remainder of the U.S. (or in the entire U.S., if this vision never occurred), we are still looking for economic gains that the Civil Rights movement mostly failed to produce. Indeed, that was where Dr. King was trying to go, but that campaign was tipped off the rails first by an increasing abandonment of his practice of nonviolence with the outbreak of riots, and then the derailment was completed by his assassination, further exacerbated by the African American response to his death: riots in more than 100 American cities. When King was shot in Memphis at 6:01 p.m. on his balcony while talking with aides, one of them, Andrew Young, checked King's pulse and told Ralph Abernathy, "Ralph, it's all over" (White 2003: online). King's death was also the death of the Civil Rights movement.

His murder killed the interracial efforts to achieve an ongoing national coalition of victims of the war system, something he was working on especially hard in the final year of his life. Had he been able to successfully do what only he could — bring together a massive coalition of poor whites, African Americans, Hispanics and others — we might have seen that economic equality so painfully missing from our nation. We might have seen enough of that to reduce the chances that, more than 35 years later, we see a worsening of the income and wealth gap, not an improvement. Nobody could speak across all the lines like King and we need now the will to do so, and the training and discipline to continue to do so in our communities. Without that, without dialog in our communities, we will not work together but we will instead see a deeper allegiance to identity groups, to nationalism and to the culture of war and individualism. King talked and wrote of crossroads and we are at another one now.

CHAPTER 6

Treaty Rights

When I was just 17, freshly graduated from high school, I went to the black community and learned to listen to how they felt regarded — or, most often, disregarded — by the dominant culture.

When I was in my early thirties I began to work alongside more and more Native Americans in various struggles in the north of Wisconsin. Of course, growing up in Minneapolis — one of the two largest urban Native cities in North America — I met and at times worked with Native Americans. Friends Paul Heinrich and Sue Pope and I, along with my son, Lee, went to the Black Hills Survival Gathering in the summer of 1980, which was a tetramerous confluence of tribal activists, safe energy and sustainability activists, anti-development ranchers, and early anti-globalization activists. Tribal leadership at that four-pronged event was significant and both local and national, since it was in the shadow of the Black Hills. I saw and heard Russell Means and John Trudell and met Floyd Red Crow Westerman; it was a truly meaningful step in my appreciation of that leadership. The movement against the globalization of Native resources was a part of that gathering and of the analysis put forth cogently by the Black Hills Alliance, which informed the safe energy movement (Black Hills Alliance 1981, 64). This helped me stitch together my worldview on tribal coalition partners.

I had to learn more, to realize that ways of understanding varied a great deal from culture to culture, from society to society, within the shell of the dominant culture. This went far beyond the relatively small changes between the suburban culture in which I was raised and the working class culture into which I transited after high school. Native Americans have a culture that retains some great rootstock. Understanding the context — very high on most reservations — is the greatest challenge. Power differentials are not simply greater or lesser, they are radically different in many ways. Time is altered. Tact is achieved in ways that are in or out, achieved by knowledge and respect for knowledge, or not achieved even when offered sincerely in some cases. Like a member of the dominant culture attempting to work well with any other culture, I was forced to learn that respect and disrespect are very culturally specific in most cases (Ting-Toomey 2002, 53).

When I brought a friend from the peace movement to the radio station, WOJB (Wisconsin OJiBwa), I confidently showed her around, and then, confidence still high, brought her over to the tribal offices and introduced her to the tribal chair, saying something like, "This is the tribal chairperson." I was soundly and immediately corrected, "Tribal chair-*man*." It was almost like boxing my stupid ears. Duly and permanently noted. Every time I gratuitously failed to honor who a tribal person was, that person would help me get it right. It was a rich learning experience.

My mentors were many, from Walter Bresette, a Red Cliff charismatic leader, to Joe Rose, Medewin religious man and Director of Native American Studies at Northland College, where I first studied and where I eventually directed the Peace and Conflict Studies program. Great Lakes Indian Fish and Wildlife Commission biologist Neil Kimisek was an advisor to me on Native American relationships between science and traditional values. Most of all, Larry Cloud Morgan — Whitefeather of the Ojibwe — taught me Native Nonviolence.

When I was involved in the peace movement in Minneapolis, I ran into Larry, a Cass Lake and Leech Lake Anishinabe. Larry was a spiritual leader, a holy man focused on his own way of being, a way that was compassionate and generous. Larry was a Catholic Worker, a mental health worker and an Anishinabe practitioner of pipe and smudge ceremonies. There is one photo of Larry conducting a mass in St. Paul's Cathedral in Minnesota, half the ceremony in the normal Catholic fashion and half in a Native pipe fashion. Larry was loved by virtually everyone he ever knew and spent years in federal prison for his direct disarmament action on Armistice Day 1984, when he hammered on a live nuclear weapon silo lid in the missile fields of Missouri. When I got the call on March 27, 1985, that Larry was sentenced to eight years, I immediately knew I would do a plowshare action. Mike Miles called me, crying, that night at WOJB, where I was working on a production of a radio program on the February trial, and I tried to absorb the news as I returned, in tears myself, to the studio to work on the audio piece.

Walter Bresette was a treaty rights activist and a speaker of consummate charismatic skill. He was program manager for WOJB radio when I met him in 1980, a voice of calm outrage and intelligent critique. He co-founded *Masinaigan*, the "talking paper" of the 13 bands of Lake Superior Ojibwa. I had a three-hour weekly peace and justice program on WOJB for some years and I wrote for *Masinaigan* for some time. But mostly I worked with Walter on special projects he dreamt up, on treaty rights struggles and on countering the many environmental threats we faced in northern Wisconsin. Walter was political, he was a campaigner and he gave a great deal to each individual with whom he worked.

More than anyone, Walter helped me see the connections between resources, hyperconsumption, environmental disaster, native lifeways under threat, and treaty rights. It was his idea, for example, to take the fish speared in the annual walleye run, put them in 55-gallon barrels, label them "toxic waste" and deliver them to the state capitol building for legislators to consider. It was Walter who first told us all — environmentalists, hunters, those who hated treaty rights and those who simply supported Anishinabe human rights — that the treaties would be our best friend if we wished to protect the environment. Of course, many scoffed. Of course, he was exactly correct. I saw that in campaign after campaign, from oil and gas drilling to mining to incinerators to the U.S. navy's thermonuclear command facility. The tribes were gaining in legal power and the environment was thus protected. We learned to love treaty rights. Walter and GLIFWC took the so-called symbolic violence out of the multicultural education we were all getting (New and Petronicolos 2001, 8) by making treaty rights clearly in the public's enlightened self-interest. While academics quickly constructed language that excused racism on the part of working class students, the ultimate conclusion that gives a robust strength to multicultural education is that it is good for all of us, on the ground, in real life. We did not have to be urbane or liberal to learn this. Treaty rights taught us that in Wisconsin in practical terms, even as they taught native kids that sovereignty meant much more than symbolism or political notice; those rights put a real dent in the historic poverty and unemployment problems. This was true across the nation as tribes reasserted sovereignty (Johansen 1978, 205). Superficial opponency was, at times, transformed into a win-win classic conflict resolution victory, only at the expense of predatory elites who profit from racial tension and division. The few who clung to overt racism were increasingly regarded as rhetorically flatulent, not as defending the interests of the hard-working whites.

Joe Rose, Director of Native American Studies at the small college from which I earned my Peace and Conflict Studies degree, is a Medewin Medicine Man, and mentored me in the Anishinabe way, which is centered, balanced, and uses nonviolent communication and persistence to engage in conflict. He introduced me to Grandfather stones — small concretions rounded to spheres by the action of Lake Superior and findable in the littoral waters of the Bad River reservation. He assured me that if I picked up a Grandfather stone in "a good way," that it would be permissible. I asked humbly and put down tobacco as I walked and waded the shoreline by Joe's home and kept a Grandfather stone as a talisman, a small smooth sphere representing a peaceful way to engage. It now sits on an altar in our Whitefeather Catholic Worker house, a sort of a shrine to Larry Cloud Morgan, and is no longer in my feretory medicine bag for just me, but available to all who come through our door. It tells me to focus, to remember the wisdom of Whitefeather and his ways of resolving conflict, even when provoked by the brutality of the state or of specific people. It reminds me that the Anishinabe way won the hearts and minds of the people in Wisconsin by nonviolence and dogged persistence. It serves as a mnemonic that connects peace and justice to the laws of the land and behavior of a people.

In the master narrative, nonviolence makes wethers of rams, geldings of stallions, capons of roosters, eunuchs of real men. This disrespect of one's manhood is a problem for some in the history of social struggle, especially for those uncertain of what manhood is. The stories of warrior and warrior-culture men and women using nonviolence in powerful ways can reach into our master culture and offer an alternative to boys and girls. They can admire a different kind of warrior, a warrior who wins victories with and for the people, but not by creating new classes of victims and not by shedding other people's blood. This new warrior is a powerful example, one worth shining lights on. The master narrative can be countered vigorously and the warriors can be understood in new ways. "The history of Chippewa Treaty Rights is a story about identity, sovereignty, and political resistance" (Loew 1997, 713). The nonviolent warriors preserved and enhanced identity and sovereignty through a combination of traditional and political resistance, evolving in the process and making the new synthesis even more powerful.

Questions of law and nonviolence weave in and out of most of these stories, as legality is a poorly understood construct by many people. The tension in the law, the unresolved questions, persist and, in many of these campaigns, provide the opportunity for nonviolent actionists to enter the legal world via the door of criminal defense to an act that they didn't believe was illegal. If we break a good law for a good reason, or if we break a bad law, we have entered the world of the law and we may, if we are competent, brash, tenacious and sacrificial enough, change the law. When Rosa Parks sat down and was arrested, it took a year, but the U.S. Supremes found in her favor. When the ancient chiefs signed treaties, their people only benefited some seven generations later. When the U.S. signs and ratifies international rules of war, those dispositive laws find their way into the U.S. military code of justice and into the laws that govern rules of warfare in every branch. All these laws are available to the nonviolent resister. And so, for example, last evening I risked arrest at a local military recruiter while I was holding a poster that depicted a poor little Iraqi girl, foot blown off by an American bomb, in the arms of her uncle. If I go to court I will cite U.S. rules of engagement and will note that civilian casualties are out of bounds, and that a little girl is a complete civilian, since the U.S. military law rules that civilians who perform roles that have "no parallel" in civilian life may not be protected (Haig 2005). This little girl and all her fellow wounded and killed Iraqi children are protected by our military's own laws, just as Rosa Parks was protected by her country's laws, but it wasn't that way in practice until someone took it into the courts via acts of nonviolent civil resistance. Indeed, this is a great deal of what motivated Daniel Ellsberg as he realized that the war in Vietnam was mostly killing civilians and was being reported as killing enemy combatants (Ellsberg 1972, 237).

So those connections go far beyond northern Wisconsin, of course. When the Shuar and Achuar indigenous nations of the Ecuadorian Amazon sent delegates to Washington, DC, and Houston, they brought a simple, elegant, clear message about these connections, part of which was, "the Shuar and Achuar people of the Ecuadorian Amazon want it to be know that the position of our communities is no to oil exploration, no to dialogue and negotiation, no to deforestation, not contamination, and no to all oil activities" (French 2004, 144). Wonderfully, this resistance is not only growing, it continues to advance toward robust and effective nonviolence. Indeed, the natives from Ecuador in particular have become so powerful as a large (30 percent) minority that, even from the economic bottom of their nation, they have helped destabilize four governments between 1997 and 2005, three of which have fallen (Reuters 2005, online).

These stories belie the image of the bloodthirsty savage so integral to the master narrative. Nonviolent power feeds into these stories and these stories enhance nonviolent power. Even the cremains of these old master narratives are corrosive to humankind; it is helpful to show them false again and again by reading new stories into the record. The record, of course, is made in families, in schools, in the media and in society's background gabble, so we are each a part of the corrective process as we spread these stories of native nonviolence versus imperial brutality as they occur.

This issue is global, this issue is about each of us and this issue is as basic as issues get in our world. It is a struggle between two worldviews and they are mutually exclusive. If we support the Shuar and Achuar peoples, the Anishinabe, the G'wichin and other indigenous peoples, we will change our lifestyles, our political programs and our very laws. This is at the heart of it all and, in the beginning, I thought it was only about a few walleyes. Movements all over the world continue to learn from the accounts of events and thinking of the American Civil Rights Movement; there is still a motherlode from which we can draw sustenance, strategy and success (Festle 2004, 10). We can all grow into an understanding and into activism that can make the transition to a world we want. The stories give us the power and resolve.

Sources for Part Two

Black Hills Alliance. *The Keystone to Survival: The Multinational Corporations and the Struggle for Control of Land.* Rapid City, SD: Black Hills Alliance, 1981.

Carawan, Guy, and Candie Carawan. *Sing for Freedom: The Story of the Civil Rights Movement Through Its Songs.* Bethlehem, PA: A Sing Out Publication, 1990.

Chernus, Ira. *American Nonviolence: The History of an Idea.* Maryknoll, NY: Orbis Books, 2004.

Durham, Michael S. *Powerful Days: The Civil Rights Photography of Charles Moore.* New York: Stewart, Tabori & Chang, 1991.

Ellsberg, Daniel. *Papers on the War.* New York: Simon and Schuster, 1972.

Environment News Service. "Nobel Peace Laureate Urges Congo Basin Forest Conservation." http://www.ens-newswire.com/ens/may2005/2005–05–18–02.asp, 18 May 2005.

Festle, Mary Jo. "Listening to the Civil Rights Movement." *Gay & Lesbian Review Worldwide,* Nov/Dec2005, Vol. 12 Issue 6, p10–15, 5p.

French, Hillary. "Linking Globalization, Consumption, and Governance." In: Worldwatch Institute, *State of the World 2004.* New York: W.W. Norton, 2004.

Gregory, Dick. "Nonviolent Protest or Eyetooth Revolution?" In: Estey, George, and Doris Hunter, *Nonviolence.* Waltham, MA: Xerox College Publishing, 1971.

Haig, Lieutenant Commander Clyde A. "Discretionary Activities of Federal Agents Vis-à-Vis the Federal Tort Claims Act and the Military Claims Act: Are Discretionary Activities Protected at the Administrative Adjudication Level, and to What Extent Should They Be Protected?" *Military Law Review,* Spring2005, 183 Mil. L. Rev. 110, LexisNexis: proxy.lib.pdx.edu.

Harding, Vincent. *Martin Luther King: The Inconvenient Hero.* Maryknoll, NY: Orbis Books, 1996.

Hastings, Tom H. *Nonviolent Response to Terrorism.* Jefferson, NC: McFarland, 2004.

Johansen, Bruce. "The Reservation Offensive." *Nation,* 2/25/1978, Vol. 226 Issue 7, p204–207, 4p.

Jones, LeRoi. *Blues People: The Negro Experience in White America and the Music That Developed From It.* New York: William Morrow, 1963.

Katz, Michael B. *The Undeserving Poor: From the War on Poverty to the War on Welfare.* New York: Pantheon, 1989.

King, Jr., Martin Luther. *Strength to Love.* New York: Harper & Row, 1963.

Lewis, John. *Walking with the Wind: A Memoir of the Movement.* San Diego: Harcourt Brace, 1998.

Loew, Patty. "Hidden Transcripts in the Chippewa Treaty Rights Struggle: A Twice Told Story Race, Resistance, and the Politics of Power." *American Indian Quarterly,* Fall97, Vol. 21 Issue 4, p713, 16p.

Nagle, John D., et al. "Overcoming Wilsonianism: American Conflict Resolution and Ethnic Nationalism in Eastern Europe and the Former Soviet Union." In: Byrne, Sean, and Cynthia L. Irvin, *Reconcilable Differences: Turning Points in Ethnopolitical Conflict.* West Hartford, CT: Kumarian Press, 2000.

New, William, and Loucas Petronicolos. "Spear Fishing in Wisconsin: Multicultural Education as Symbolic Violence." *Race, Ethnicity & Education,* Feb2001, Vol. 4 Issue 1, p5–27, 23p.

Reuters. "Ecuadorean Police Beat Indians back from Congress." 17 Nov 2005, online: http://www.alertnet.org/thenews/newsdesk/N16639383.htm.

Schock, Kurt. *Unarmed Insurrections: People Power Movements in Nondemocracies.* Minneapolis: University of Minnesota Press, 2005.

Simon, Paul. "Social Significance of Non-Violence." *Presidents & Prime Ministers,* May/Jun2001, Vol. 10 Issue 3, p3, 2p.

Ting-Toomey, Stella, and John G. Oetzel. *Managing Intercultural Conflict Effectively.* Thousand Oaks, CA: Sage, 2001.

Umoja, Akinyele O. "1964: The Beginning of the End of Nonviolence in the Mississippi Freedom Movement." *Radical History Review,* Winter2003 Issue 85, p201, 26p.

White, Jack E. "Killing the Dreamer." *Time Europe,* 3/31/2003, Vol. 161 Issue 13, pA40, 1/3p, 1bw.

Part Three

Gandhian Nonviolence; or, Industrialized War Meets Mass Liberatory Nonviolence

I believe it is much more, that it is a "one-edged philosophy" which cannot easily be used to defend or advance injustice, and which is of value only if tested in the real world. When I came into the pacifist movement in 1948 the concept of nonviolence as a method of change was new to the United States, the direct result of Gandhi's teachings and actions in India. Historically nonviolence had been seen either as an expression of the Gospels, or as a variant on the stoic philosophy of Marcus Aurelius. But neither the Christian nor the stoic teachings gave us a method to deal with injustice except through endurance. This was fine if I was the one suffering, but it did not provide a way to stop you from inflicting injustice on a third party. The Christian could choose to endure great injustice — but what of the non–Christian who had done nothing to merit the suffering, and sought relief from it?
— David McReynolds

Is nonviolence merely a Western construct, a legacy from the peace churches that sprung up across Europe some four centuries ago in response to the endlessly destructive wars on that continent? After all, the backbone of many peace and justice initiatives in the U.S. is its Quaker, Mennonite and other peace church rootstock. While this egocentric view is understandable, the roots of nonviolent struggle come to us at least equally from Eastern thought and action. Indeed, the joining, weaving strands of

Judeo-Christian tradition, ancient Greek philosophy and various Eastern spiritualities have produced a confusing but effective synthesis for those seeking a method of conflict management that can work, even against state terrorism and tyrannical domination.

In *The Republic*, a bedrock of Western philosophy, Plato has Socrates, in accord with Glaucon, determine that, most assuredly, "we have arrived at the conclusion that in the perfect State wives and children are to be in common; and that all education and the pursuits of war and peace are also to be common, and the best philosophers and the bravest warriors are to be their kings" (Plato, 291).

Gandhi offered the world significant alterations to these assumptions.

First, no kings. He — for all his charismatic leadership — struggled to cast himself out of the individual leadership role, one he regarded as a poor paradigm. Indeed, one might argue that he was the template for the most recent form of research into a productive and transformative leadership style that has been associated with vision and charisma. Transformational leadership seeks to change the individual, not merely prompt obedience or followship (Northouse 2004, 169). This was always Gandhi's goal and style.

Second, war would no longer be possible for the people who subscribed to a Gandhian philosophy. Conflict, yes. Struggle, assuredly. Campaigns for justice, frequently. But not war.

Third, gender roles would be done away with.

Plato and Socrates dreamt up ways to control others; Gandhi dreamt of each controlling herself and himself even as one submitted to the will of the community, the ashram, the village of compassionate relatives and neighbors. His wisdom, though emanating from a culture even older than the ancient Greeks, was indigenous. He certainly saw the weaknesses in himself and in society, in all religion and in philosophy. Most ironically, he was the industrial revolution's answer to industrialized warfare. He industrialized peace even as he spun cotton at his wheel a half-hour each day. He industrialized nonviolence even as he berated the Indian princes to their faces at the opening of Banaras Hindu University in 1916, saying that freedom for India could not come until after they had stripped themselves of their illusions of power, of their jewelry, and hold it all in trust for their countrymen (Sood 2002, 16). Then, unlike many other philosophers, he put his notions into play.

Further, from *Crito*, Plato's further dialectics that honored his mentor Socrates, he has Socrates saying, *Why, my dear Crito, should we care about the opinion of the many? Good men, and they are the only persons who are worth considering, will think of these things as they happened* (Plato 2002, 19).

Gandhi, on the other hand, cared enormously what the masses thought, since they were his only hope for the success of nonviolence in the face of British arms and control. Gandhi was interested in persuading, motivating and mobilizing the masses. He cared not at all that he may have been opposed in his initial beliefs by masses as long as he was able to continue to outreach to them and to act to prompt them to think and to act themselves. He had little interest in saving his own spiritual self if he could not bring along his people and if, indeed, his people weren't just wealthy Hindus, weren't just wealthy Hindus and Muslims, weren't just Hindus and Muslims, but were in fact all Indians and even all British. Unlike Socrates and Plato, Gandhi was even more ethically demanding of the individual, that s/he not only act properly and nonviolently, but that s/he convince others to do so as well. This moves theory to action and back again, forming a praxis the world had not previously seen.

The greatest historical figures of East and West seem to come at times of greatest societal upheaval and they are the individuals who somehow develop the skills to sense the incoming waves and ride them in. The Surfer Royalty. This is not to claim that these individuals do well for themselves in terms of wealth or power, but that they grasp the movements aswirl and sense the patterns and the power and give humanity the ability to understand the world in both its permanence and its morphing power. There are those who seem to somehow get the meaning of really important concepts, trends and historically significant occasions, even as they generally ignore the fashion, the shallow, the fleeting and fluffy.

Industrial war system versus mass liberatory nonviolence

The dawn of the industrial age — or, some might say, the start of the sunset of humankind — was, we are all taught, at or around 1750. By 1793, Napoleon brought masses to war with his levee en masse, the first universal conscription. Then came the Maxim gun, and the Gatling. Just as the industrial age with its various internal combustion engines had made society ripe for the mass production that Henry Ford would discover and develop, and just as masses of workers were drawn to the new factories, war, too, took on the aspects of industry. And just as the individual conscience challenged the warriors of East and West, and challenged the religious East and West, so too did the thinking about peace naturally move from the lone soul refusing to fight others to the notion of mass liberatory nonviolence. To all this was added the asymmetry of the invaded indigenous peoples in their homelands struggling for dignity under the boot heel of the industrialized war machines of the empires. The colonial system must have looked nearly impervious to those who closely examined its overwhelming firepower.

Elihu Burritt, an American craftsman and auto-didact, was a member of various peace societies that were wrestling with the onslaught of industrialized war machines and the mass conscription that provided the manpower to run them. He founded the League of Universal Brotherhood as the Mexican-American War began in 1846. Burritt proposed, in the mid–19th century, that people power could stop war, even the U.S. Civil War. Indeed, membership in the LUB required a pledge to withdraw support from *any* war (Bennett 2003, 32). He didn't call it people power; he used the language of the day and asserted that an international union of Christian workers could, through the strike, stop the horrific wars that had plagued humanity — and Europe, and the nascent United States for such a long time. Europe had been tearing itself apart and the U.S. seemed to be following in the European model, at war with the indigenous tribes, at war for liberation, at war again with the Mother Country, at war with Mexico, still at war with various tribes, at war with itself, at war with the tribes again and again — clearly the model of conflict management was anything but different, and it was getting worse. Burritt saw the Gatling and he saw mass conscription; he saw the U.S. act as empire in its ripping of territory from Mexico, and he proposed a religiously inspired and oriented peace alternative of massive noncoöperation.

His proposal was duly noted.

Later, his work would come before Tolstoy, who noted its influence — and wondered why Americans were so little influenced by such a thinker. Influence, however, works in mysterious ways. Burritt may have been ineffective in his day, but his fine idea passed through the Tolstoy filter to Gandhi, who essentially modified it and applied it to his struggles in South Africa and then India, calling it satyagraha and *hartal*— soul force and mass noncoöperation. The thetic best from several threads of tradition, then, wove into a fabric the world had hitherto not seen.

Leo Tolstoy was something of a contemporary of Gandhi's, older but actively offering his observations to the world as Gandhi was most hungry for such thinking. In another great society, Russia, which was also on the cusp of massive change, Tolstoy struggled to influence what he accurately perceived to be a sea change in the old monarchical system now ever-more irrelevant and outdated in his beloved homeland. He felt the needs of the oppressed vitally, sharply, accurately enough to write cogently about them, and he yearned for changes that would enable them to be treated with dignity, yet he sensed that the changes would likely produce as much indignity and oppression as he saw in the land of the czar. He hoped to teach the people that they already knew how to treat each other well, that they already had compassion and faith, and that they could choose non-violence.

In one of his short books, *What Men Live By*, we might find clues to Tolstoy's success and his failure. His stories within stories were a master-ful use of the art of the storyteller's craft and he engaged the world in his tales. This little book is, in the end, a book about the angel Michael, how he falls from his incorrect knowledge of divine will, and of his redemp-tion and his lessons at the hands of humanity (Tolstoy 1886, 50). Tolstoy's peasants and working people teach the mighty of heaven about love, com-passion, and about limitations on freedom and license. Tolstoy wished to use his literary abilities to show his fellow Russians that they had the abilities to do things in God's way and to make them both effective and ethical.

He hoped that, and he wrote stories with that moral, with that com-mon person point of view, but in the end he failed to convince his coun-trypeople. He watched the aborted revolution of 1905 turn violent, get crushed and drive even more deeply into the scarred psyche of the lead-ership. Gandhi observed from afar, as he contemplated his role in South Africa, as he discerned what Russia might teach him about approaching massive social change.

Albert Schweitzer, science and civilization

A bit younger than Gandhi, who was born in 1869, Albert Schweitzer was born in 1875 in Alsace. Schweitzer threw his lot in with the most belea-guered of humanity, with the most trampled of the Earth, and yet he was culturally accomplished in every important European way; he was a world-class pianist, a medical doctor and a philosopher. When he and his wife were relatively new to Africa in 1914, war broke out in Europe, he was essentially a prisoner of war, ludicrously, and was actually forbidden to practice his medicine. He wrote. He discoursed on the progress of civi-lization, which, he saw, peaked with the beginning of science and also began a decline, now manifest in the outbreak of war. Little did he know at that time that World War I, ugly and industrial as it was, only showed the world a dress rehearsal for the main act, which was to break out 21 years later with the Nazi attacks on Poland and other invasions.

Schweitzer wrote in 1914 that humanity had benefited from the achievements of the generations but was in the process of squandering that intellectual and especially philosophical and spiritual capital — and the Great War was an obvious marker of that trend (Schweitzer: 146). One might argue, in fact, that Schweitzer was ahead of Gandhi in his expressed antiwar attitudes.

Gandhi, just leaving Africa for home in India, was still in his nascent-to-middle stages of political and philosophical development during the war, and actually stopped his resistance to the British empire during the war in order to play fair. The British, of course, responded to the increasing restive yearnings of the Indians with the despised Rowlatt Acts, which codified and worsened the oppressive wartime conditions just as India was expecting relief. Gandhi controlled the explosion by transforming it to nonviolence, and still the British failed to appreciate that he was saving them. Indeed, when just three British colonists were killed, General Dyer responded as so many lazy warmongers have done in history: he killed the most vulnerable, the nonviolent, the available civilians. He ordered the massacre at Amritsar. The timing was abysmal and India was in full revolt. It was the first time Gandhi told them to just leave, to drop their mendacious rhetoric about India's inability to self-govern. He called for *hartal*, a full noncoöperation and a cessation of societal functioning. He was so impressed with the total strike that he made a rare claim that if the *hartal* were complete, nationwide, and absolutely nonviolent, India would be free within the year. Of course, the nonviolence broke down, as it always does in just enough dribs and drabs to contaminate the campaign and provide the oppressor with the excuse for a crackdown. Gandhi eventually called off the campaign until such time as Indians were ready to act in concert, with nonviolence.

Gandhi's legacy: his greatest achievements

Eulogizing Gandhi, a French diplomat offered the prophetic: *His greatest achievements are yet to come.* From the use of nonviolence in gaining against apartheid in South Africa to liberating India, Gandhian nonviolence has gone on to achieve an enormous legacy that will continue to grow. The liberation and creation of Ghana, Zambia, Tanzania, the American Civil Rights movement, the liberation of the Philippines, the Velvet Revolution, the Baltic states and the fall of Slobodan Milošević all contained major elements of Gandhian mass liberatory nonviolence. And in innumerable smaller struggles around the world, we the people continue to act inspired by Gandhi's example, sometimes successfully and sometimes without discernible progress. We learn. We study our mistakes and our victories and we try to incorporate those learnings and improve. It all began with Mohandas Gandhi and he was fast to note that nonviolence for each of us, and for each society, is a different proposition than for any other individual or society: *Nonviolence of two persons occupying different positions will not outwardly take the same shape* (Bartolf 2001, 60).

In one little campaign in northern Wisconsin, as we tried to shut down the thermonuclear command center, we offered nonviolence where it had never been offered before. We tried to learn about Gandhian methods and we reflected on our efforts and the results, though the reflection process was not as significant as was the planning and execution of the next action, which I believe was an error that kept that campaign stuck and less effective than it could be. But the history of that issue — Project ELF (Extremely Low Frequency) — goes back to the 1950s and the offering of nonviolent resistance goes back to the summer of 1983.

At one of the early nonviolent resistance actions — Palm Sunday, 1984 — we planned to use a ladder constructed by Mike Miles, patterned after the ladders used at women's peace camps to scale fences around bases. The ladder was hinged and could be brought to the fence and flipped over. I had arrived earliest and was walking around, preparing for our get-together. Paul Bergschneider, the man who ran the facility as a civilian contractor, approached me and said grimly and threateningly, "I'd advise you to stay away from that fence today, or you'll get hurt worse than you can possibly imagine." With that, he turned and walked back into the compound.

This was a man who, when we had brought a rope that was as long as a Trident submarine and used it to encircle the compound, confiscated the rope and handed me back a few feet of it — tied into a hangman's noose. He had gone out of his way to be both personally and professionally unpleasant over the years, making statements such as, "I don't want my grandchildren to be speaking no Russian." His threats were somehow quite credible.

I wondered if we would get beaten, shot, or what, and his threat was with me as everyone arrived, as we assembled and as we went forward with our planned service and act of nonviolent resistance. I didn't share his threat with anyone else, not wishing to dampen the sweet tone of gentle, joyous confrontation of the war machine, but it stayed, working in my emotional background, worrying me more and more. It wasn't a phobic — irrational — fear, but felt healthy. After all, psychiatry even names a fear of feces — coprophobia — which seems more like a sensible fear, but has no phobic condition named for fear of arrest or fear of incarceration. That is normal; a fear of getting grabbed, wrestled into submission, painfully handcuffed and shoved into a police car seems to be such a deep and common fear that people will allow their governments to commit mass murder of innocents rather than risk such consequences. I grew more determined to do the best nonviolent outreach I could.

Six of us planned to climb over the fence. When Mike and Jimmy Miles brought the ladder out and flipped it over the fence flawlessly, I butted in line to be first, not wanting anyone else to take the risk that Bergschneider's warning had elevated, especially since I hadn't shared it with anyone and was thus, I felt, bound to take the announced risk, whatever it might be. I scanned the buildings and their roofs, looking for snipers — this was the height of the Reagan Cold War and paranoia wasn't entirely out of line, especially with a snarled warning.

I went over the fence, climbed down the other side, and was simply cuffed and stuffed into the "pony" — the word the deputies then used for their squad cars. No shots, no beating, just an arrest as we had been assuming all along. I was quite relieved and joyful, a feeling I hadn't expected from getting arrested, and it was quite a lesson to me about expecting the worst, hoping for the best, and being thoroughly grateful for minor consequences when major disasters were logically expected.

What Bergschneider did for me was to give me what felt for a long while like a life *lagniappe*, days of grace that set me much more free. I didn't die or get hospitalized, and was given the gratuity of a longer life, which liberated me to give much more, since I had felt internally as though I was risking everything in going over the fence. In fact, I am not sure I would have entertained the notion of a plowshares action at all had he not mortally threatened me that day. Surviving existential threat is probably always similarly liberating and, in some senses, only deepens the power of nonviolent resistance it is meant to attenuate. Dave Dellinger spoke of experiencing something similar in Danbury prison, as he grappled with his fear of always being in such trouble and taking such risks, finding himself failing at normal life because his conscience would always be dragging him back into harm's way. He went deeply into himself and eventually made his peace with that, calling it such a watershed survival event that "I called all the rest of my life my bonus years," he concluded.

The good September 11

Gandhi went through his long night of despair and discernment when thrown off the train at Maritzburg, in South Africa, in 1893. By the time he was organizing toward his first act of mass nonviolent resistance, it was just after the bitter turn of events in Russia, when the partially completed nonviolent revolution against the czar was ruined and ended by the actions of those convinced of the necessity of violence. Gandhi had been watching that attempt at liberation as closely as he could from his remove in South Africa, and had made some serious decisions about nonviolence that no one had made before, based on who he was and the world in which he found himself.

And so, when the odious South African laws regarding Indians were passed — that all Indians more than eight years old must register, be fingerprinted, carry passcards and submit to police invasion without warrant — he and others called a meeting on September 11, 1906, at the Imperial Theater in Johannesburg, which was packed with Indians from all regions of the homeland and included many religions and castes (Fischer 1963, 73). They were enraged and Gandhi got them to promise two things, a promise he kept with confidence. First, to resist these laws of a government that "has taken leave of all sense of decency," even to the death. Second, to do so without killing anyone else. The promise was an oath taken before Allah, before God. As his character put it in the Attenborough Hollywood version of his life, "I'm willing to die for this, but there is no cause for which I'm willing to kill."

This was crucial to me many times during the long rural resistance to Project ELF, when I was approached several times, for example, by backwoods government haters who talked boldly of shooting out the ELF lines and perhaps some of the navy personnel or anyone else who worked on behalf of the navy to run that nuclear command facility. I was much more able to answer them with the benefit of Gandhi's summation in mind. It was not a more radical or serious step to kill someone, rather, it was a failure in the proposal, and I was able to convey that to those various individuals. I have no way to know if any might have otherwise engaged in that kind of activity, but more than one seemed quite credible to me at the time.

Before our very first act of nonviolent resistance at the Wisconsin ELF site we invited folks to come up a day or two ahead of time and camp on the Larson's farm — Jeanne and Lynn Larson are two wonderful peace activists from Cable, a tiny town in the far north. Marv Davidov came up and offered nonviolence training from his long experience, which had begun in the Deep South during the Civil Rights movement. He even demonstrated the SNCC position.

As we prepared for the Labor Day 1983 event I worked with Howard Liebhaber, editor of *Northern Sun News*, tying orange survey ribbons we had removed from the ELF survey line in Michigan onto the Trident rope. As we counted out some 408 survey ribbons — one for each potential thermonuclear warhead on each Trident submarine — Howard talked about writing for peace and I was a wannabe writer, so I listened closely. He was witty, endlessly engaging and wonderfully patient with a hippie homesteader with zero formal post–high school academic education. Little did I know this joyous spirit would be robbed from us just nine years hence, October 25, 1992. Howard told one meeting full of paranoid young anarchists who were heavily into the security culture to the point of near-paralysis, "Listen, I'm Jewish, I'm a progressive radical and I'm gay. I think if I can be open about what we are doing, you can too." Howard was not afraid but they got him. His rabbi father found him roped to his kitchen chair, gagged and strangled to death by some sick attacker. I miss him still. Each year some activist is awarded the Howard Liebhaber Human Rights award in Minnesota and his memory is alive in many hearts.

Baby steps away from emnification

During the mid–1980s my father, who was in his late 50s–early 60s, joined me in Washington, DC, for one peace walk to call for an end to the nuclear arms race. I was then doing many nonviolent trainings, including for those who intended to risk arrest the following day at the White House. As always, I was very concerned with the tone and relationships of the event.

As we walked along from the Lincoln Memorial to the Capitol building along Pennsylvania Avenue amidst thousands of others, the youth were mostly joyous in the hot May weather, many wading in the fountains. While thousands of police lined the walk route, the exuberance of the majority seemed to defuse any negative dynamic, which is important for the success of the event. Others in the protest event were less joyful, and a pack of young men came up from behind us in leather and steel, one of them yelling "Pigs go home! Pigs go home!"

"I'll be back in a minute," I said to my father, who needed a hip operation and was walking slowly indeed. He continued to fall behind as I approached the knot of young belligerents.

"Hi!" I chirped at the fellow who was in the center of the young men and who was the one yelling. He paused a half-second in his chant and I asked if I could just talk with him for a second.

"Yeah?"

"Well, my friend, I'm wondering if you are pissed at the cops?" I asked.

"Always," he said, "They're fucking pigs."

"OK, here's the big favor I'm going to ask of you," I said. "I'm one of the people supposed to watch the vibe here and I am worried that some of the cops are rogue cops who might beat or arrest people for no reason. I am wondering if you might consider toning it down a little, since one of the cops might decide that now he's pissed and he's gonna head to a fountain and start kicking ass and hauling hippie kids to jail for a month."

The fellow thought about it. "I don't care what they do to me," he said.

"Yeah?"

"But if you think these assholes are gonna go bust heads I could probably tone it down."

"Thanks, brother," I said. "I gotta go find my father, thanks." I was very pleased with myself, thinking, man, you really worked a miracle on this tough hoodlum. So I turn to walk the "wrong" way back to find my father and, as I step away by just a few feet, the young man starts a new chant, his tweak of his old one that he, I guess, reckons is a major improvement: *Pigs,* **please** *go home! Pigs,* **please** *go home!*

Baby steps, baby steps, I say to myself.

Founder of the field

Mohandas K. Gandhi was the founder of the field of mass liberatory nonviolence and one of the co-founders of the field of conflict resolution. The essential connection at the level of general conflict resolution to Gandhi's work is that he not only practiced good conflict resolution communication, he exposed and confronted latent, structural conflicts, i.e., conflicts that produced casualties but not battlefield deaths. Usually, those conflicts included an elite, often British, class of wealthy and powerful and a poverty-stricken, exploited number of Indians. Gandhi's gift is that he dealt with these conflicts in a manner that didn't itself set off another cycle of violence (Miall 1999, 41).

Nonviolence and conflict resolution

Nonviolence comprises a certain set of actions, beliefs, communication competencies and principles. Conflict resolution comprises its own. Subsets of conflict resolution include negotiation and mediation, and both can overlap significantly with the militant assertive nonviolence. Good nonviolent communication overlaps both almost entirely and, to the extent those skills are employed the efficacy of all is enhanced.

Nonviolence can be conducted using adversarial approaches, and can certainly involve coercion. But if it is coercion that doesn't bluster, that uses excellent nonviolent communication skills and that doesn't attempt to physically harm anyone, it can overlap with conflict resolution. When it is approached as a strictly technical tactic meaning simply a lack of physical harm, it barely qualifies as nonviolence and doesn't overlap with conflict resolution, which has a skill set that assists in achieving nonviolent progress anytime it is employed.

Within the circle of conflict resolution, mediation relates most distantly to nonviolence, or has the least overlap, but certainly a nonviolent campaign designed to either respond to or lead to a mediation is a significant relationship, just as is a nonviolent campaign that leads to or is in response to a failure of negotiation.

Gandhi used I messages, acknowledgement, cultural sensitivity, face-preservation, all available listening skills and a great deal of empathic communication, even as he fielded hundreds of thousands of nonviolent warriors to confront injustice and foreign rule. The relationship between his campaigns and negotiation was clear: "Efforts were made to effect a settlement before resorting to direct action" (Bondurant 1965, 72). This first-rate nonviolent communication helped to set both fields in the firmament of usable styles of conflict communication, even though much of the rest of the world continued — and continues — to frame conflict in language that belittles, personifies and attacks. This kind of language is maladaptive and produces a reaction that is almost guaranteed to prolong rather than resolve conflict. Gandhian language works better.

Of course, his successor in the U.S., Dr. Martin Luther King, said precisely the same kind of thing with regard to negotiation and nonviolence in his famous Letter from Birmingham jail, written there in 1963 in the midst of exactly the kind of interplay about which he wrote: "You may well ask: 'Why direct action? Why sit-ins, marches and so forth? Isn't negotiation a better path?' You are quite right in calling, for negotiation. Indeed, this is the very purpose of direct action. Nonviolent direct action seeks to create such a crisis and foster such a tension that a community which has constantly refused to negotiate is forced to confront the issue." And, in response to failed negotiation: "In any nonviolent campaign there are four basic steps: collection of the facts to determine whether injustices exist; negotiation; self-purification; and direct action" (King 1986/1963, 290–291).

This connection between and nonviolence and negotiation is missed by some, which is scarcely believable but, sadly, understandable, when an adversarially oriented party simply seeks unconditional surrender, the only exception to the connection between negotiation and nonviolence. Gandhi actually had a word for that kind of approach, distinguishing it from his *satyagraha,* or truthforce: *duragraha,* meaning an obdurate clinging to nonviolent action with no hope of negotiation, often based in rage or sullen bitterness, not hope and win-win intent.

Indeed, negotiation is the only path to a peace accord except with unconditional surrender, which offers some insight into how so-called terrorists (often actual terrorists, but not more so than the rulers of nation-states using the term in most cases) are transformed overnight into negotiators from a "political wing" of an organization. This sprucing up of the image only comes, of course, when peace is the goal. As long as bloody, destructive conflict is the unstated (or differently stated) goal, everyone on the other side is a terrorist, and is evil either by overt labeling or implication. Gandhi, like his successors, generally strove to create the image of himself separate from terrorists, but needed to be sensitive to his countrypeople's emotions and would occasionally honor those who engaged in violent resistance to British occupation. This was apparently inconsistent of him, but he was also dealing with enormous pressures from multiple directions on a daily basis, often with screaming urgency and often apparently irreconcilable. That he expressed pleasure at being included in the company of violent insurrectionists in the courtroom of a British judge is not surprising if one thinks of the British imperial presence as utterly objectionable and Gandhi's understandable feelings of being loathe to condemn an Indian independence fighter who was risking life and limb to free India.

Negotiation is always easier, of course, when one comes into the session with a combination of power and yet nonviolence. When violence is associated with strength, more emotional baggage drags down the likelihood that negotiation will proceed smoothly. For example, imagine a Palestine Liberation Organization that had been run by a Palestinian Gandhi instead of Yassir Arafat, and the nascent negotiations for a Palestinian state. Yes, the Gaza Strip and West Bank had been occupied for 20 years by the time the first intifada broke out in December 1987. Yet India had been occupied for more than 150 years by the British, beginning in 1610 with their first outpost as the British East India Company, which assumed total control of the subcontinent by 1769 and, following the Sepoy Rebellion of 1858, all authority was taken by the British government (India, online 2005). It could hardly be said that Indians in general and Gandhi as an Indian had fewer reasons to be violent or angry than did Palestinians at the founding of the PLO in 1964. Gandhi led the Indians to independence with dignity, without hatred for the foreign occupiers and he did it with very few casualties.

Contrast that with the fear and bitterness naturally engendered by the violence on all sides of the Israel-Palestine conflict. Uri Savir, one of the primary negotiators for Israel in the Oslo Peace Process, wrote about meeting, for the first time, his Palestinian counterpart, Ahmed Qurei (Abu Ala): "I wondered whether this man had been directly involved in any of the PLO terror operations against Israel. The profile didn't suggest it, but I couldn't help speculating on whether he had known about the plan to kill Israeli athletes at the Munich Olympics, or about the attacks on Israeli schools in Ma'alot and Kiryat Shmonah, where scores of children had been murdered" (Savir 1998, 9).

Naturally, the PLO negotiators were not only intimately acquainted with the "iron fist" policy of Israel, but had individually suffered on many accounts at the hands of those Israelis, who had completely failed to win many Palestinian hearts and minds over the years. Palestinians suffered through humiliating imprisonment, detention, interrogation, travel restrictions, curfews, closures of educational institutions, unjust taxes, economic hardships and much more (Abu-Amr 1994, 53). Indeed, the later Oslo process talks were held in Israel and one day of them was postponed because Abu Ala was detained for a long time at a checkpoint. Beginning on that footing makes progress slow, if not improbable, for quite some time. Applying the counterfactual, then, and imagining a nonviolent struggle for freedom for Palestinians from Israeli domination and occupation makes such negotiations seem not only more smooth and efficient, but possible much earlier. Nonviolence, applied with Gandhian strength and determination, and using updated lessons from around the world, may conceivably have begun years, if not decades, earlier. Had nonviolence been used exclusively by Palestinians, it is entirely possible they would have been a totally sovereign nation with UN membership long before the turn of the millennium.

In any negotiation, those who negotiate must be clear on whom and what they represent and in whose interest they are negotiating. An activist in a peace, justice or environmental group is not merely negotiating for a concept or a cessation of a bad or harm; she or he is also creating a presence for a group, a coalition or some other organization. A lawyer privately employed is negotiating for her client and for her firm (Mnookin 2000, 296). This double service tells all parties how to approach the negotiator and needs to be acknowledged properly, fully vetted and incorporated into the understanding of interests represented at the table, or the process suffers from potentially hidden surprising developments that can derail progress suddenly.

This is precisely why it is inappropriate, for example, for the U.S. to pretend to broker peace in the Mideast when it is the largest arms supplier to the region. This is why the Oslo process needed to exist independent of the official U.S. negotiator and actually needed to progress past the point where the U.S. interference could push the process back. By the time it was a *fait accompli,* the U.S. could look involved and even appear to be playing an important role; the decision to shake hands on the South Lawn of the White House with the Great White Father Bill Clinton was a smart move, giving apparent credit to an authority who had no authority to make peace, as a bit of insurance against that powerful authority blowing up the process. Had the real table been inclusive to the real power-down groups, the rest of the excellent decisions might have produced an agreement robust enough to withstand spoilers.

Nonviolence is so strange in the Mideast that even rudimentary training is often missing for those who use it. The International Solidarity Movement, for example, trains volunteers only a bit before sending them in harms way, and does not, apparently, advise their volunteers to always tell the truth as a matter of nonviolent philosophy. Thus, for example, our friend for whom we all collected a few thousand dollars and who is the most gentle, nonviolent and fearless man I can imagine, was told, presumably, that Israel would not let him in to be an ISM volunteer if they knew he had been there before. He lied to Israeli customs officials as he was attempting his second stint for ISM in late July 2005 and they turned him away as a security threat. This is *prima facie* evidence, of course, and simply psychologically inappropriate and ineffectual. Basic nonviolence training should always include an instruction for honesty, if not in overt announcements, certainly in response to questions of those in power, with whom one must negotiate. Lying will produce mistrust, the opposite of what nonviolence produces. Our friend lied harming no one and intending no one any harm; indeed, he lied in order to be able to risk his life protecting innocent Palestinians as he had done the previous summer for several months in absolutely heroic disregard for his own safety and a remarkable understanding of the Israeli Defense Force. He came home to talk to my students within 36 hours of his return from Nablus and we literally were crying and we surrounded him to support his own spiritual crisis at the violence and disregard for life he had witnessed first hand. He is a natural nonviolent interpositioner and yet ISM failed to offer him the most basic lessons in getting into the country for the second time. It could be said that Phil would have been turned back for telling the truth, yet, as one nonviolent actionist said when she heard about it, *How much worse could it be?* In other words, how would have telling the truth hurt more than the double damage of telling a "white" lie, getting turned back, and establishing that ISM could not be trusted? How is this going to redound on ISM volunteers in the future? Trust is easy to break and very difficult to repair.

CHAPTER 7

Blood, Oil and Nonviolence

When the first Gulf War erupted, Michele Naar-Obed joined a growing group of peace activists who began to focus on the connections — now painfully obvious — between oil and conflict.

Oil has had a relationship to blood, to conflict, since the advent of the internal combustion machine and the growing need for imported oil. The increasing connection to the addiction to the biggest proven supplies in the world — those in Saudi Arabia — has proceeded from supplying the King with military assistance so he could suppress his own rising tide of popular discontent with whatever violence necessary, to the attacks on the U.S. by al-Qa'ida. Indeed, the boots on the ground of the infidels during Desert Shield, Desert Storm and after led to Osama bin Laden's declaration of war against the U.S., and then even against civilians in the U.S. He declared that *fatwa*, he said, for their apathetic refusal to slow and stop their government's acts of injustice against Palestinians via the billions of dollars in U.S. aid to Israel, the killer sanctions against Iraq (during which Saddam never missed a meal and the poorest died from lack of medical care and rudimentary sanitation), and the massive aid to Saudi royals and other corrupt rulers in the Arab world.

As long as the U.S. is pathetically dependent on the 262 billion barrels of proven Saudi reserves, and as long as it can get away with chasing after oil with its military, it will go to war for oil. That trend is worsening, that trend is made deeper and more vicious with each act of violence committed by the U.S. against Muslims, who are more and more convinced that the only hope for their independence from the U.S. juggernaut is more war, more insurgency, more sacrificial attack on the U.S. military. Further, since the U.S. uses its military to slaughter Muslims, any means used by any group acting against the U.S. will be acceptable to more and more people; the opposite is true when violence is used against nonviolent or virtually nonviolent forces, whether governmental or nongovernmental. Indeed, when the Front de Libération du Québec kidnapped and executed Québec Labor Minister Pierre Laporte in 1970 their popularity went from a majority to scant, as the Canadian government was not seen as a brutal oppressor (Carter 2000, 51). But attacks by al-Qa'ida are seen as just retaliation in the Muslim world more and more.

Into this dynamic, then, a control rod of temporary short-term fixes might be lowered to relieve the pressure, the hot conflict, and it might buy time for our society to become sustainable in both its energy usage, resource distribution and conflict management — tall orders each, but crucial all.

Energy conflict researcher Michael Klare describes the need for a paradigm shift that will enable our nation to take constructive steps to handle our energy needs with nonviolence (Klare 2004, 187), and there are more specifics that would contribute to that potential transition. A short list of these fixes might include:

• increased subsidies for public transport
• increased subsidies for bicycle use (individual consumer tax deductions and rebates, path construction)
• increases in gasoline taxes
• increased purchase taxes and annual fees for each vehicle based on inverse relationship to mpg and converting externalized costs to internalized
• end to foreign military aid entirely
• end to all aid to governments sanctioned by UN for human rights violations
• end to U.S. military forward basing, foreign basing, power projection
• increase in funding for utilizing available principled conflict managers in peace negotiations
• increased funding for peace and nonviolent conflict management research and development

Looking at conflict with an open eye on resources can reveal a history rich in lessons and altered in perspective, mostly because ideology has papered over the true motivations. For example, examining the events that led to the 1967 war in the Mideast might convince the student of history that it was actually a war over water. Israel had designs on the entire Jordan River basin, including the tributaries, and other nations — Syria in particular —

were making moves to control the flow. Indeed, the minor conflicts that broke out leading to that war were almost entirely over water rights that each nation interpreted as favoring itself (Hastings 2005, 106).

Like H. L. Mencken's dictum to follow the money — which has helped to look more honestly at campaign finance reform in the U.S.— that viewpoint regarding material resources may help us resolve conflict much more easily than looking at ideology.

International regimes and nonviolence

Regimes of international laws, treaties, protocols, conventions, accords and agreements are being researched and understood, both from an effectiveness standpoint and a regime-building perspective. These regimes can operate as multistate agreements, bilateral treaties or global law. The lawless heads of American jurisprudence are making a mockery, literally, of international law — one has only to read Attorney General Alberto Gonzalez's infamous 25 January 2002 Memorandum to the President, in which he called the Geneva Convention on the Treatment of Prisoners of War "quaint" and "obsolete" to understand the true depth of U.S. juridical depravity on this (Gonzales 2002, 131).

One could argue for this and many other reasons that it is increasingly important to involve non-state actors in these agreements as the war on terror is replaced with a nonviolent approach to all terror activities. The history of such regimes regarding international and transnational relations is something that could benefit from an examination of Gandhi's final dream, the *Shanti Sena*, or global peaceforce. He died days before a planned conference to begin the regime of practices and institutions that would have produced just that.

Conflict over environmental problems, trade issues and armed conflict has produced a large corpus of such regimes over the past century or so, but what makes some robust and enforceable and some mere paper tigers or even piles of scoria — slag left behind by the triumphal reassertion of hypernationalism we see on so many sides, led by the U.S. reaction to 9.11.01? Shifferd suggests it is the lack of regimes that meet the interests of armed conflict management that prevents a vigorous regime of armed conflict prevention. Gandhi showed interest and intent in meeting those needs, or at least some of them, with his *Shanti Sena* dream. Other elements of such a regime include the entire corpus of international agreements that proscribe war, certain arms, configurations of arsenals, use of some kinds of weapons in certain fashions, and provision for available negotiation environments and services to conflictual parties.

Missing also in many hoped-for results in controlling and replacing armed struggle is the so-called bicycle theory of updating agreements to make them work better and better as conditions teach and morph (Sjöstedt 2003, 91). Why did the ban on war passed in 1929 fail? It was not tested until it was too late; when Italy invaded Ethiopia, the world failed to enforce the pact against war and that incipient regime failed. Nonviolence can make it work much better because it offers the hope for alternative methods of group-to-group conflict, something which will happen whether it's banned or not.

CHAPTER 8

Philippines, Timing and Training

Few cases in the history of nonviolence offer such clear lessons on the counterfactual of violence and on the efficacy of training as does the example of the February 1986 People Power revolution in that country.

Ferdinand Marcos had been promoted by the U.S. and supported in exchange for Marcos's support for the U.S., especially in the form of allowing the U.S. to keep ongoing ports and airports for the forward-based U.S. military. Clark Field and Subic navy base were the gateways to the Pacific Asia theater and Marcos was defended stoutly by the U.S. for more than two decades.

During his final decade, he became more and more militaristic and oppressive to his own people, at times declaring martial law and generally suppressing all dissent. All that decade, the Filipina nuns and others were doing nonviolence trainings that were preparing the Filipinas and Filipinos for liberation. Some 90 percent of the population there are Catholic and the primary social struggle for the decade preceding liberation was led by nuns and others who kept it nonviolent. Of course, the New People's Army, a communist guerrilla group, had been attempting violent revolution for years and Marcos swatted them down easily.

But the hundreds of thousands on the *Epifamio de los Santos Avenue*, the 10-lane arterial thoroughfare in Manila, interposed between the Marcos army of tanks surrounding the presidential palace and the tanks of General Fidel Ramos, who had announced his opposition to Marcos and who had begun his own violent uprising after the crooked election that even long-time Marcos supporter Ronald Reagan was forced to condemn

(Diokno 1991, 24). The interposition, conducted by a population versed in nonviolence, was completely successful, with no mortalities. It was evidence that training and discipline could overcome violence on all sides, even between two sides spoiling for a fight.

CHAPTER 9

Modern Buddhism and Gandhian Nonviolence

In ancient Buddhism, the names of Gautama the Buddha and Asoka, Buddhist philosopher king of India, are two standouts for nonviolent leadership. Asoka's amazing governance was the high point for India back in 268 BCE, all the way until Gandhi's nonviolent revolution. Asoka had battled his way to the crown and ruled with nonviolence, ordering the construction of stellae inscribed with rules of *ahimsa*, even including vegetarianism — beginning with himself (Esler: 62).

Like Jainism, Buddhism subscribes to a version of *ahimsa*, or harmlessness (Gier 2004, 52). Moving that further toward Gandhian nonviolence means helping to stop violence and promote nonviolence, very different, actually, from merely refusing to participate in violence. In the Buddhist view, nonviolent resistance is a holding action, meant to say no to hurtful practices, while activists also repent for those practices, and while they unpack the root causes of those practices, and as they attempt to reclaim a moral culture through transformational work in a social context from the grassroots (Kaza: 85).

Like Dr. King's essay from a Birmingham jail, this notion of a phased process of transformation is one that might correspond to a plan for a change in culture — or, perhaps, only the change of one practice. It does seem to have the advantage of the promise of an alternative, though, interestingly, the alternative comes after the resistance instead of ahead of time. To the extent that these steps can inform each other as they are approached concomitantly, each will be more effective.

The idea that the entire campaign begins with repentance is logical. Thus, offering a compilation of offerings of repentance, or developing a common statement of repentance, or holding a repentance ritual may be clear and helpful places from which to begin.

Then, as the engaged Buddhist analysis describes, it is time for an offering of nonviolent resistance. This may take the form of a blockade, or a refusal to coöperate, or any creative interference with the offensive practice. If, say, the practice involves cutting trees in an ancient forest, the resistance may involve a treesit. If the offensive practice is the readiness of a nuclear arsenal, the resistance may involve physically, carefully dismantling a component of that arsenal. If the practice is racial hatred, the resistance might include a mass of joyous singers interfering with the message of hate, or it could include a silent blockade of the radio studios of a station carrying programs that promote hate. The resistance options are limited only by the creativity of the human mind, which is essentially boundless.

Counter-recruitment

As the Bush regime wades into a bloody second term, it is becoming increasingly clear that activity must grow and grow more serious. To that end, the Portland Catholic Worker is starting to act like a CW community — we are vigiling at one of the recruitment centers. Another CW and I made a leaflet to give to recruiters. The title is "Truth in recruiting: an appeal to conscience," and the front cover includes military coffins and a recovering soldier with a prosthetic leg. We give them to anyone heading into the station, including potential recruits. The inside text and photos contrast the recruitment message (happy, camaraderie, macho fun) with photos of little Iraqi girls, one of them crying confronting two U.S. soldiers, one of them in pain, missing her leg. It's graphic, it's meant to directly counter the recruitment message and it also contains a panel with a message directly to recruiters:

to recruiters
Call to conscience
   When you joined the military, you were younger, more naive, more easily led (just like the youth you hope to recruit into military "service").
   By now, you are well-informed about the atrocities associated with war. You have friends, buddies, tight companions who have been ruined by violence. We can agree that our national policy with regard to Iraq is much like that of Vietnam and is a major error that is needlessly and shamefully costing both nations the flower of their youth. Most of the people on Earth agree that the occupation is immoral and unhelpful.

There comes a time when the violations of our consciences are too overwhelming to ignore. That point is painful. That point involves questioning basic relationships in our lives. That point almost always means contemplating huge personal changes in order to feel good and right about ourselves.

That point is now.

Please think of your spirit, of your relationship to your own sense of what is proper and right. We stand prepared to help you. Declare your independence from a corrupt administration that is sending off wonderful young Americans to do very dirty work and to die or be wounded psychologically, spiritually and perhaps physically. We want to honor you. Help us do that.

Resign recruitment and tell truth.

Once I leafleted in the snow in Eau Claire, Wisconsin, for an hour before and during morning shift change, and again at the end of the day shift, at a large construction company that had been awarded a contract to construct buildings and upgrade old buildings at the thermonuclear command post in the northwoods. I stood many hours in the frozen cold, snow drifting down, hands losing feeling, hands hurting, and I thought of Jim Wallis's essay on commitment and conflict management methods he wrote in his introduction to his book, *Waging Peace.* He wrote of a soldier sitting in the cold on a hill thousands of miles from home, prepared to die for his people, and asserted that it was hard for him to imagine how to convert to a peace system until peace people displayed that kind of commitment, that level of sacrifice, for nonviolence. As I thought of that, leafleting in the snow was not so difficult. Similarly, handing a message of challenge and hope to a military recruiter is not hard when one considers the alternative: more of the same. That is a very poor alternative indeed.

Sources for Part Three

Bartolf, Christian, ed. *The Breath of My Life: The Correspondence of Mahatma Gandhi (India) and Bart de Ligt (Holland) on War and Peace.* Berlin: Gandhi-Information-Zentrum, 2001.

Bennett, Scott H. *Radical Pacifism: The War Resisters League and Gandhian Nonviolence in America, 1915–1963.* Syracuse, NY: Syracuse University Press, 2003.

Bondurant, Joan V. *Conquest of Violence: The Gandhian Philosophy of Conflict.* Rev. ed. Berkeley: University of California Press, 1965.

Carter, Neal, and Sean Byrne. "The Dynamics of Social Cubism: A View from Northern Ireland and Québec." In: Byrne, Sean, and Cynthia L. Irvin, *Reconcilable Differences: Turning Points in Ethnopolitical Conflict.* West Hartford, CT: Kumarian Press, 2000.

Diokno, Maria Serena I. "People Power: The Philippines." In: Anderson, Shelley, and

Janet Larmore, eds., *Nonviolent Struggle and Social Defence.* London: War Resisters' International, 1991.

Esler, Anthony. *The Human Venture: The Great Enterprise: A World History to 1500.* Englewood Cliffs, NJ: Prentice-Hall, 1986.

Fischer, Louis. *The Life of Mahatma Gandhi.* New York: Harper & Row, 1963 (original 1950).

Gonzalez, Alberto R. "Memorandum to the President." In: Brecher, Jeremy, Jill Cutler, and Brendan Smith, eds., *In the Name of Democracy: American War Crimes in Iraq and Beyond.* New York: Metropolitan Books, 2005.

Hastings, Tom H. *Power.* Lanham, MD: Hamilton Press, 2006.

India: http://www.geographia.com/india/index.html.

Kaza, Stephanie. "Keeping Peace with Nature." In: Chappell, David, ed., *Buddhist Peacework: Creating Cultures of Peace.* Boston: Wisdom Publications, 1999.

King, Jr., Martin Luther. In: James Melville Washington, ed., *A Testament of Hope: The Essential Writings and Speeches of Martin Luther King, Jr.* New York: HarperSanFrancisco, 1986.

Klare, Michael T. *Blood and Oil: The Dangers and Consequences of America's Growing Petroleum Dependency.* New York: Henry Holt, 2004.

McReynolds, David. "Philosophy of Nonviolence." http://www.nonviolence.org/issues/philosophy-nonviolence.php, accessed 29 June 2005.

Northouse, Peter G. *Leadership: Theory and Practice.* 3rd ed. Thousand Oaks, CA: Sage, 2004.

Plato. *The Republic.* B. Jowett, M.A., trans. New York: The Modern Library, unknown.

Plato. "Crito." In: Mallick, Krishna, and Doris Hunter, eds., *An Anthology of Nonviolence: Historical and Contemporary Voices.* Westport, CT: Greenwood Press, 2002.

Savir, Uri. *The Process: 1,100 Days That Changed the Middle East.* New York: Vintage Books, 1998.

Sjöstedt, Gunnar. "Norms and Principles as Support to Postnegotiation and Rule Implementation." In: Spector, Bertram I., and I. William Zartman, eds., *Getting It Done: Post-Agreement Negotiation and International Regimes.* Washington, DC: United States Institute of Peace Press, 2003.

Sood, Madhu. *Gandhi: Messiah of Peace.* New Delhi: Roli Books, 2002.

Tolstoy, Leo. *What Men Live By.* Mount Vernon, NY: The Peter Pauper Press, unknown, original 1886.

Part Four

Radical Disarmament; or, Plowshares-Style

And he shall judge among the nations, and shall rebuke many people: and they shall beat their swords into plowshares, and their spears into pruninghooks: nation shall not lift up sword against nation, neither shall they learn war any more.
— Isaiah 2:4

The steady increase in the destructive capacity of small groups and individuals is driven largely by three technological advances: more powerful weapons, the dramatic progress in communications and information processing, and more abundant opportunities to divert non-weapon technologies to destructive ends.
— Thomas Homer-Dixon (Homer-Dixon 2004, 135)

It was a cool morning, May 28, 1985, when I awoke in my car. I drove an old '76 Ford Pinto and was sleeping in the back, when I still had keen hearing. There were perhaps 20 of us sleeping in vehicles, tents and in bags in the woods, awaiting the dawn of our next step toward disarming the U.S. nuclear machine — beginning with our little piece of it in our backyard. It was an unlikely place, in the far northern boreal forest of Michigan's Upper Peninsula amidst the balsam fir, black spruce, hemlock, cedar, quaking aspen, balsam poplar, white birch, white spruce and white pine. Even more unlikely was that we were at a U.S. navy facility some 40 miles south of Lake Superior in the middle of the state forest in the middle of the Upper Peninsula of Michigan in the middle of the continent of North America — a long way indeed from the oceans hiding the nuclear submarines with their omnicidal cargo of thermonuclear weaponry.

Project ELF — extremely low frequency — was the command facility that the navy was expanding from Wisconsin into Michigan. With the ELF transmitter operational, the U.S. could orchestrate a nuclear first-strike against the Soviets. Without, the U.S. could not. A decapitating first-strike capability, of course, was inherently unstable, making the worst disaster on Earth more likely. When an opponent is operating with weapons of highest value completely vulnerable to an offensive attack, there is a powerful logic to use 'em or lose 'em. With a first-strike capability pointed at them, the Soviets were essentially forced to be prepared to launch their nuclear arsenal in the event of a launch — or perceived launch — of U.S. nukes.

This makes the entire world more at risk from the arsenal built by U.S. taxpayers' income tax, an arsenal begun in absolute secrecy without democratic consultation, which went from merely in violation of international law to literally the primary threat to life on Earth. That threat is hidden in silos and bombers and mostly on board submarines under the command of this facility in our woods. We could not let that stand. The moral leadership of the world had been calling the leaders of nation-states to disarm nuclear weapons for decades by then — Albert Schweitzer spoke from Africa, Jawaharlal Nehru was insistent from Asia, and Women Strike for Peace founder Dagmar Wilson told the Seventeen-Nation Committee on Disarmament in the Palais des Nations in 1962 that they were "constantly concerned with national security, national sovereignty, national prestige. All these outmoded ideas must be abandoned.(In your hands lies the fate of the human race" (Swerdlow 1993, 198).

In 1969, when the system was first built in Wisconsin over the objections of the citizens, the navy promised to "dismantle and remove" the entire darn thing "as soon as testing is completed." During the 1970s, no politician in Wisconsin favored it. When Reagan was elected, there was a concerted effort to get it upgraded into Michigan, bucking the more than *80 percent* of the citizenry who had voted against it in every county in the Upper Peninsula in referenda. We felt as though we had the backing of the electorate as we continued to act to stop this atrocity against life, against decency, against democracy.

Earlier, the year before, in 1983–1984, we had one-by-one pulled each and every survey ribbon and survey stake placed in the forest of the UP by the navy-hired surveyors. Some areas had been desurveyed several times. We were serious, we were nonviolent, and we were determined. People from Michigan, Minnesota and Wisconsin had joined weekend after weekend and the dismantlement went on and on. Children were pulling down ribbons. Elders were wading soggy ground and yanking up stakes.

A "stakeout" community was formed and out of that grew a community of blockade and trespass and finally a community of disarmers.

I could barely hear the sound of distant motors, but I knew they were coming to us in the back country on those gravel roads. I jumped out of my bag, out the back hatch of the Pinto and walked over to Charlie Turvey's van and knocked. "Charlie, I hear them coming." I heard some rustling inside, a little groan or two, and the sound of the door mechanism fiddling. The door opened a little and a blond shock of rumpled hair poked out. "I hear vehicles," I said. Charlie nodded and Joey, his wife, said, "Oh dear." They were all tucked into the van, Charlie, Joey and their two sons. Charlie was planning to risk arrest and Joey was not looking forward to Charlie's capture and confinement.

Joey, Charlie and many others had already been opposing that nuclear navy command center for years. We weren't just going out on a whim or an urge and risking arrest willy-nilly. There were those who had been working against this Bad Idea for some 16 already.

I walked on, waking up everyone and, as they got up, got out, stretched and shivered in the early morning mist as the rising sun burned in slantwise through the pines, the vehicles started arriving.

Charlie, Kurt Miron, John Sherman-Jones and Jeff Leys had built a roadblock at the drive to the navy facility, which was nearing completion at the end of the new half-mile drive. The roadblock was composed of some aspen poles placed into holes and repacked. It was a symbolic effort, fashioned from sticks we cut from trees that the navy's contractors had cut to build this nuclear command facility, the Michigan portion of the world's largest radio station. It would have taken a worker probably 15–20 minutes to dismantle, at the most, if he had simply gripped one, moved it forcefully back and forth to loosen it, and taken it out of the hole, and then repeated for the six or seven poles, none of which were more than six inches in diameter and all just set in soil with no concrete.

Instead, the lead vehicle, which was a tow truck, decided to make a dominant, forceful impression on us all as we wandered up to the symbolic "peace antenna." He turned around to back in and rammed the poles with his thick metal rear bumper. It wasn't his most brilliantly conceived plan.

The truck broke off a couple of the poles and, because he was moving against them so hard, the driver actually managed to make the truck jump a bit. As it churned backward violently, one of the aspen poles broke off higher and the truck rammed up over it, grinding to a halt on top of the pole, tires spinning in midair as uselessly as all the arguments for nuclear weaponry. The tow truck was stuck, unable to go back or for-ward. The driver and the navy officer both cursed and the sheriff deputies tried to look uninvolved. It was not the most impressive U.S. nuclear forces moment. Their assault on the passive peace antenna was literally hung up.

In a while, they had jacked the truck down off the broken pole and the four peace fellows stood quietly in front of the remaining peace poles, which were strung together by string festooned with photos of loved ones and messages of peace.

During all this, I tried to outreach once again to the navy officer, telling him that the facility, after all, was in violation of international law and that we were only being good citizens — our very own government was the scofflaw, not us. We were only calling out that tension in the law. During those days I did a three-hour per week peace and justice radio program on WOJB (Wisconsin OJiBwa, a tribal station) and frequently on that program referred to one or another element of the campaign to shut down this navy nuclear command facility. The naval officer inter-rupted me as I was offering this explanation to say, "I know your argu-ments, I get tapes of your radio program every week for my listening enjoyment."

The lieutenant commander from the navy then asked the deputies to arrest our four peace antenna builders, which the deputies did, and our friends were taken to Ishpeming, Michigan, for booking and jailing. The rest of us, who had been up late around a roaring campfire together, went to Republic, Michigan, for breakfast.

After our meal together, I told Mary, Gerard, Stella, Metta, Joe, Bubby, Crystal, Greg and the others that I was off to do some reconnais-sance and I'd cut down one of the navy poles the next day. Everyone hugged and we parted, everyone but me toward their homes in Michigan, Wisconsin and Minnesota. The Michiganders would care for the jailed resisters after they were booked.

This was my first act of direct disarmament in the context of a move-ment. I went out to the woods, looked around, and cut down one of the poles that the U.S. Navy had planted in an 56-mile giant F-shaped configuration through portions of four state forests in the Upper Penin-sula, back in 1985, on Memorial Day. I just couldn't bear to wait another day. Happy holidays.

It was a ceremonious event for me. I first found a pole that, once felled, wouldn't be across a road or put any cable on a road. It was back into the woods enough to be isolated. I donned my ribbon shirt made for me by friend Sandy Lyons and my Guatemalan headband from friend Paul Heinrich and I prayed to the Creator to give me the strength I would need. I planted some Mandan corn, variegated colors and sacred to Native Americans, in a circle around the pole. I sang some peace songs and began to cut with my trusty swedesaw, a quiet 36-inch blade handsaw I had used to buck up countless sticks of firewood for my cabin over the years. About halfway through I heard a scout plane and bucked it for the woods, reaching the jackpines in this high ground just seconds before the plane flew on its security run down the line. I continued the cuts, dropped the 45-foot pole in a great crash, which made the cable strain and literally plow a furrow as the 18-inch butt end was dragged back from the tension of the line, which was thick as my wrist. Nuclear swords into plowshares.

I cut off the top six feet of the pole, which, once decapitated, snapped back right over me to straighten out the cable, bowling me down the hill and bruising my shoulder. I was thrilled not to be decapitated myself. I packed out with the pole over my shoulder, saw in hand, and stowed it in my old Pinto and drove to Marquette to friends. There I cut up the pole into pieces and gave them out as souvenirs, saving three (one of those three sits on my library bookshelf in Oregon now). Leaving the pole pieces, I drove back to Ishpeming and did jail support for the four friends, all of whom were still being processed. The deputy was a funny northwoods cop who put the guys in the hallway and went back to his office. He poked his head out once and said, "Hey, you guys, don't forget I've got you surrounded!" We all laughed. I softly told them that I had already cut the pole down and generated some raised eyebrows and big smiles. I had to leave the lads in custody after it was determined that the judge couldn't be reached until the next day for bail determination. I went back to the friends in Marquette where we finished the day in Presque Isle Park on the Big Lake, drinking beer and eating great pizza. The next day I went to the congressman's office, plunked a piece of the pole on the desk, told what it was, and said, "Don't bother calling the sheriff; I'm on my way there now," and did the same just a few blocks away at the sheriff's office. This was all new to me and enormously frightening and liberating all at once.

My lieutenant investigator, Cookie, had a fine time with me after he realized that I was serious about waiving my Miranda Rights, which he tried to read to me every few minutes, as he looked up from taking my statement. He'd say something like, "Are you sure you want to be telling me all this," and I'd say yes. He excused himself finally and when he reentered the office I said, "They didn't know about it yet, did they?"

"No," he answered, realizing that I had guessed he had called the navy to check on my story. "Would you mind heading out there with me?" he asked. We drove out in his car and walked in to where I had cut down the pole. On the way, I showed him where the fallen logs, covered with moss, spanned the soggy bottom of a tiny valley between poles. We walked to the downed pole and Cookie took photos. For one photo I put my foot on top of the top of the pole, just like a safari hunter with his foot on the downed lion. I kidded with Cookie, "Got my buck." We laughed. We saw the navy fellows, three of them, arrive at the top of the hill and I shouted to them where they should walk to avoid getting soggy. Of course, this meant that they couldn't go that way, or they'd be taking the advice of a peacenik hippie enemy.

They all arrived with wet shoes, soaked socks and stained dress whites. It was pollen season for the jackpines and thus their wet shoes and soaked whites were glued with yellow dots.

The lieutenant commander was furious, naturally. He assured me they would prosecute to the full extent of the law and I said I was counting on it. We all parted and Cookie took me out to coffee on the way back to Marquette. I never wore cuffs or felt as though he regarded me as a "real" prisoner; clearly the mood of the people of that region was anti-navy for the most part, since the navy had run roughshod over the notion of process and democracy. I've certainly been treated like a criminal when arrested elsewhere.

I cycled in and out of jail as I awaited trial and worked that summer as the wilderness guide at a Jewish camp in northern Wisconsin. After returning from a trip to the Boundary Waters Canoe Wilderness Area I found a letter from Phil Berrigan, whom I had met some time earlier and who was a part of my inspiration to try one of his plowshares actions.

The letter began with a *wie geht*'s friendly introduction, chitting and chatting, and then got into the real substance — what was up with my action? What was my spiritual basis? What moved me to do this? Did I consider myself part of a movement? Who was I, after all? I smiled through the entire letter and wrote Phil in return, letting him know that I had no real Plowshares pedigree, that I was just challenged by him and by the Silo Pruning Hooks, and had undergone some radical changes when those four good people were sentenced to 18, 18, 10 and 8 years in federal prison for their act of hammering a nuclear spear into a pruning hook on Armistice Day, 1984. I told Phil that my act might be more analogous to the jar of pickles that says "kosher-style," instead of kosher. I was plowshares style, not a real Biblically based Plowshares actor with a history of radical Abrahamic roots and motivation. As a born-again treehugging pantheist, it seemed to me to be the best I could do. As a student and attempted practitioner of nonviolent rhetoric, I deeply appreciated Phil's approach *and* hoped to expand the message, carefully, to make it a bit less exclusively Abrahamic and a bit more friendly to the humanist, the secular, the Buddhist, the Sufi or whomever. I especially wanted to join Phil in building ties between rhetoric and just power, between the symbology of language and nonviolence that he and Dan had done so well, and that is all too rare (Gorsevski 1999, 446).

Phil, his brother Dan, and six other radical religiously driven peace actionists had begun the movement on September 9, 1980, with their foray into the General Electric nuclear nosecone manufacturing plant in King of Prussia, Pennsylvania, where they had smacked down a nosecone for the Mark XII warhead destined to be installed in missile silos in the high plains of the western U.S. (Laffin 1996, 48). Their act initiated a wave of such copycat actions worldwide, a key difference between their action and most others.

Like the draft board raids initiated and conducted by the Berrigans in opposition to the war in Vietnam 12 years earlier, the Plowshares actions not only spurred others to do similar high-risk actions, but also inspired others to take smaller risks in the name of peace and even disarmament. While it is foolish to assume or really even to hope that such an act of symbolic damage is going to take away physical power from the warmakers or move political power to the peacemakers, it is important to realize how much potential power there is in such an action; when I did my first Plowshares action in 1985 I was keenly aware that the first one had prompted the nonviolent resistance campaign to shut down the military side of Honeywell. Of course, power comes out of a combination of money, might and popularity (Barry 2000, 158). The act of taking a risk of many years in prison — and, in some cases, physical risks of beating or even lethal force — can rally others to throw their best actions into the mix, into the campaign. Indeed, when I joined Donna Howard in another act of direct disarmament 11 years after my first, one of the organizers said, in reaction to hearing the plan for the first time, "Well, this will destroy the trespass campaign." I didn't think it would and I challenged us all to make the act more inspirational and invitational than scary and alienating.

I think we generally succeeded. Like a little burst of ignition, a Plowshare action is a bit of fuss without much direct power. But if that ignition can engage the slow but sure worm gear of nonviolent mass action, a longer but much more powerful process has been launched.

My first act of direct disarmament was the 14th, and my second was the 57th. The first I did alone, though not by choice, and the second I did with one other person, though we sought others during our months of discernment. Sure enough, two others did the same action in the same place some three years later.

The plowshares movement is ongoing with some 80–90 actions to our credit as of early 2006, and will probably not cease until either weapons of mass destruction are gone from Earth or the human conscience is gone from Earth. Learning how awful the potential is in each of these weapons — and then trying to comprehend an entire arsenal of them — will thoroughly engage anyone who dares to do so. Daniel Berrigan once wrote of them that *In Germany, they brought the people to the ovens. Now we propose to bring the ovens to the people.* Kathy Kelly served a year in Lexington, Kentucky's, federal women's maximum security prison for her acts of going over fences at five nuclear missile sites in Missouri in 1988 and planting corn. At sentencing, she told the judge that she would not comply with the state as it planned and threatened mass murder of civilians, surely Kathy's contribution to the war on terror. She said nuclear missiles, each of them, were the functional equivalent of "Auschwitz to go" (Kelly 1988, 132).

Hopefully, the movement will continue until *all* implements designed to kill others are eliminated from our world. After all, nuclear weapons are only the most efficient killers potentially; small arms kill approximately half a million people annually around the world and wound another 1.5 million (Renner 2005, 123). This ongoing death rate dwarfs all weapons of mass destruction to date. While the need to prevent the use of a single WMD drives many of us in the Plowshare movement, several have used hammers on small arms as well. Our agenda ought to be unambiguous — no guns, no bombs, no explosives, no military weaponry of any kind is acceptable. Sculptor Esther Augsburger, Washington, DC, grandmother of two, did her legal version of a plowshares action on these small arms that commit large harms, gathering more than 3,000 handguns, more than a few of which had actually been used to commit murder, and welding a massive plowshare from the guns, which is on display in Washington. Most of the guns she worked with were the result of a 1993 gun turn-in program in that city. The NRA and others condemned her and her project and she went deeply into her faith to perform her art education activist project, as there were even death threats against some of the police who gathered the guns for her (Lowell 1995, 39). Those invested emotionally in any weapons seem irrationally attached to them and quite threatened by those who would disarm the world.

We violate our consciences each day we don't dismantle another weapon or component of an arsenal. This stark realization may not bring us into the field of action directly, but it at least removes the denial and psychological numbing that Yale University Psychiatry Research Chair Robert Jay Lifton described in his early work on our collective and individual relationship to the overwhelming questions surrounding the use and possession of a nuclear arsenal by our own government (Lifton 1982, 101). Discussing the notions of personal responsibility for our portion of our culture's, or our government's, actions and policies is rare, involves guilt, and must involve strategies by which we can break through, break up and sweep away this numbing. Doing so ought not make it impossible to go on without taking huge risks, but it ought to make it impossible to go on without acknowledging that taking those risks may move us forward faster.

The motives of the Plowshares community remain constant from war to war and identify it as part of the peace movement even more strongly than the antiwar movements, which is part of why it remains marginalized by mainstream media and dismissed by leftists, who support some wars and some armed struggle. In the last interview he gave, the late Elmer Maas — one of the original Plowshares Eight resisters — told the *National Catholic Reporter* that the members of the plowshares movement who were marching in New York along with some 300,000 others in August 2004 were doing so for reasons that included but preceded and went beyond the current movement to end the war in Iraq. He identified global dominance by the U.S. with its array of arsenals in the ocean, on land, in the atmosphere and even in space as the ongoing targets of the plowshares movement and noted that three nuns hammered on one of the many thousands of nuclear weapons in late 2002 to expose the fact that the U.S. still had live weapons of mass destruction at the ready while Saddam Hussein had none (Lefevere 2004, 5). Confronting the hubris of empire, challenging the Manifest Destiny that has been routinely updated since its 19th century belief that the U.S. is destined to control the lands stretching across the continent, extending to the Pacific ocean, and ending all Native American full sovereignty (the Manifest Destiny that now includes Earth and is more complexly described as control by the U.S. military and government for the benefit of transnational corporations) — these are the core of plowshares' motives. Dominance by the few is what the U.S. and its weaponry stand for around the world and the plowshares movement is one of the few movements that explicitly rejects both that hegemony *and* the armed struggle that is seen by many as its alternative. It is one of the even more rare communities that rejects all that and is willing to engage in nonviolent resistance to both at a level that risks a great deal. It is the *only* movement that does all this and enters the bunkers, bases and corporate sources of those arsenals to directly begin what governments ought to continue and finish — the disarmament of all weaponry.

Looking at the government's attitude toward the movement and those in it, one is tempted to ask about the state of freedom and ethical values in the U.S. When Plowshares movement co-founder Phil Berrigan was in prison in September 2001, the attacks on that day allowed the government the excuse to throw this peace elder — he was 77 years old then — into solitary confinement and deny him visitors and even phone calls or written communication. This treatment of a nonviolent old man hurt our hearts, but also filled them with a recommitment. Phil couldn't have issued a more articulate plea for peace in reaction to September 11 than the government did for him. His wife and fellow felon for peace, Liz McAlister, was prophetic then when she described who Phil was and that stripping him of all prisoner human rights immediately following these terror attacks was "the end of all we say and value as a nation" (Duffy 2001, 10).

Using international law to showcase the rogue nature of nuclear weapons and using the illegality of nuclear weapons to promote international law is a natural outgrowth of the work to directly disarm from a logical perspective instead of a religious mandate. The religious mandate is taking its cue from higher laws, divine law, obedience to God, while the rest of us answer to the logic of morals, ethics and, handily, international law as it outlaws various classes of weapons that do objectionable things. Poisonous weapons, weapons that hurt cities, weapons that target protected populations such as civilians are all illegal under treaties that the U.S. has not only signed, but ratified, thus making those laws dispositive in the U.S., second only to (and defined by) the U.S. Constitution. Without international law and the respect it should engender transnationally, peace between and amongst peoples and nations will be much less likely and much harder to achieve and maintain.

Promoting the respect for international law uniformly and multilaterally can operate to change the emergence of positive peace movements and can set a new tone for such struggles (Hartz 2005, 258). When Milošević operated outside international law in the former Yugoslavia, for example, the U.S. was in an inferior position to underscore Slobo's invalid actions, since it was committing its own violative actions. Upholding international law in the U.S. will make enforcing international law around the world much more likely and viable, thus making peace more achievable and sustainable.

Thus, it is likely that using international law might make the direct disarmament movement not only potentially more effective inside the U.S., but might strengthen the respect for that law domestically too. It is so threatening to some that it is forbidden in court to even say the words international law in cases where citizens challenge the military. The aversion of the military to international law is well noted when it does make its way into court cases in respectful, competent ways. That willingness to go to the rules, to go to the very laws under which nonviolent resisters are prosecuted, and to figure out ways in which to focus the attention of the jury on the conduct of the state, is potentially a huge advantage for the direct disarmament movement.

Indeed, when Captain James (no relation) Bush took the stand during my last Plowshares trial and told the jury that, while he skippered a nuclear submarine it gradually became clear to him that he was operating in violation of international law, the air in the courtroom changed. A former commander of a nuclear submarine willing to tell a jury of good Americans that our nuclear weapons are in violation of international law, and that such laws trump local and state laws in the U.S., makes quite an impact.

If enough Plowshares resisters became serious about using international law, the stable of lawyers familiar with that corpus of law would grow and become progressively more effective, presenting a more serious cognitive dissonance face to America with each action and trial.

Staughton Lynd was another person who came to the trial of Donna Howard and me in September 1996, following our act of cutting down three wooden poles that supported the unsupportable — the nuclear command antenna transmitting the Extremely Low Frequency signal to all the nuclear submarines. I had been reading Staughton and Alice Lynd's 1995 edition of *Nonviolence in America: A Documentary History*, updated since Staughton wrote the original in 1966, following his involvement in both the Civil Rights movement — including co-directing Freedom Schools with Robert Moses during Freedom Summer in 1964 in Mississippi — and the antiwar movement — including his arrest at the Assembly of Unrepresented People that met in Washington, DC, August 6–9 (Hiroshima-Nagasaki), 1965 to declare peace with the people of Vietnam (Lynd and Lynd 1996, 12). Staughton and Alice were two of my models and intellectual activist mentors — though neither knew it until I wrote them from the Ashland County jail in the late spring of 1996, inviting Staughton to come testify as to the probability of success using nonviolence.

My thinking on inviting Staughton went like this: If an expert testifies in court, the jury must weigh that evidence. Staughton is certainly an expert in nonviolence, certifiably, with all his degrees, positions, professorial experience and publications. If we were able to conduct what is called a necessity defense (the need to commit a lesser crime in order to avoid a greater crime or a disaster, such as breaking and entering a burning home to save a child you can see crying in the upstairs window, even though there are "No trespassing" signs posted around the home), Staughton could supply the evidence that it was entirely possible that our action might have succeeded in helping to inspire enough civil resistance and political pressure to shut down Project ELF. Key to any successful necessity defense is proof of some likelihood of success and who better to offer that testimony?

When Staughton was an activist history professor in the 1960s, he was blacklisted and could not retain or obtain teaching positions, so he went back to school and became a lawyer. Who better to come help navigate the tricky waters of such a legal case?

I also invited Francis Boyle, renowned professor of international law and author of a book on the elements of mounting a legal defense using international law during civil resistance trials, as well as aforementioned former sub captain James Bush, former Lockheed submarine launched ballistic missile designer Robert Aldridge, attorneys Kary Love (a Boyle protégé and colleague) and Katya Komrisaruk (former plowshare resister who served her time and blasted through Harvard Law School to work as a movement lawyer). Finally, to convince the jury that I had the knowledge necessary to legally act on that nuclear arsenal component, I asked Dr. Kent Shifferd, my mentor at Northland College, to testify as to what I might have known as his student in his Peace Studies program. They all testified, except Staughton, who arrived ready to do so but after one day at the trial said, "They will never allow me onto the stand." Everyone else did get to testify and the judge, a most unctuous man who was ever-hostile to all ELF resisters, forbade only Staughton. It seems that nonviolence was the only frightening aspect of all the expert knowledge.

Boyle, his shock of canescent hair and incandescent legal eagle stare clearly outranking the judge, offered brilliant testimony despite all obstacles thrown in his path by prosecutor and judge. He clearly detailed how this nuclear facility was in violation of the U.S. navy rules of warfare. When Captain Bush and Robert Aldridge supplied the rest of the technical knowledge, the case against nuclear weapons was airtight; they are offensive, not defensive, and this component — ELF — made that capability possible. Therefore, we did not interfere with the nation's defense, committing no sabotage.

When the jury heard it all, they acquitted us on sabotage and found us guilty on destruction of property, as we were not permitted to present our defense to that charge, which was simply that ELF, as criminal instrumentalia, was not property at all, but rather much like contraband, and therefore property destruction was not committed. The sentence was three years, but the sabotage carried a 10-year possible sentence, so the lawyers and experts carried the day by all accounts.

CHAPTER 10

The Nonviolence Just Conflict Doctrine

In the Just War doctrine, several criteria must be met before it is acceptable to wage war. In the world of nonviolent struggle, several conditions would be analogous before one engaged in risky civil resistance or other consequential action (doing something that might well cause a loss of a job is certainly sacrificial nonviolence, even though it may not entail risk of physical attack or incarceration). Dr. King alludes to some of these steps in his *Letter from Birmingham Jail.*

•Is there enough of a violation of conscience to make such risk-taking more imperative?

•Have other means of opposition been seriously attempted?

•Is the action contemplated directed at the proper actor or institution?

•Is there a chance for success?

•Will the intended action harm anyone?

•Is the action proportional to the harm being opposed?

Plowshares resisters approach these questions in one of several fashions. Some have tried many paths to protest, for example, nuclear weapons, weapons which are such a profound blasphemous violation of conscience: letters to congresspeople, to the President, to editors; joining groups that oppose these arsenals; petitions; lobbying; persuasion; education; electioneering; civil suit; public dialog and much more. Then they cross the line and kneel to pray for peace on a military base or in the lobby of a weapon manufacturing corporation, or some other act of nonviolent civil resistance. Finally, they take a hammer in hand and ding some nuclear missile component or a warplane or some other component of some arsenal. They are careful to be sure that they are the only possible casualties and to be sure to set it up so there is some reasonable chance of success. Mostly, they know that nothing less robust is even remotely proportional to the violence perpetrated by nuclear weapons; writing letters to the editor about imminent danger from the nuclear arsenals is most appropriately done *after* arrest and incarceration, since it is so hard to imagine a truly proportionate response to an existential threat to all of humankind.

Not even a Plowshares prisoner, but rather a whistleblower, Israeli Mordecai Vanunu can attest to the practice of paying a serious civil resistance price for even calling attention to the existence of nuclear bombs in a country such as Israel. Vanunu, a former nuclear technician, blew the whistle on Israel's secret program and spent 18 years in Ashkelon Prison as a direct result, a dozen of those years in solitary confinement. It strained his very spiritual center and affected his mental and emotional health quite negatively, but he was released, at last, 21 April 2004. If the world had 1,000 Vanunus it would be very hard to run these arsenals. If the world had 10,000 Vanunus, the unthinkable arsenals would indeed be unthinkable, at long last.

As it is, the longer we can claim to wash it from our thoughts, the more firmly does a new image flow in, then. To mark Hiroshima Day 2004, the 59th year since the incineration of a city full of civilians by one bomb, Lisa Hughes and I chalked outlines of her body on several corners surrounding the center of Portland, beginning on the beautiful brick sidewalk across from Pioneer Courthouse Square, in front of Nordstrom's department store. Lisa had made a paper cutout of her body and we had a few big pieces of chalk. We were assigned to a four-block area as part of the Shadow Project, organized by Eric Bagai, and we made perhaps a dozen of these renditions around our area. Each was an outline with chalk rays coming out, representing the shadows of those poor souls in Hiroshima who were vaporized instantly by the bomb and whose shadows were, in that moment, etched into iron, into concrete, into marble, in the positions they were in when that atomic device exploded right where it was aimed: at the civilian center of town. Lisa then wrote *Hiroshima 8/6/45* and I wrote *Never Again* in large chalk letters. As we were doing these, we were met with varying reactions, some excruciatingly telling. Several young people, in their twenties, did not know the reference, some, in fact, claimed that they had never heard of Hiroshima. If there were ever validation for doing these Shadow Projects and continuing this discussion, that ignorance — a direct reflection on the paucity of substantive content in U.S. education, since Hiroshima was the first time atomic bombs were used intentionally on humans — that lacuna in those young people's education was a serious legitimation of this Shadow Project and any other that raises consciousness about the issue. As this nation ponders funding a new generation of nuclear weapons, it cannot efface the facts of its culpability in the use of the original arsenal.

Still, the officials try. Educators are guilty, as are those who have an agenda and run our official intellectual organizations, such as the Smithsonian Institute, which houses the Air and Space Museum, which owns the Enola Gay, which is the airplane from which the original nuclear bomb was dropped over Hiroshima on that fateful August morning in 1945. Stephen Kobasa writes that this airplane, the one in history that represents ultimate evil and homicidal mania, now sits in this museum, its fuselage as scrubbed as its deeds. He and two others properly marked it eight years ago, with their blood and some ashes, for which they were, of course, arrested. "For a brief moment," Kobasa noted, "the plane was like one of those legendary sites of murder which ooze the evidence of the crimes committed there" (Kobasa 2004, 1).

My generation — I was born in 1950 — was raised in the political and moral shadow of that attack. When Roosevelt ordered the Manhattan Project, which produced the first bombs, he did so without even consulting Congress (Thomas 1977, 8). His wartime powers were becoming absolute and the $2 billion spent on developing the first three atomic bombs (the first, Trinity, blown off on 16 July 1945 to test it) was serious money in those days. The only people's representative asked was the president, who made this unilateral decision that still stands prepared to end life on Earth. The Vatican and at least some others immediately reacted to the Hiroshima bombing news with horror and anguish, and we might legitimately assert that, had humanity (or, possibly but doubtfully, even the American people) been asked, this arsenal would never have been developed. And if we had looked at the elements of racism involved — from the first uranium mining to the use on Japanese to the testing in the South Pacific and so forth — we might have rejected the bomb at several key points of realization (Hastings 2000, 31).

It seems we are called to continue to display and describe the evidence or we may slide toward a repetition of the outrage that took an estimated 75,000 human lives in an instant and another 75,000 or more since from the effects of that poison, burning bomb. Every Hiroshima Day is an important marker, like 50 September 11ths. Peace education is obviously more crucial than it seems; we cannot rely on either mass public education or mass media to do what needs to be done.

CHAPTER 11

When Officials Fail Long Enough

From 23 May to 30 June 1978, 149 nations met in the United Nations Special Session on Disarmament, the most sincere effort to disarm since 1932 (General 1979, online). Proposed in 1961 because leaders of many nations were increasingly concerned about the level of international weaponry and the burgeoning international transfer of weaponry, the SSOD took some 17 years to actually happen, during which time the world experienced the Cuban missile crisis, the Vietnam war (during which the U.S. threatened to launch nuclear weapons at North Vietnam unless the North Vietnamese caved in the Paris Peace Talks), and was inching closer to a nuclear showdown first in the Mideast and then on the subcontinent. Stockpiles of nuclear weapons increased from hundreds in 1961—alarming indeed—to scores of thousands by 1978, at which point the entire world was both nervous about superpower relations and justifiably enraged that two nation-states arrogated unto themselves the power and control over the possible end of life on Earth. Not unrelated, world starvation and malnutrition rates are high and have been for decades. In the last part of the 1990s, the sheer number of people starving or suffering from some form of food insecurity had risen to at least 576 million and possibly as high as 1.1 billion (GAO 1999, 2). Possessing nuclear weapons in the light of those kinds of numbers is a crime against humanity even if none of them polluted, even if none were ever fired. We, as a species, simply do not have the right to allow so many to suffer so grievously when massive monetary and other resources are poured into annihilatory weapons of mass destruction. People know this worldwide, with the exception of the U.S., which is particularly troubling and particularly alienating. What right does the

U.S. have to threaten planetary destruction as it burps its way along in chubby hyperarmed self-satisfaction while so many innocent children and others suffer so terribly for lack of simple staples? The people of the U.S. simply do not have those rights and the rest of the world knows that.

While the world achieved zero disarmament as a direct result of the 1978 six-week gathering, the event did alert the citizenry of the world to the danger once again. The previous time that the people of planet Earth had become agitated over nuclear weapons was as a result of the fallout from open-air nuclear testing, something that put radioactivity into the various levels of the Earth's atmosphere as fireballs shot more than 30,000 feet into the air from ground bursts and even more dispersed from air-bursts of these weapons, many as large as megatons each. In fact, the worst, a 58-megaton weapon, actually, finally, seemed to scare the weaponeers and they began to reduce the size and increase the accuracy of the delivery vehicles.

When, in August of 1963, Kennedy and Khrushchev signed the Partial Test Ban Treaty, the peace movement promptly rolled over and played dead until after the UN Special Session of 1978, at which point the most radical of the movement, the Atlantic Life Community in the eastern U.S., began to refocus from the post–Vietnam War stance to the anti-nuclear stance that led to the first Plowshares action. Thus, the dialectic between the people's movements and the global leadership, one motivating and driving the other in cycles that counter the elite profiteers' endless acquisition of more weaponry, more destructive power, more and deeper death culture. Without the peace movement, it is entirely likely that we would not be alive, or that those of us who were would live in abysmal, post-apocalyptic conditions much worse than the Stone Age.

Plowshares and any war anywhere

> It was a great time of challenging Irish complicity in this terrible war (in the court, on the streets, public meetings and celebrations.
> — Ciaron O'Reilly, on the Pitstop Plowshares witness
> (2005 letter to author)

When a country is at war or coöperating in war, plowshares acts are more risky but more necessary. The need to challenge George Bush's war attitudes and assumptions is interesting; the critical necessity of confronting an apathetic and disengaged American conscience is the true battle-ground. Thinking like a terrorist will draw actionists to attempt maximum damage; thinking like a disarmament actionist will bring us to the front lines to wage quixotic yet real battle. The founders of the Plowshares movement, including the Berrigans, are motivated not just by WMD, but by the same logic ascribed to Simone Weil, which is that war is irrational by any standard other than that which serves the elite and which serves society's bizarre image of itself as controlling its universe (Broderick 1991, 110). Plowshares asks us to reassert humility and faith-based human agency. War is evil, twisted, satanic, and the weapons by which it is waged do not belong in human hands. Plowshares attacks violence with robust nonviolence, with varying affect depending on the individuals and small groups involved — some with considerable *brio*, some with sincere somber sobriety — offering direct, transparent challenges to war and to the instruments of war. This is obviously paradigmatic in the context of war.

Homer-Dixon — quoted at the top of this chapter — also notes that, like any complex network, the high-tech becomes more, rather than less, vulnerable to a sabotage component of terrorism, yet one might argue that thinking like a disarmament actionist — thinking about saving lives — means we ought to be less symbolic and more real, taking out more and more of the high-tech weapons and arsenal components in the most vulnerable places. If, for example, we take the ELF actions as a case study, it was literally impossible for the U.S. to launch a first strike nuclear war until they could repair the downed system. Thus, for 24 hours, approximately, there was little or no confidence in the U.S. ability to initiate a nuclear war against any opponent with serious retaliatory capabilities. That, according to virtually all analysts, changes the equations of power and diplomacy, economy and projection around the world. It is possible that the plowshares movement might be better able to initiate discussion and even move to the negotiating table if it got more serious about discovering the choke points — the complex nodes — in the network of military offensive capacity.

But the more universally compassionate plowshares model is opposed to preparation for any war anyplace with any weapons. The plowshares resisters who bang on bombs are addressing mass destruction, but so are the few who hammer on individual rifles, since those individual rifles, taken in aggregate, have almost certainly killed more humans than have bombs. The sheer number of those guns and the ease with which they are used in many conflicts militate a person of conscience toward addressing those weapons of slower-but-mass destruction.

CHAPTER 12

Peace Journalism Prepares Society

The idea is that survival in the nuclear age may well depend on the ability of Americans to muster contempt for official secrecy.
— Sam Day (DeVolpi 1981, 239)

Sam Day was a peace journalist. He was also an antinuclear resister and chronicled much of that resistance. His career as an antinuclear resister began with the famous case of the Morland article, when a young man, Howard Morland, wrote an article describing how a nuclear bomb is made. Sam was his editor at the *Progressive*, a Madison, Wisconsin, monthly magazine of alternative journalism, often investigative. The Department of Justice visited Sam and Erwin Knoll, editor-in-chief, and threatened to arrest the both of them. "They told us that what we had done was tantamount to treason and that, until recently, treason was a capital offense and we should just think about that. So we thought about that and decided to continue our efforts."

In the end, after the magazine weathered a court injunction to stop the presses and other serious assaults on the First Amendment, the higher courts threw out the government's case. Sam's primary point is that secrecy ought to be resisted if we wish to see an electorate — a citizenry — operate in a democracy. To the extent we demystify the military we can control it from a standpoint of informed electorate making wiser decisions. To the extent the military dictates what may and may not be revealed, they arrogate unto themselves the dominant rights to decide. Nowhere is this more polarized than in the nuclear arena and Sam took on the nuclear establishment — military, political, corporate — directly and vigorously.

106

He served time in several jails and a U.S. prison in his "second career as a criminal," as he phrased it.

In a sense, peace journalism launched Sam's nonviolent civil resistance life. In another sense, his peace journalism contributed toward the recruitment that the movement needed and needs, a movement that waxes and wanes as journalism changes the threat perception of the public. As a peace journalist, Sam was on hand for the Silo Pruning Hooks act of Armistice Day 1984 and took photos, later writing a story for *The Progressive* about the act, the trial and the draconian sentencing. Sam might have easily been punished with many years in prison for this risky journalism, but he did so with an anonymous courage that ought to instruct journalists nowadays. Sam began his nonviolent resistance as he was easing out of workaday journalism — his first arrest was on Hiroshima Day 1981 in Chicago at Union Carbide corporate offices. Union Carbide manufactured components of nuclear weapons (Day 1991, 183). Sam was then a year into retirement from his lifelong career as a journalist — including editing the *Bulletin of Atomic Scientists* and *The Progressive* — but before his work with Nukewatch. He would remain a writer until his passing, and some would say he never really retired from being a peace journalist, but rather became a full-time nonviolent resister and a part-time journalist.

When I approached Mike Simonson, a journalist at Wisconsin Public Radio, and told him that he would want to be on hand for an exclusive radio report at a peace activity at Project ELF in northern Wisconsin, I assured him the event would be newsworthy. He knew how transparent the entire nonviolent movement had been at Project ELF — none of the cute surprises that other campaigns seem to enjoy springing — and so he knew that my ambiguity really meant newsworthy. He covered that plowshares action himself and won an Associated Press award for his coverage. I took my cue in some ways from the Jean Gump model, in which she and her co-actionists brought a much bigger media outfit with them to their plowshares on a Missouri missile; a 60 Minutes crew, including Mike Wallace. That segment helped raise the plowshares movement to the national conversation by taking some time on it, rather than simply reporting it briefly in passing.

The misinformation and lack of context is a huge challenge to peace journalists. Greenpeace did a survey and found that the more TV news watched, the more misinformed about Gulf War I. FAIR did several studies showing the same and a study of UK citizens showed that their mainstream-media-informed citizenry often believed, for example, that the settlers referred to in the Palestine-Israeli conflict were Palestinian. They often completely missed the meaning of occupation, assuming it simply meant the land was occupied and had a much stronger picture of Palestinian violence even though most of the casualties were Palestinian (Lynch and McGoldrick 2005, 11). A great deal of what Amy Goodman does on her Democracy Now! program is simply provide context by her choice of topics, interview subjects and questions. Peace journalism can help kick open the doors allowing the voices of nonviolent dissent to be heard accurately for once. When people know a greater perspective than that which has passed muster in the commercial media they are more open to the changes we need for peace, justice and ecological security.

Plowshares inclusivity

While the direct disarmament mode of nonviolent resistance is quite robust and certainly meets the proportional response component of the Just Conflict Doctrine of nonviolent engagement, it is still manifestly inclusive.

Elders can strike a symbolic blow for disarmament — indeed, Sam Day advocated that all elderly peace activists begin a post-retirement criminal career in the nonviolent service of peace.

Plowshares resistance is gender-inclusive, just as all nonviolent conflict methods are. Barbara Deming called nonviolent actions inherently androgynous, fostering the strongest feminine and masculine qualities of the actor (Deming 1984, 229). Thus, plowshares can help not only with inclusivity in the sense of bringing people together, but can change people to become more inclusive themselves.

While the direct disarmament movement has been largely white, the few people of color who have engaged in it have been valorized immensely; indeed, I live in a Catholic Worker house named for Silo Pruning Hooks resister Larry Cloud Morgan, Whitefeather of the Ojibwa.

The plowshares movement has also practiced political inclusivity; there have been socialists, Democrats, and many anarchists. While it is true that all Republicans are former Republicans, that is hardly unexpected when the Republicans have been as pro-nuclear and pro-weapons as almost any group ever has been.

Sources for Part Four

Barry, Jan. *A Citizen's Guide to Grassroots Campaigns.* New Brunswick, NJ: Rutgers University Press, 2000.

Broderick, John. "Uncommon Martyrs: The Berrigans, the Catholic Left, and the Plowshares Movement (Book)." *Library Journal,* 4/15/91, Vol. 116 Issue 7, p110, 1/7p.

Day, Samuel H. *Crossing the Line: From Editor to Activist to Inmate—a Writer's Journey.* Baltimore, MD: Fortkamp, 1991.

Deming, Barbara. *We Are All Part of One Another: A Barbara Deming Reader.* Philadelphia, PA: New Society Publishers, 1984.

DeVolpi, A., et al. *Born Secret: The H-Bomb, the* Progressive *Case and National Security.* Elmsford, NY: Pergamon Press, 1981.

Duffy, Claire Schaeffer. "Berrigan Segregated; Wife Says it's Punitive." *National Catholic Reporter,* 10/5/2001, Vol. 37 Issue 42, p10, 1/6p.

General Accounting Office. "Food Security: Factors that Could Affect Progress toward Meeting World Food Summit Goals." March 1999. Online: GAO.

General Accounting Office. "United Nations Special Session on Disarmament: A Forum for International Participation," 3 July 1979. Online: GAO.

Gorsevski, Ellen W. "Nonviolent Theory on Communication: The Implications for Theorizing a Nonviolent Rhetoric." *Peace & Change,* Oct99, Vol. 24 Issue 4, p445, 31p, 1 chart.

Hartz, Halvor A., and Laura Mercean with Clint Williamson. "Safeguarding a Viable Peace: Institutionalizing the Rule of Law." In: Covey, Jock, Michael J. Dziedzic, and Leonard R. Hawley, eds., *The Quest for Viable Peace: International Intervention and Strategies for Conflict Transformation.* Washington, DC: United States Institute of Peace Press, 2005.

Hastings, Tom H. *Ecology of War & Peace: Counting Costs of Conflict.* Lanham, MD: University Press of America, 2000.

Homer-Dixon, Thomas. "The Rise of Complex Terrorism." In: Martin, Gus, ed., *The New Era of Terrorism: Selected Readings.* Thousand Oaks, CA: Sage, 2004.

Kelly, Kathy. Sentencing statement, federal court, 1988. In: Day, Samuel H., ed., *Prisoners on Purpose: A Peacemakers' Guide to Jails and Prisons.* Madison, WI: Nukewatch, 1989.

Kobasa, Stephen Vincent. "More Lies from a Machine: Revisiting the Enola Gay." *The Nuclear Resister,* 134, 1 August 2004.

Laffin, Arthur J., and Anne Montgomery. *Swords into Plowshares: Nonviolent Direct Action for Disarmament...Peace...Social Justice.* Marion, SD: Fortkamp, Rose Hill Books, 1996.

Lefevere, Patricia. "Catholic Antiwar Activists Join Protests." *National Catholic Reporter,* 9/10/2004, Vol. 40 Issue 39, p5, 1/2p.

Lifton, Robert Jay, and Richard Falk. *Indefensible Weapons: The Political and Psychological Case Against Nuclearism.* New York: Basic Books, 1982.

Lowell, Piper. "A .38-Caliber Plowshare." *Christianity Today,* 10/2/95, Vol. 39 Issue 11, p38, 2p, 3bw.

Lynch, Jake, and Annabel McGoldrick. "War and Peace Journalism in the Holy Land." *Social Alternatives,* First Quarter 2005, Vol. 24 Issue 1, p11–15, 5p.

Lynd, Alice, and Staughton Lynd. *Liberation Theology for Quakers.* Wallingford, PA: Pendle Hill, 1996.

Renner, Michael. "Disarming Postwar Societies." In: Worldwatch Institute, *State of the World 2005*. New York: W.W. Norton, 2005.

Swerdlow, Amy. *Women Strike for Peace: Traditional Motherhood and Radical Politics in the 1960s*. Chicago: University of Chicago Press, 1993.

Thomas, Gordon, and Max Morgan Witts. *Enola Gay*. New York: Stein and Day, 1977.

Part Five

Eroding the War Machine; or, Boycotting War

The next time you hear a politician use the words "billion" casually, think about whether you want that politician spending your tax money. A billion is a difficult number to comprehend, but one advertising agency did a good job of putting that figure into perspective in one of its releases: A billion seconds ago, it was 1959. A billion minutes ago, Jesus was alive. A billion hours ago, our ancestors were living in the Stone Age. A billion dollars ago was only 1 hour and 20 minutes, at the rate Washington spends it.
— War Tax Resistance listserv

Draft resisters have known "insult, outrage, suffering." The movement has been opposed actively by Congress, the courts, the executive branch, and mainstream public opinion. Almost 10,000 anti-war conscientious objectors have been imprisoned. A handful have died. Thousands have been permanently scarred from the effects of imprison and the stigma of a felony conviction. Yet over the years the movement has survived, grown, and blossomed into a force that seriously imperils the very existence of a draft in the United States.
— Stephen M. Kohn (Kohn 1986, 140)

CHAPTER 13

Who Will Pay to Kill Kids?

The handful of war tax resisters stood shivering in the April 15 chill. Most of us, fully clothed, were perfectly warm. Then again, the resisters were wearing barrels and little else. They sported signs on their barrels that made various observations about the Bush budget:

- *Stripped of health care*
- *Stripped of environmental protection*
- *Stripped of human rights*
- *Stripped of civil liberties*
- *Stripped of jobs*
- *Stripped of natural resources*

The barrels were cardboard, the signs were hand-lettered, and the group was somewhat motley, which was the intent. They all carried leaflets or song sheets, which they passed out to passersby and the curious in Pioneer Courthouse Square, the main downtown Portland city gathering place for those who might wish to speak to the public. A high volume, anything-goes square — punked-out kids and random homeless, businesspeople studiously focused on cellphone power meetings, flower vendors and miscellaneous voyeurs — Pioneer Square draws the most pluralistic crowd downtown. It is where people protest and hold forth, where lovers sit on the many steps that double as amphitheater bleachers, and where Very Important People take their downtown powerbreaks in the sun, should there be any sun in this rainforest town.

The contrast between the mass peace rallies, where people say they oppose war, and the tiny demonstrations of the war tax resisters is hard to ignore. Where are the tens of thousands who came out as Bush prepped to invade Iraq in 2003? Working and paying taxes dutifully, for the most part. This demonstration clearly separates protest from resistance. The portamento, easy tonal change from protest to resistance that can occur when a movement is fully integrated and committed to nonviolence is missing in Portland, where civil disobedience is seen as violence, as bricks through windows, as "throwing down" with the cops. The sadness of this can best be appreciated by attending an event where the transition is smooth and the large protest crowd transforms into support for resistance. Being at those events brings a new charge, a frisson of challenge and empowerment, to a protest event that cannot occur when there is no real resistance.

But there is no mention of that at this war tax resistance gathering and annual ceremony in Portland, and certainly no vibe of smug righteous radical superiority one finds in the black bloc actions on occasion; these people know humility because they are pariahs in many ways. They are not the sit-in-the-roadway, mass action brave civil resisters who block shipments of guns in a sea of support. Rather, they are the people who have careers, who have jobs, but who cannot in conscience pay for a regime to bomb and shoot others. They resist by refusing to pay for death and then redirecting their taxes to life-affirming causes instead. They move beyond opinion to belief; belief entails sacrifice, whereas opinion, by contrast, is easy.

And though they stand together on tax day in small demonstrations around the nation, they go out alone when they battle the IRS quietly. Some live around places like Portland, where there is an actual community of war tax resisters; many more live where there is none, and yet they continue to quietly defy the government that demands and seizes the fruits of our labor to pay for war. For those who feel alone, as I have on occasion, it is helpful to reflect on Ammon Hennacy: "When I have been picketing the tax office I did not need a committee to coördinate or regulate me, for I can organize myself. This is what a one-man revolution is supposed to do" (Hennacy 1994, 435). The power of one can be regarded either as immaterial or as the most relevant power of all.

Some practice voluntary poverty, choosing to earn less than taxable income so that they can resist paying for war legally. They didn't drive; they biked or took mass transit. To pay for a private vehicle in Portland, where the cost of living is quite high, is impossible unless one is earning more than the taxable minimum.

Most, however, earn more than that minimum and use a variety of means and methods to resist. Some withhold only the portion of their taxes that the federal government spends on the Pentagon. Some are determined to keep the war machine from obtaining one *afghani*, one *zloty*, one red cent. Some are quite public in their resistance. Some are low profile, preferring to make the IRS earn their convictions — just as we all earn our convictions, so to speak.

My own record is spotty; I infrequently have the courage to be very public about the years I refuse to pay, simply because war tax resistance might cause me to lose my teaching job and thus might drastically affect the life I've worked so hard to create. Of course, this is precisely true for all those who are much more public in their resistance than I; they are braver, or they are thinking ahead better. Marv Davidov, the old Jewish communist radical from Minneapolis who did so much good organizing for Civil Rights, against the war in Vietnam, and against nuclear weapons and landmines, described the difference between protest and resistance as not so much bravery as planning. *If you want to live in resistance, you have to craft a life that allows for that,* is what Marv declared, and he's right. Still, whether we resist from our personal *kivas* or on the public stage, we are answering to that inner tyrannical conscience in the best way we can.

The choice to resist war taxes never occurs to the vast majority of people — even those who are attracted to a belief in peace, and even including activists — in part because it appears to be a given that, if it were to be an effective tool, more would surely be using it. We are deterred by our fear of the IRS, by our fear of an open-ended invitation to the government to suddenly and without warning intrude rudely into our lives to seize us, confiscate our property, send us in chains to the dungeon. The omnipotence of the IRS is assumed, as though they have computer files that track each dollar and each person and pop up a list of those in violation, which results in consequences of grave and drastic proportion. With that level of knowledge about the dangers of war tax resistance, the choices between being victim or executioner narrow and diminish. We are caught like collaborators in the headlight of our own train of conscience, unable to decide on risky nonviolence and unable to easily coöperate with making war. Feeling as though opposition to war is all or nothing, we find solace in what poet Linda McCarriston declares: *So if you'll excuse me, I'm going to do some psychic maneuvering here, off to the side, and ally myself with the animals* (Moyers 1995, 279).

WTR meets DV: in tents experience

Part of war tax resistance is to choose to fund other struggles engaging in nonviolent resistance to injustice, since the intention of the war taxes are to fund a violent force that is nominally meant to achieve justice. Indeed, as one conscientious objector to the war in Vietnam put it: "The best part of the antiwar movement came out of the Civil Rights movement and merged into the women's movement. Stopping the war was just one part of a broader movement against racism and sexism and economic inequality and environmental shortsightedness" (Tollefson 1993, 209). Redirecting war taxes toward such movements says that we are prepared to fund a different method of conflict management. In Oregon, we've given funds to groups working for indigenous rights in Colombia, for example, in symbolic counterpoint to the U.S. government's massive military aid to that repressive government. Other redirected war taxes have gone to support nonviolent struggle for Palestinian liberation; there are more foreigners involved in nonviolent direct action in Palestine than in any other time in history (Rubenberg 2003, 412).

Another part of what the war tax resistance movement can be about is to connect to other movements that are *for* something, not merely against military spending. That dovetails perfectly with the WTR movement at the instance of redirection.

The first year I moved to Portland we held our war tax resistance meetings in the winter of 2001, preparing to do our April 15 action in Pioneer Square, and I became familiar with the process, which I admire. First, the veteran resisters asked, which local group is doing the most interesting, robust work outside the system for justice? The war tax resistance community had learned about Dignity Village, an intentional community of homeless who were fighting for the simple right to have a night's sleep without being rousted, driven away from wherever they were managing to catch some rest and all the other indignities of life on the streets.

First staking out tents along the waterfront of the Willamette River that runs through downtown Portland, and then moving *en masse* beneath a high freeway bridge as it spanned the river and came into downtown, DV was an exercise in creating pride in being human. The collection of bums and beggars, ill and healthy, quiet and noisy, beaten and straight-backed, were just people. Gathering was easy; street people had been told they were human beings since Genny Nelson founded Sisters of the Road Café in 1979. After establishing that culture of nonviolent communication and conflict resolution in the transient population, eventually, Dignity Village was inevitable. Many others picked up the idea and as people saw that these homeless possessed an analysis about their condition, that they maintained a legal site with no drugs or alcohol, no minors, no violence and that they kept it more picked up than many yards in our city, the sympathy for the villagers increased. It was a long battle, however, and the Oregon Department of Transportation — owner of the land on which DV had squatted — was aggressively moving to get them out of that location. Wherever DV might move, it would cost money for many things, including portable toilets, website maintenance, food, public transportation and so forth. We in the war tax resistance community in Portland decided to offer our resisted funds to DV.

I volunteered to attend the next DV meeting and explain our offer to them. They told me to be in a parking lot at 7 p.m. the next Wednesday, which I did. There were about 25 in attendance, representing about a quarter of the population of the village. Some were clean and decently dressed; most were rough-looking, obviously vets of the street life. All were involved and all were courteous and respectful of group process; they ran the meeting as well as or better than does the peace movement.

At that meeting I met Tim, a young African-American fellow who helped found Dignity Village. He put me on the agenda and when it was my turn I told them that we were a group who weren't paying federal taxes because the money was going largely to fund the military rather than the vital social needs that Dignity Village so clearly represented. I said that we were gathering this money and would award it on April 15 in Pioneer Square and that I would be back next week to learn their decision. They told me the next week's meeting would be in Boxcar Bertha's, just some three blocks away.

When I entered Boxcar Bertha's the following week, most of those who had been in attendance were back, with a couple missing and a few added. When my item came around on the agenda, I quickly recapped and then asked for questions again. A slender man of about 40 who was well dressed for a homeless fellow asked if the money was legal. I said that this was exactly why some groups declined the funds, that the IRS might come and say, well, this isn't your money, it's ours. Someone else asked how often that happened. Not ever, to my knowledge, I replied. Another asked if there would be penalties or arrests if the IRS decided to come after the funds. Not for the recipients, that I know of, I said, just for those of us who redirected our monies. Finally, one woman asked how much we thought we would be offering to Dignity Village.

"$6,000," I said. There was a long pause. Then a homeless man with an eye patch lurched to his feet, a man always struggling, I expect, to find his balance and depth with only one eye. Gripping the arm of the chair, he looked around the room with his one eye and said in his gravelly voice,

"Sounds like a no-brainer to me," looked around at the nodding heads and then at me.

"We will see you at 4 p.m. on April 15 in Pioneer Square," I said. "I'm glad to meet all of you." Tim was the man they chose to receive the check and we had a good ceremony, also giving $600 or so to an Oregon group promoting peace in Colombia. DV used the redirected funds, in part, to relocate from ODOT land to their permanent permitted home on little-use city land.

WTR and Dorothy

In 2005 the Oregon War Tax Alternatives Committee presented two checks to the Portland Catholic Worker to honor the hospitality and non-violence of the Worker in general and the mission of the new community — less than a year old — specifically. The two checks were made out for $2,400 (my redirection) and $1,600 (a portion of others' redirections). The checks were offered to our core community member, Gail Skenandore, who spoke on behalf of the CW community and thanked all the war tax resisters in Oregon who had contributed to making peace instead of war.

Dorothy, we believe, would have been supportive, and even a little pleased with all of this. No one keeps track of national redirections, but it is a safe bet that other worker communities receive some of the funds, since the notion of offering resistance to war taxes is utterly resonant and consonant with the values of the Catholic Worker. Most of the workers live below taxable income in no small part precisely because to pay federal taxes is to pay into war, and the rest of us try to resist the taxes on our incomes as best we can. Many in the WTR movement are CWs, so the connections are powerful in many mutually reinforcing ways.

DC, WTR and the IRS

The international community of those who oppose military taxes had a conference in Washington, DC, in July 2000 at Catholic University. We heard from Germans and Brits, Africans, Indians and more, and we were privileged to hear from James Lawson, the African American who helped begin the most serious phase of the nonviolent Civil Rights movement in the U.S. Lawson discussed the power of economic resistance and linked our tax struggle to the Montgomery bus boycott, the grape boycott, and other pressure tactics, but noted that war tax resistance is special because it moves past legal boycott into civil resistance. And while Quakers refused war taxes from the earliest days of the nation, our most famous war tax resister remains Henry David Thoreau, who spent a grand total of one night in jail for his resistance. His writing, however, was what gave legs to his resistance, and his essay, "Civil disobedience," remains a classic in American literature and political discourse. Judges cite it and resisters cite it. Politicians cower before its challenge: *Any man more right than his neighbors constitutes a majority of one already.*

During one of the conference days we set up a penny poll by the Washington monument, leafleted passersby and then did a peacewalk to the IRS building, where Juanita Nelson led a small delegation of war tax resisters up the stairs to confront the IRS and to declare publicly and to them that all of the delegation members were war tax resisters and were turning themselves in. The armed guards pondered this, went into their building and came out to fetch Juanita, a then 78-year-old African American woman all of five feet tall. She and her husband, then 91-year-old Wally Nelson, had been resisting war taxes since 1948. Juanita went with the guards and we hoped she'd come back out swiftly. She was in the IRS headquarters for what seemed like forever before finally emerging and announcing to the little crowd of perhaps 100 or so gathered with signs and flags, *They don't know what to do with us, so they asked us to go to customer complaints, two blocks away.*

We all laughed. The IRS, who absolutely will pound down the door and charge in at 4 a.m. if you are scamming them with some lame *I don't have to pay taxes because it doesn't mandate it in the Constitution* line, did not wish to appear unfair or like jackbooted thugs out to get ordinary working Americans. Snatching tiny Juanita and a handful of Mennonites and Quakers who are all professedly and provably nonviolent wouldn't do much for the IRS image, so they bailed on the opportunity. This is part of the power of nonviolence. When done right, its vulnerability can be its protection.

Betsy, Randy and home fires

During the war in Vietnam, war tax resistance became somewhat popular; my father was teaching then at a community college in Minneapolis and refused to pay for war. Eventually, the IRS came to him and said, pay up or go to prison. It may or may not have been an empty threat, but my father was, at that time, still supporting my youngest sister and helping to support my mother as they underwent a painful breakup, so he elected to make a deal with the IRS and paid up. This helped me clarify my thinking about the value of resisting and then caving in. I believe there is a great deal of value in that.

How many might resist war taxes if they understood that they might be able to negotiate with the IRS in the end? That is not the popular perception of dealing with IRS agents, after all, who practically smell like slamming metal doors on cages that hold you for years in dank prison cells, beaten once in a while for fun, while your family falls into poverty, your wife finds another man or your husband another woman, your children hate you and your career possibilities slide toward stablehand or bedpan cleaning. If, however, 1,000,000 people resisted and 1,000 cut a deal once the IRS came calling, that would leave 999,000 incomes untouched by the war machine. That would be effective. That would be a movement rather than a cult of conscience. I think there is a great deal of potential value in resisting until the question is called and then choosing to pay up into the war machine. Naturally, that is hard to reconcile with the urgent and nagging demands of conscience, but we ought to be contemplating practicalities from time-to-time. I know of no case to date where the IRS has refused to negotiate with a tax refuser who does so from a principled basis. They have no compunction about imprisoning a Pete Rose, or any other greedy person who has sought to avoid his fair share, but it is much less likely that someone will give away thousands of dollars publicly — the Portland, Oregon group gave away something like $15,000 in 2004 to various groups — and will not be able to discuss a payment program of some type with the IRS if it comes to that.

In the end, obviously, the examen — the daily examination of one's conscience — will crack the intradictatorial whip for those who subject themselves to such a routine, but when we can explore these questions in detail and assess both short and long term effects of actions, we can answer to both conscience and practicality in many cases. Often the self-saving is very different from the self-serving, though the beginner can fail to account for scale and degree in many cases.

Why resist?

Even for hardcore nonviolent adherents like me, I need frequent reminders, here in the land of the free, why it is a bad — unacceptable, in fact — practice to pay federal taxes.

I think big. I think of the U.S. military presence in 150 nations with 800 DoD installations around the world (Johnson 2003, 323). I know that wars are longer when they are intervened on (Hironaka 2005, 130). I know that U.S. military aid to Israel is more massive than to any other nation and that, in order to maintain its strategic power in the Mideast and thus its access to oil, the U.S. will continue to unconditionally fund Israel's own imperialism over Palestinians. I know the U.S. funds the largest nuclear arsenal on Earth.

Then I think small, in the particular. I recall the photo of the old Iraqi carrying the dying young girl, foot blown off by an American bomb, that galvanized the Arab world during the invasion of Iraq. I think of Rachel Corrie; she could have been my student. All the big stories are composed of tiny stories and each one is crucial, as Reverend Bucky Beach, a war tax resister, reminds: "As I write this, someone somewhere is grieving the loss of a child — American, Iraqi, or Afghani. I don't want to be responsible for financing the reasons for their loss" (Beach 2005, 8).

Resistance is ethically mandatory. It is required, at some level, if we ever wish to replace the war system we have with the peace system we dream about. Indeed, it may legitimately be a component in what peace researcher Robert Irwin called nonviolent direct law enforcement (Irwin 1989, 147). When we are being coerced into paying for illegal activity, and when the UN or its courts have found the U.S. in violation (or any government), its citizens may with some validity make a claim that to pay war taxes is to participate in illegal acts.

It is hard to get around the challenge. Recently, I was asked to moderate a discussion following a few films about Palestine. Watching the films made me more and more distraught; it was so clear from the footage that the Israeli Defense Force was generally convinced that they were doing the right thing. It was clear that they were murdering civilians, even children, even committed nonviolent activists such as Rachel Corrie and Tom Hurndall. And it was clear that the violent Palestinian resistance was giving the IDF all the moral purchase they needed to continue, unabated and without apology, the practices of wrecking homes, wrecking lives, and taking that which was not theirs.

Watching the masked gunmen amongst the Palestinians was painful; how do locals stand up to them?, how do the women tell them please, stop, you are wonderful young men but you are not truly protecting us?

Somehow, this has become the international rallying point for pro–Palestinian activists, and is as dysfunctional as it is tragic. Rocks hurt. Anyone knows that and wonders who might be getting hit in the head by these rocks. Watching footage of young men — some little boys, some older teens, some men in their 20s — throw rocks at tanks and at IDF soldiers, is watching one reason the Palestinians cannot generate sympathy amongst other peoples to the extent they should be able to do so. Some of the young men also throw petrol bombs with the obvious intent of burning up tanks and IDF troops. It is war, waged completely asymmetrically, but waged with deadly intent nonetheless. Does anyone honestly think that it's a long leap mentally to imagine any of these young men — who appear to be in the majority of Palestinian youth — strapping himself with explosives and making a deal with Hamas, Islamic Jihad, or al Aqsa, and making his way into an Israeli dance club, pizzeria, or family celebration to murder himself and another dozen, or 30, or 50 people?

Palestinians who throw rocks, it is sad to say, make it less likely that Americans are going to engage in war tax resistance in support of the clearly vulnerable, the harmless, the victims, the nonviolent suffering ones. And yet, seeing the little Palestinian girl in her hospital bed in one of the films, blinded by a bullet from the Israeli Defense Force, crystallizes for me the necessity of war tax resistance and makes me angry at those who profess opposition to U.S. funding of the IDF and yet who pay their federal taxes. "Let them march all they want," said Alexander Haig, "as long as they pay their taxes." Just so.

The little girl, sweet and open-eyed but unseeing, was in her school when she was shot. Guerrillas had been firing on the IDF from near her school and the IDF periodically shot in the direction of the shooters, justifying themselves with computer imagery of such shooters, recorded and visible to anyone. The little girl was in a war zone. The IDF officers interviewed by the filmmaker claimed to be amazed that Palestinians would allow their civilians to be put into war zones, even though the war zones were the neighborhoods in which these civilians lived. The Palestinians were surprised at the inhumanity of the IDF soldiers, who could treat them barbarously. It was like the Merchant of Venice, in which the Christians treated Jews contemptuously, Jews took their revenge in usury and finally in the threat of the pound of flesh, and everyone suffered on all sides, hatred grew between the peoples, and misery generalized by this hate. Everyone's right and justified and hatred and revenge produce a lose-lose scenario.

It is the little girls who pay for the testosterone poisoned vengeance on all sides, and once revenge is in the air, everyone gets infected. War tax resistance is one ethical out; simply stop paying for bullets, for policies that kill, for the weapons that take blood and shear limbs, that put out eyes and blow up babies on all sides.

Marshall Rosenberg, who is Jewish, does some work in Palestine and Israel with his specialty, nonviolent communication. He is clear throughout his work that punishment isn't adaptive; it changes motivations and wounds human hearts. At one workshop in Switzerland, Palestinian and Israelis learned nonviolent communication together and one Sufi Muslim Palestinian, Nafez Assailey, locked his thumb onto Rosenberg's and said, "I kiss the God in you," and kissed Rosenberg's hand (Rosenberg 1999, 185).

That is disarming. Assailey does more good for Palestine and the aspirations of her citizens than do all the fighters who head out at night with rocket-propelled grenade launchers. My insignificant act of war tax resistance was prompted by Rachel Corrie's murder and made more firm by the image of the blind girl. To know that our tax dollars pay more foreign military aid to Israel, a prosperous nation, than to any other on Earth, and to know that the vast majority of the IDF is funded by U.S. taxes, is to understand where culpability lies. Assailey gives me hope that something good could come out of this. As we transition away from the era when only men could claim to be combat warriors, we will experience a shift in combat as a testosterone manifestation to combat as a total commitment, de-gendering violence (Ehrenreich 1997, 230), but also furthering the paradigmatic change toward nonviolent combat. This will change our notions of both "real men" and of combat itself.

General reasons to resist war taxes

Our military is busy in so many internal conflicts globally and thus is making so much more misery around the world that it becomes increasingly crucial to bring these findings to light and to demonstrate their importance by our resistance.

Christian war tax resisters such as the late Phil Berrigan and William Durland are clear in their motivation: they regard militarism as demonic and are aghast at the possibility of supporting such blasphemy (Durland 1987, 113).

Peace scholars have an obvious mandate and obligation to demonstrate behavior that would tend to lead toward more peace. This makes it imperative that those of us who teach peace also practice it to the best of our abilities. And, once we accept the logic that war tax resistance is a possible path to peace, and once we begin to practice it to some degree, we make it much more likely that others will follow. This kind of dialectic makes teaching peace both more powerful and more personally risky. Those risks pale alongside those of a Palestinian child in a Gaza town under occupation by the Israeli Defense Force paid for by U.S. taxes. Those risks are tiny when we consider the awful situation and suffering of a baby in Falujah, a town leveled by U.S. military attack. And our minor risks are kept in proportion in our minds when we recall the indigenous Colombian villagers under siege from U.S.-sponsored government troops determined to keep oil and other resources in corporate control irrespective of the human cost. The list is immensely longer than these examples, not even considering the enormous impacts domestically on U.S. soldiers and their families or upon the military-impacted environment. One of the most invisible and egregious examples is the research the Bush regime is launching into biological warfare, research that is in direct violation of the 1972 Biological Weapons Convention and which makes it vastly more likely that U.S. citizens (and others) will be exposed to lethal, and usually weaponized, untreatable scourges that will kill civilians (Boyle 2005, 12). The list needs to be kept and updated so people never forget why they are called to resist.

Jimmy Carter recently told the world that we are doing bad things to prisoners that help fuel the fires of terror: "I think what's going on in Guantánamo Bay and other places is a disgrace to the U.S.A.," he told a news conference at the Baptist World Alliance's centenary conference in Birmingham, England. "I wouldn't say it's the cause of terrorism, but it has given impetus and excuses to potential terrorists to lash out at our country and justify their despicable acts" (Associated 2005). We could stop paying for torture. I think of when friends Jan Shireman and Gerard Grabowski were arrested for the mere act of climbing the fence at Project ELF in Michigan in nonviolent, open, public, daytime resistance to that navy thermonuclear command site. They were handcuffed behind their backs, made to kneel in sharp gravel, and kept for the entire rest of the day and into the night, thirsty, in pain, bitten by hordes of mosquitoes, hungry and tired. It was totally outrageous and if we think of the orders of magnitude more cruel that the punishment has been at Guantánamo, why does Jimmy Carter help fund it with his taxes? Why do any Americans of goodwill continue to pay for torture and murder? Where is our national conscience? Indeed, flirting with an aroused and angry IRS is dangerous to our material well being, but isn't that part of the point? How dearly do we value our material possessions in comparison to our conscience? The line is different for all, and should be, but at the least this ought to be a national question.

CHAPTER 14

Sanctions, Boycotts and Results

If twenty-five people die in a plane crash in the U.S. it makes headlines. But five thousand Iraqi children?(how is it possible that the deaths of five thousand children in a month is not burned into our minds?"
— Diana Abu-Jaber, *Crescent* (Abu-Jaber 2003, 288)

When a person refuses to shop at a small store and that person is an influential member of the community served by that store, the little business is affected negatively. If the refusal is made known and is based on logic and justice, the storeowner and all the employees are wise to adjust the store policy. Even one influential person can hurt a small business. Discouraging others from doing business with a store that practices some form of injustice is very possible if attempted by that influential person. When the refusal to shop in that store becomes more generalized to the community, it can become a serious, potentially damaging, boycott.

That kind of boycott changed public policy in Montgomery, Alabama, in the mid–1950s, when African-Americans and others of good will boycotted buses. It worked again in Nashville, Tennessee, in the spring of 1960 as the sit-in movement was first persecuted and then victorious. The boycott of downtown helped make that victory happen much sooner.

By the same principle, boycotts and other sanctions can change the behavior of nation-states. It was a critical part of the end of apartheid in South Africa. Sanctions have helped to make armed struggle unnecessary and are regarded as vital tools — perhaps the most effective tool — in the nonviolent tool chest.

But other cruel sanctions have besmirched the reputation of that instrument. The U.S.-instigated UN sanctions program on Iraq in the

1990s was so harmful to the general population and so irrelevant to the rule of Saddam Hussein that sanctions were dismissed by many. That is decidedly correct in the case of Iraq and absolutely wrong in many other cases. David Cortright and George Lopez of the Fourth Freedom Forum have done remarkable research and analysis of the power and potential of sanctions, including two monographs of substance, one before 9.11.01 and one after. In the former they note that those in favor of sanctions cite the positive effect on freedom and justice of the sanctions on South Africa's apartheid regime, and those who oppose sanctions often cite the failure of sanctions in the cases of both Angola and "Iraq, where sanctions are seen as purely an instrument of punishment against a civilian population, with no hope for changing the leadership or its policies" (Cortright and Lopez 2000, 7). They state categorically that sanctions must hold to strict ethical standards of non-harm of civilians and that the UN sanctions on Iraq "grievously violated ethical standards" (25).

In the latter book they go to the elements of a nonviolent response to terrorism that involve the economic sanctions on terrorism that might alter behavior, if complemented by other behavior by nation-states.

As they point out, the "dominant trend in UN policymaking has been the shift away from general trade sanctions toward more targeted and selective measure. Since 1994, all UN sanctions have been targeted. Financial sanctions, travel bans, arms embargoes, and commodity boycotts have replaced general trade embargoes as the preferred instruments of UN policy. The sweeping counterterrorism measures adopted in SCR 1373 (2001) continued this trend, imposing targeted financial, travel, and other restrictions on terrorists and those who support them. In each of the categories of selective sanctions — financial, travel, arms, and commodities — the Security Council has introduced important innovations" (Cortright 2002, 202). These kinds of innovative, sharply targeted UN smart sanctions are complex and underappreciated, and, thus far, do not include grassroots sanctions such as war tax resistance.

Like many other initiatives that have great potential to substitute nonviolent alternatives to violence, the fundamental problem is the conflict of interest between the purveyor of arms and violence on the one hand and nominal use of a nonviolent tactic on the other. Thus, the imprimatur of the U.S. contaminates much of what it touches, and people on the ground who see the results of some U.S. policies logically reject it all as bad faith. This has been true of the trial of Slobodan Milošević, which is rightly called "victor's justice" by many Serbs, it is true of the trial of Saddam Hussein, it is true for the role of the U.S. in the Israel/Palestinian conflict and it was true for the U.S.-prodded sanctions on Iraq. The questions are basic and become watershed for many. *How can the largest arms supplier in the Mideast be an honest broker of peace? How can democracy be forced at gunpoint? How can an oil-crazed U.S. design sanctions on a country with so much oil? How can a nation with more WMD than any other act to sanction any other nation for their relatively tiny amount of WMD?* Every time a U.S. weapon is used to kill a Palestinian child, that is a calefacient on the emotional core of the conflict, a source of great heat, great rage, great determination to harm the imperious and self-assured impervious U.S. That source of white hot rage will make calm appreciation of the justice of sanctions moot to most people in the region. It is precisely backward from the sanctions on South Africa, for example, when the people there and in the U.S. forced the U.S. to comply and to eventually participate. But the Iraq sanctions were irretrievably damaged by the U.S. pressure that created them.

The UN is clearly afraid of the U.S. and unlikely to seriously sanction even massively rogue behavior such as invading a nation utterly unprovoked, but those interested in the power and utility of sanctions to substitute for such invasions do well to argue on behalf of such methods.

Kathy Kelly and her compatriots in Voices in the Wilderness have shown how to boycott the sanctions themselves, when they are killer sanctions employed by a government to the detriment of the innocent civilians, which was exactly what the U.S.-initiated UN sanctions on Iraq were. Her approach — visiting those who are affected by the sanctions and assessing the direct human costs — prescinds the problem of a negative view of sanctions by using personalism and investigation. Kelly's group broke the embargo on medicine and did so openly and forthrightly, nonviolently, demonstrating what a *real* sanction should look like, if we wish to regard sanctions as a nonviolent tool for waging struggle for justice, instead of a weapon that complements and is enforced by guns and bombs. Indeed, the promotion and creative improvement of nonviolent technique is driver and core to Kelly's philosophy: "There's nothing I'd rather be doing in my work or my personal life than trying to be part of the further invention of nonviolence" (Roberts 2000, 32).

Appropriately, the power of sanctions can best be demonstrated by the organizing of individual acts of participation into a collective action that can nonviolently force governments to stop violence (Schaeffer-Duffy 2005, 16A). Beyond resisting war taxes, citizens can organize others to commit nonviolent acts of civil resistance, such as occupation or blockade of offices, military bases, or key warmaking facilities (such as certain roads or commandeered airports as happened to Ireland with its Shannon airport used as a staging area by U.S. military during the invasion of Iraq). These citizen sanctions are only limited by citizens' creativity and are best applied to nonviolently coerce behavior, just as all sanctions are designed to do. We can best show the efficacy of nonviolence by practicing it; the people, once they've seen the power of nonviolence to coerce a government to behave better, tend to understand that even nation-states could use this kind of nonviolence. It can be a feedback loop with ever-escalating good result, if done in an atmosphere that frames it that way. It is crucial to the success of nonviolence that it not have a flaccid, loppy image of insipid pusillanimity, but rather that of a determined, disciplined and forceful potential.

CHAPTER 15

Not My Body

The ultimate demand, even more direct than requiring money, is when the government orders a person to prepare to kill other people. This has been an enormous problem for humanity especially since Napoleon introduced the *leveé en masse*— universal conscription — in 1793, his industrial response to the industrial age, his contribution to industrializing war by industrializing the human side of war. Indeed, looking at the numbers of people in the armed forces in Europe before and after Napoleon, one can see the end of the era of the elite warrior and the beginning of the mass army. The apotheosis of that era, really, was World War I, when a war of attrition simply slogged on for four years in the trenches in France and, exhausted and bloody, Europe tried and failed to learn. During that period many Europeans migrated to the land where there was no universal conscription — except during its tragic civil war — the U.S.

When I turned 17 just before Vietnam's Tet Offensive, I knew nothing about conscientious objection and only found out by a referral to the Twin Cities Draft Information Center, where I was educated by some young men barely older than I, all of whom were in college and all of whom were risking imprisonment for their resistance to the draft, even though they all had student deferments. They burned draft cards. They dropped out of school. They publicly denounced the war and declared their nonviolent resistance. They all went to prison eventually.

The tradition in the U.S. includes some of the finest minds in many fields, people who resisted conscription and went on to live well, to learn and teach, to write and produce ideas that have affected U.S. social norms, including Dave Dellinger, Gordon Zahn, Bayard Rustin and other World War II resisters (True 1995, 75). Indeed, it was a World War II resister, Chester Bruvold, who advised me on my rights as I pondered what to do about that war of my youth, Vietnam. Bruvold, a Minneapolis lawyer, gave his time to many young men as they resisted that war. He argued David Gutknecht's case all the way to the U.S. Supreme Court and won. Gutknecht, a young Minnesota man, had burned his draft card and Selective Service punitively revoked his 2S status, making him 1A, or immediately eligible. Bruvold won that case eventually, affecting the cases of perhaps 30,000 young men who had taken similar measures and had been treated thusly. By the principles of *stare decisis*— settled precedent — then, the Supremes have rendered the vengeance of any future retributive-minded Selective Service harder to effect. This is how the law has advanced for conscientious objectors over time, war-to-war, sacrificial draftee to sacrificial objector.

Gutknecht's case was but one of many advances and effective outcomes of the peace movement during the Vietnam War, some or possibly most of the American peace movement spurred by a combination of conscription and the clarity of the unjust nature of the war. Other accomplishments of that peace movement include, for example, the demystification of the draft; local organizers could count on national groups such as AFSC, Women Strike for Peace and others to provide reliable information on negotiating the maze of Selective Service laws (Elmer 2005, 227). Most important, perhaps, was that, for the first time, the peace movement succeeded in placing a serious value on the lives of U.S. soldiers, sailors and marines. Despite the military-generated imagery of antiwar protesters throwing vials of urine on returning troops, spitting in their faces and calling them babykillers, the truth was that we in that movement were saying loudly and to all concerned that these young men should be brought home safely. At the troop level, they understood that widely during the war, as the myriad connections between the antiwar movements in and out of the military attested. At the brass level, the propagandists then and now continue to pollute the historical memory with isolated or fabricated incidents of such behavior, portraying that as the norm, casting themselves as paternally concerned, and so the battle for hearts and minds over the Vietnam War continues.

The dance of the religions around this draft issue and related concerns — e.g., capital punishment, taxes, legislating abortion law — is one that is painful to observe. One sect of Christians proclaims taxes entirely legal and proper but military service as against God's law by their interpretation of the Bible. In short, they are willing to pay others to kill, especially since nonpayment of taxes is going to affect the material well being of their believers when the IRS seizes homes and bank accounts. One pontificating Christian author even claims that the apostles clearly recommend capital punishment in order to keep citizens "secure," and that there is "nothing to be gained in protests" or demonstrations and yet he writes that military service is against Christian values because when a government conscripts it "requires a person to sacrifice their life [sic] for the country they reside in," and thus "the state is usurping authority over life which only belongs to God" (Shubin 1999, 41). This awkward attempt to apply the Bible to pacifism only gives ammunition to those who disparage actual conscientious objectors, as the level of hypocrisy is entirely evident to all critically thinking observers and certainly to those who believe in both capital punishment and war. Further, the focus on the risk to the draftee and not on the potential victims of the future soldier is clear and again lends itself to a rejection of that logic — even though it may make acceptance of it more likely at the draft board level. As a young man looking at religion and the draft, I was unimpressed by anyone except those who not only rejected military service but who rejected all violence by the state. I retain that analysis in my advancing old age.

Gutknecht was one of my draft counselors and helped me think about my personal responsibilities. While I never had the nerve to go to prison at that time, accepting my conscientious objector status instead of resisting, his case and that of George Crocker — another of my counselors — affected me forever. I believe it was the challenge they laid down to me in my youth that worked on me and prepared me to do two plowshares actions later.

When peace conversion is late: soldiers grow consciences

Thursday 17 November 2005
Statement made at Fort Benning, GA

My name is Katherine Jashinski. I am a SPC in the Texas Army National Guard. I was born in Milwaukee, WI and I am 22 years old. When I graduated high school I moved to Austin, TX to attend college. At age 19 I enlisted in the Guard as a cook because I wanted to experience military life. When I enlisted I believed that killing was immoral, but also that war was an inevitable part of life and therefore, an exception to the rule.

After enlisting I began the slow transformation into adulthood. Like many teenagers who leave their home for the first time, I went through a period of growth and soul searching. I encountered many new people and ideas that broadly expanded my narrow experiences. After reading essays by Bertrand Russell and traveling to the South Pacific and talking to people from all over the world, my beliefs about human-

ity and its relation to war changed. I began to see a bigger picture of the world and I started to reevaluate everything that I had been taught about war as a child. I developed the belief that taking human life was wrong and war was no exception. I was then able to clarify who I am and what it is that I stand for.

The thing that I revere most in this world is life, and I will never take another person's life.

By the time the recruiter has secured the signature of the young person on the dotted line and convinced him or her to raise the right hand and take the oath, it is too late to hope for a change in attitude or in action. This is the hope of the war promoter and the fear of the peace promoter.

But it's not true.

Indeed, as historian Howard Zinn reminds us, dissension and even full-scale refusal amongst the troops is hardly a new phenomenon in U.S. history. He recounts the cases of troop dissatisfaction and even, at times, open defiance in the American revolution, the Mexican-American War, the Civil War, the Vietnam War and the invasion and occupation of Iraq in 2003 and after (Zinn 2005, *viii*).

The loneliness of a nonviolent general

How can we counsel young people to resist the draft if that resistance will likely send them to prison? How can we counsel others to resist war taxes if that resistance may result in them losing their home or vehicle? How can we in good conscience ask another person to join a plowshares group, to hammer on a weapon and face up to 18 years in prison, or worse? The chances of success may be slim and the risks of paying all the individual prices and making all the personal sacrifices and then losing the campaign are great.

On the other hand, in any nonviolent campaign the outcome is anything but certain and giving in too soon, when a more persistent push might have given rise to the conditions that produced victory — preserving or gaining property, human rights, liberation and even saving lives — may be even more tragic (Ackerman and Kruegler 1994, 317). The complexity of context and conditions, coupled with a kind of tychistic, chancy set of elements that fall beneath analytical radar, will make certain predictions impossible in most cases.

Some see leadership through rose-colored lenses. I do not. I have rarely been, and never wanted to be, a leader. When I have been perceived as such and have been responsible for successfully convincing others to engage in nonviolent resistance, my guilt over the consequences to those others has had a number of effects on me. When others joined me in non-violent resistance to Project ELF in Michigan or Wisconsin — and if I felt that one or more of them did so because of something I had written, spoken or done — I was guilt-ridden every day they spent incarcerated and forever after.

First, it made me hesitate and even attempt to convince others not to engage in resistance. I didn't want their incarceration and all the ancillary costs on my conscience. The long imprisonment of Jeff Leys — a very young man when he chose to cut a notch in an ELF pole with my saw just two months after I did so in 1985, and with a ride to the scene from me — that incarceration for that young man was painful for me and shut me up for a long while. Ironically, in the end, we won only after more plowshares actions were done on the facility many years later, but the imprisonment of someone I felt I had partially convinced to act was paralyzing for me.

The second effect, again from guilt, was to make it much more likely that I would again engage in high-risk direct disarmament, and would serve prison time and resist war with more determination, which is what I have done (in the case of my second plowshares act) and what I've tried to do with my life.

This is not to say that guilt is the primary motivating factor in my decisions surrounding my own actions and my small role in persuading others to act (or lack of that role). But it is to acknowledge the tensions that I have observed and felt, and it is to analyze how those tensions have played out for one person caught up in the actual practice of this kind of conflict management. It has taught me that sacrifice is anything but hypothetical and to ask it of anyone else is very nervy. Indeed, that is one of the astonishing facets of confronting recruiters with the results of their work — names of the dead and photos of the wounded. How can they do that?

On the nonviolent side, I still struggle. I recognize that without persuasion, few will risk anything, and I try then to ask something of others, though I do not flatter myself with the notion that they are waiting for my cogency to grow a conscience or to act on it. But, as any writer must, as any teacher must, I acknowledge the dangers of convincing others that sacrifice is called for. I wish that, before he crossed over, I had engaged in this conversation with Phil Berrigan. He asked so much and sacrificed so much. And, with the draft board raids in the 1960s and the plowshares movement in the 1980s and after, so much was achieved. His heart must have been squeezed in many directions simultaneously. He gave approximately 11 years of his life to incarceration for peace and disarmament and it is unknown how many others he inspired to sacrifice; certainly I am among them. When he and his brother Daniel were photographed praying over the draft files they had lit on fire in the parking lot outside the draft board in Catonsville, Maryland, on 18 May 1968, the image burned its path into the eidetic files of our national memory and changed many of us forever. I am comforted and frightened by these considerations. Comforted because I hold nothing in my heart for Phil except love and admiration. Frightened because he continued to sacrifice his entire life and I wonder what my "golden years" will look like? I was never in his league in either case, but the sacrifices keep coming around on the cosmic wheel and they can be daunting as age slows me down and gives me medical challenges.

When Ossie Davis died, Amy Goodman played a clip of him referring to Dr. Martin Luther King, Jr., as "my Commander-in-Chief." King, Gandhi, Chavez and other nonviolent generals and commanders-in-chief do indeed require much of us who choose to volunteer to follow them, including the ability to grow with them, to change with them, to learn with them. This critical thinking — the ability to synthesize new information with the old and to evaluate and then to reevaluate positions — is what led Gandhi to learn mass liberatory nonviolence and is what allowed King to finally, on 4 April 1967, tell more than 3,000 souls in the Riverside Church in New York City that the war in Vietnam was immoral and needed to be resisted. Two weeks later he was leading a peacewalk of thousands to the UN and was, in practice if not announced intention, fusing the peace and Civil Rights movements more than had anyone been able to (Cook and Pesick 2005, 41). This ability to form coalition and thus effect more change and offer a more powerful challenge to state power is given to few but is the most precious and dangerous dividend of a life of integrity and resistance. King earned it and he paid the price — assassinated one year *to the day* after his Riverside Church call.

When the state delegitimates, covers up and denigrates

Peace scholars Brian Martin and Lain Murray categorize the responses of the state to efforts to engage in protest and resistance against its violent policies.

First the state attempts to cover up its wrongdoing. This may take the form of failing to report breeches in behavior or active methods taken to hide or suppress its oppressive actions.

Then the state attempts to denigrate those who oppose or reveal its policies, usually by attempting to smear them with a label such as terrorist, communist or criminal.

Finally the state makes the attempt to reinterpret the facts and assign blame to any other party, if not the protesters themselves. Thus civilian casualties become accidents (even when missiles are fired directly into civilian residences) or protesters become security risks even when they are openly, avowedly nonviolent.

This kind of state approach can result in backfire when it fails, that is, when the truth is made known, public outrage over the conduct of the state is not merely made mildly more by the activities of the protesters, but increased much more by the demonstrably objectionable tactics of the state (Martin and Murray 2005, 46). Their case study was the 2005 visit to Australia by an American peace activist, Scott Parkin, who was arrested, detained and deported by the government. That became an international incident reflecting poorly on the Australian government. The goal of those who engage in conscientious objection to the conduct of the state is to stop that conduct and the possibility of this kind of backfire dynamic is one that can essentially use the power of the state against itself when the state acts unjustly. This dynamic can appeal to the sense of justice that the vast majority of citizens claim to hold.

Sources for Part Five

Abu-Jaber, Diana. *Crescent.* New York: W.W. Norton, 2003.

Ackerman, Peter, and Christopher Kruegler. *Strategic Nonviolent Conflict: The Dynamics of People Power in the Twentieth Century.* Westport, CT: Praeger, 1994.

Associated Press. "Carter: Guantánamo Detentions Disgraceful." *New York Times,* 30 July 2005, online: http://www.nytimes.com/.

Beach, Rev. Bucky. "The Choice Seems Obvious." *More Than a Paycheck,* Apr2005, p8, 1p.

Boyle, Francis A. *Biowarfare and Terrorism.* Atlanta: Clarity Press, 2005.

Cook, Erin, and Stan Pesick. "Martin Luther King, Jr.'s 'Beyond Vietnam.'" *OAH Magazine of History,* Jan2005, Vol. 19 Issue 1, p41–50, 10p.

Cortright, David, and George Lopez. *The Sanctions Decade: Assessing UN Strategies in the 1990s.* Boulder, CO: Lynne Rienner, 2000.

_____. *Sanctions and the Search for Security: Challenges to UN Action.* Boulder, CO: Lynne Rienner, 2002.

Durland, William. "War-Tax Resistance: A Christian Response to the Demons Around Us." In: Laffin, Arthur J., and Anne Montgomery, *Swords into Plowshares:*

Nonviolent Direct Action for Disarmament. San Francisco: Harper & Row, 1987.

Ehrenreich, Barbara. *Blood Rites: Origins and History of the Passions of War.* New York: Metropolitan Books, 1997.

Elmer, Jerry. *Felon for Peace: The Memoir of a Vietnam-Era Draft Resister.* Nashville, TN: Vanderbilt University Press, 2005.

Hennacy, Ammon. *The Book of Ammon*, 2nd ed. Baltimore: Fortkamp, 1994 (original 1965).

Hironaka, Ann. *Neverending Wars: The International Community, Weak States, and the Perpetuation of Civil War.* Cambridge, MA: Harvard University Press, 2005.

Irwin, Robert A. *Building a Peace System.* Washington, DC: ExPro Press, 1989.

Jashinski, Katherine, online: http://www.truthout.org/docs_2005/111705S.shtml.

Johnson, Chalmers. "Blowback." In: Yuen, Nicky González, ed., *The Politics of Liberation: An American Studies Primer*, 4th ed. Dubuque, IA: Kendall/Hunt, 2003.

Kohn, Stephen M. *Jailed for Peace: The History of American Draft Law Violators, 1658–1985.* New York: Praeger, 1986.

Martin, Brian, and Iain Murray. "The Parkin Backfire." *Social Alternatives*, Third Quarter 2005, Vol. 24 Issue 3, p46–49, 4p.

Moyers, Bill. *The Language of Life: A Festival of Poets.* New York: Doubleday, 1995.

Roberts, Tom. "On the Further Invention of Nonviolence." *National Catholic Reporter*, 9/15/2000, Vol. 36 Issue 40, p32, 4/7p.

Rosenberg, Marshall B. *Nonviolent Communication: A Language of Compassion.* Encinitas, CA: PuddleDancer Press, 1999.

Rubenberg, Cheryl A. *The Palestinians: In Search of a Just Peace.* Boulder, CO: Lynne Rienner, 2003.

Schaeffer-Duffy, Claire. "Nonviolence: Most Adaptive Response to Terrorism." *National Catholic Reporter*, 10/21/2005, Vol. 42 Issue 1, p16a, 1p, 1 cartoon, 1c.

Shubin, Daniel H. *The Conflict of Ages: A Treatise on the Dichotomy of the Kingdom of God and Military Service.* La Habra, CA: Daniel Shubin, 1999.

Thoreau, Henry David. "Civil Disobedience." In: Barash, David P., *Approaches to Peace: A Reader in Peace Studies.* New York: Oxford University Press, 2000.

Tollefson, James W. *The Strength Not to Fight: An Oral History of Conscientious Objectors of the Vietnam War.* Boston: Little, Brown, 1993.

True, Michael. *An Energy Field More Intense Than War: The Nonviolent Tradition and American Literature.* Syracuse, NY: Syracuse University Press, 1995.

Zinn, Howard. "Introduction." In: Cortright, David, *Soldiers in Revolt: GI Resistance During the Vietnam War.* Chicago: Haymarket Books, 2005 (original 1975).

Part Six

War Poverty and Peace Prosperity; or, Living Large or Living in the Little Way

The American way of life is not negotiable.
— Dick Cheney (Thiers)

Arriving early, I stood in the late day sun, watching, listening to the small group of perhaps a dozen gathered outside the door of Sisters of the Road Café on skid row in Portland. Folks were as diverse as any decent group ought to be, but this crowd was clearly a bit more dinged by life. Some were missing teeth — of course, many of us who are privileged would be missing teeth were it not for dental coverage. Some were unwashed — of course, if a run of bad luck had resulted in my living on the street, I'd often be unwashed. Some were overtly glitchy, nervous, with random, sketchy movements. Then again, some brilliant colleagues who profess in the university here are raging eccentrics with odd, visible personal quirks. Most wore the beat-out clothing of the working poor. I wore the same, but perhaps more recently laundered, as I had access to a washing machine and a few quarters, as well as an apartment in which to hang them to dry. Good luck drying your clean washed clothes outdoors in Portland between September and early July. We live in the Pacific Northwest temperate rain-forest and the air quite often contains more moisture than your laundry does. Sisters of the Road might be the Our Lady of the Cenacle for the poor, but they also need an Our Lady of the Spin Cycle ministry.

But on this evening, these were people, black and white, poor and poorer, who were waiting to party. The occasion, marked well in the storefront plate glass windows, was the 25th anniversary of the founding of the cafe, which was started by Genny Nelson and some others in 1979, with the express purpose of providing an alternative to bars, to fancy cafes, to working class cafes that required fast turnover to make profit, to the occasional church soup line that opened and closed in a hurry and with the usual patronizing religious domination. Sisters of the Road Café was meant to be a place of solace, of community, of nonviolent refuge, of gathering and rest, rejuvenation and reflection for the dispossessed of our society. The combination of a meal and a gentle personalist recognition of the humanity behind every set of eyes, in every mind, is not the same as a church's meal with a particular gospel and recruitment to belief and salvation. Sisters' salvation is simple dignity and nonviolence for all, an unguent of understanding instead of the radical surgery of religious redemption.

When Genny was honored later than evening, an African American woman who had been all scuffed up by life was given the privilege of presenting Genny with the plaque. The woman used her time to talk about how she had been helped by so many Portland organizations that provide a piece of the puzzle for poor people who are seeking some support in George Bush's America, in our individualistic, competitive world with a safety net that either goes beyond government or the body count skyrockets.

This is no exaggeration. I've ridden the rails, I've hitchhiked across the U.S., I've stayed in mission houses and I can report that privately funded initiatives save lives daily in this rich land, lives that poverty would otherwise claim much earlier. The little things that a church group does — sometimes woefully paternalistic, sometimes perfectly sensitive to everyone's dignity — may give the shelter for a night to a man at the edge of his ability to survive another night in the elements. Even in relatively balmy Portland, life on the streets is exceeding rough, unstable, driven, precarious and lethal. In Chicago or Minneapolis, it's natural selection at a much faster rate. While some glance at a homeless alcoholic lolling about in the city park in the sunshine and vow to never give a nickel to a panhandler, others image the circadian vulnerability of street people as they shiver, sleepless in the nighttime chill, literally dying for a roof and a bed during the night, and those people are more likely to give change to homeless beggars as well as work for change in government spending.

Since the year of the founding of Sisters, the wealthiest one percent of Americans have seen their personal income increase by 157 percent while those in the poorest 20 percent of our nation have lost about $100 per year in wages (in constant 1979 dollars) (Moore 2001, 52). The immediate need is growing, though Sisters and other such efforts are founded and run on a systemic analysis that attempts to address the root causes as well as offer aid in the moment. We would need many more such efforts to have the desired effect on the roots of poverty alongside obscene wealth — which is exactly where it often is, as is true in Portland, with Skid Row just a couple of blocks from the snazzy, gleaming downtown highrises of power.

Poverty is caused by a complex of factors. Many now understand that war redounds disastrously on economic development around the world (Cranna 1994, 197). Poverty in the U.S. is a particular mix, different for each victim of poverty but with discernible factors. There are some elements in the U.S. poverty picture that are arguably meaner than elsewhere — e.g., power and poverty in proximity — and some of the underlying problems are traceable to our Puritanical roots. That baseline of values is in constant competition with the other natural American value that came with rising up against empire, the identification with — or at least the cheering for — the underdog, the person who's been dealt a rotten hand by life in one way or another.

CHAPTER 16

Potpourri or Popery?
Catholic Worker Movement

Indeed, it took the rise of the spirit of the innate rights of each person to produce one of the most inspirational movements to ever come out of the U.S., the Catholic Worker movement. Founder Dorothy Day was a young radical in the days of World War I, advocating for women's right to vote, alongside the seasoned radical Quakers like Alice Paul. Day, however — as many young people are still — was attracted to the politics of the left, to socialism, to the rhetoric of the rise of the working class, and she took to the streets as an advocate journalist, writing stories about the activism of which she was a part. It was an era of advocate journalists, from Ida Tarbell to Lincoln Steffens, George Seldes and Upton Sinclair. It was a popular ferment of progressive writing and Dorothy fit right in — until she didn't. She wrote for a socialist newspaper, but grew disaffected with some of their tactics, both journalistically and in the streets.

As the rough-and-tumble 1920s gave way to a squalid, impoverished America of the Dust Bowl and unemployed 1930s, Dorothy grew restive at the rhetoric and rage, the action without compassion, the screaming of the masses of poor in the Great Depression without the effort of community care that could provide for the common welfare when the government didn't. Dorothy converted to Catholicism in 1927 and maintained a deep faith but a troubled relationship with the church for the rest of her life. In 1933, she began the Catholic Worker, a home for homeless men, and she started a paper by the same name that went from a circulation of a few hundred to 100,000 in a short time. Her synthesis was to provide the human works of mercy so absent in the radical struggles of the left and to offer resistance to the war system so absent in the charity model offered by the church. She shared the best of both — the structural analysis of the socialists and the hospitality of the faith-based communities — and rejected what she felt were the dysfunctional components of those models, including violence.

Dorothy began something unique, but not unconnected to other social phenomena of the day. Her relationship with socialism and communism continued throughout much of her life, even as she moved deeper and deeper into Catholicism and nonviolence. Indeed, she and some other delegates from the peace movement, including A.J. Muste, attended the 1957 Communist Party convention as non-communist observers, primarily to discern whether the broader peace movement could regard the American communists as free from Moscow and Soviet direction. Naturally, FBI Director J. Edgar Hoover filed a report with the U.S. Senate Internal Security Subcommittee that these peace movement subversives were "handpicked" and often fronted for communists (Hentoff 1982, 163). Dorothy was used to traducement from the right and left; she simply followed her own lights. Her insistence on nonviolence seemed like a near-clinical cataphasia to the Soviet-Lenin-violent revolutionaries — most of whom are so unfamiliar with nonviolent theory that they grow irritated at hearing about nonviolence — and like a phony front to many FBI-types, but since she represented a discounted social norm it was necessary to repeat her commitment frequently.

Community cross-culture connective tissue

The comparison of the life of a Catholic Worker to that of the ashram member who worked with Gandhi is fascinating, as Gandhi concomitantly formulated his notion of what a real, worthy life might be. He was operating under very different conditions, coming from a very different cultural matrix indeed, and yet the life of his ashram member and the life of a Catholic Worker, at times, would be very similar. Both stressed simplicity and community self-reliance. Both stressed noncoöperation with government if that government was acting unjustly or violently. Both stressed some form of service to — and nonviolent defense of— poor, vulnerable, oppressed populations of people, and both held a deeply spiritual set of core values even while both were at least tolerant of— and in some cases openly embracing — other religions' expression of resonant values. In later years, a portion of the movement Gandhi began and which survived him, the Shanti Sena movement, would set all their activities in light of helping the poor and oppressed, acting in nonviolent resistance to their government when it acted violently, thus practicing "resistance and assistance" (Weber 1996, 162). Dr. Martin Luther King called Gandhi "inevitable" and perhaps Dorothy Day was as well.

She tried to be worthy of the hopeful and sometimes arrogant Latin claim, *annuit coeptis,* God has favored our undertaking. With humility but steely determination, she built a movement on principles and hard work, favoring the Little Way, the humble approach, the foot-washing-of-the-poor *peu à peu,* little by little.

More than 185 Catholic Worker communities still operate around the world with some version of Dorothy's vision and practice, though a part of her ideology was anarchism, so few practices are regarded as obligatory. There are two, however, that stand out.

One, active nonviolence, by which is meant the practice of nonviolent resistance to militarism and the roots of poverty and misery. This means that, in some cities, the epicenter of nonviolent resistance to the government may be in the Catholic Worker communities. While our U.S. culture seems obsequiously determined to propitiate the god of war, the Catholic Worker will always serve the God of Peace.

Two, works of mercy, or service to the victims of a system that not only causes poverty but refuses to end it. The kinds of such works are varied, from a soup line to a house of hospitality for homeless families, from a home near a prison which provides housing for poor people traveling to visit incarcerated loved ones to a community that serves many meals to many of the poorest every day.

Some of these communities favor a balance more toward the beans and blankets and less toward the leaflets and pickets, as some say. *Potage,* not pamphlets. Some of these communities are more involved in resisting injustice than they are in shelter or soup. Each has some kind of balance between the two. Some of the communities have individual members who focus on one or another of these primary missions, which allows for the anarchical order so typical of the CW movement.

While Dorothy was a Catholic, the Worker communities are inclusive, some more, some less. A very few expect that all core members will be Catholic. Most don't, though virtually all have some kind of spiritual approach to the work. The roots of the movement are much more about challenge to the church than about absorption into it. Indeed, Dorothy's partner in many of her initial efforts, Peter Maurin, wrote in one of his "Easy Essays" about the better hospitality practiced by Muslims. Near the conclusion, he wrote, "Mohammedan teachers tell us that God commands hospitality. And hospitality is still practiced in Mohammedan countries. But the duty of hospitality is neither taught nor practiced in Christian Countries" (Forest 1997, 64). One of the couples living in the Dorothy Day house in Washington, DC, when I first began visiting there in the 1980s was Mary Grace and Sebastian, a Catholic woman and Jewish man, both of them Catholic Workers. Whencesoever the spirit of nonviolence, justice and service to the victims of militarism might come, it is welcome in the Worker.

This way to the ogress... no surrender Dorothy!

Though Dorothy maintained her loyalty to the church, she challenged the pope directly on some issues and is credited by many with influencing the Vatican and the bishops in their 1960s stances for peace and against nuclear weapons. She had another, more constant challenging relationship to the very conservative, hawkish, American patriotic Cardinal Francis Spellman of New York, who often attempted to curtail Dorothy's work and tried to get her to remove the word Catholic from her newspaper, if not her house of hospitality and in fact the entire movement. She played that to the edge many times, maintaining both her principles and keeping the direct wrath of the Cardinal from her community.

One Catholic Worker who stumbled into the movement despite his non-religious tendencies was Ammon Hennacy, who had been arrested for speaking out against the draft at the beginning of World War II, and who spent the entire war locked down in federal prison in Atlanta. He edited the prison newspaper and actually put the famous Thoreau quote, *In a corrupt society the only honorable place for a man is prison*, on the newspaper masthead. When the warden — a man quick to oppress any prisoner for almost any infraction — saw that, he complimented Hennacy on the choice. Hennacy was dumbstruck, realizing the warden actually thought it was a pro-prison, pro-rehabilitation admonition to inmates.

Hennacy spent much of his prison time in solitary confinement for his refusal to give in to prison policy and especially his refusal to give names. While in the hole he had only one piece of reading, the Bible. He later wrote that he had become something of an expert on the book, since he had time to read it at least three times, and that, had he only been given the Chicago phone book instead, he would have been quite an expert on that.

When Hennacy happened to meet Dorothy Day, he was smitten and made numerous attempts to woo her, all to no avail whatsoever. Still, he became a Catholic Worker, and even briefly a Catholic in his vain attempt. He vacillated between an uxorious devotion to her and near disdain, hesitating to call her much of a hero since "she could chicken out any time." His working class autobiography, *Book of Ammon*, is a testament to the power of one determined nonviolent anarchist and, more than any other document, reveals the inner strength and stubborn streak necessary to achieve a completely pacifist stance in the face of a war zeitgeist and in the midst of a violent society.

Dorothy and the Portland CW movement

While Lisa Hughes was in prison for her nonviolent resistance to the export of U.S. militarism, we corresponded. I had been restless about the idea that, for all my hippie homestead experience, for all my involvement with the Catholic Worker movement, and for all my appreciation for community in so many ways, I had never lived in community as my primary residence. Lisa had lived in community; she was a community nurse in El Salvador for more than five years in the 1990s, much of it during the final years of the bloody civil war. She went to Georgia with thousands of others to offer nonviolent resistance to the School of the Americas and spent a half-year in prison in Pekin, Illinois.

Lisa had a much more intentional, purposive attitude about living in a Catholic Worker community than did I, which is exactly what was necessary for it to work. She was in prison with Corbin Streett, a young woman from Mississippi who was otherwise inexperienced in activism but whose good heart put her in harm's way and who was one of the random "lucky" ones to be prosecuted to the full extent of the federal trespass law, thus serving her half-year in Club Fed as well.

Lisa organized the three of us, then, as the initial core of what would become the Portland Catholic Worker, a family home in Northeast Portland that offers hospitality to single women who have experienced homelessness, or who might be living in intolerable conditions of abuse, or who may be just coming out of prison. As I drafted these words on New Year's Day 2005 I was in my basement office in the Portland Catholic Worker with my little basement bedroom just a few feet away. Lisa and Hanna were asleep on the 2nd floor. Gail was flying back from her visit to her home reservation and I planned to pick her up at the Portland airport in the afternoon. Mary Kay was flying back the next day from her visit home to Dubuque, Iowa and I picked her up as well, as the only one in the community with a car. I was listening to Andrew Vasquez playing *Shadow*, a Native flute song of contemplation and depth of reflection. A year later, just onto New Years Eve 2005, I am at the same desk — but in Whitefeather House, the second CW house in our Portland Catholic Worker community. This experiment is one that teaches and offers great rewards and challenges.

As Lisa and I first engaged in discussion and then in mutual and joint discernment about starting a Worker community, I had concerns — well, honestly, fears. She got out of prison and traveled to Corbin's and then elsewhere to visit, eventually coming to roost in Portland at Ann and Bruce Huntwork's home for an extended stay while we worked toward starting a Worker. The Huntworks have lived a life of service and radical peace and justice involvement — including a total of more than a decade offering service in Iran, and Ann went to prison for a 6-month bit before Lisa, also for SoA resistance. I visited Ann in the women's prison at Dublin, California, another version of women's community that also comes out of imperial America. Ann and Bruce are probably the most vital of our crucial close circle of support in Portland.

My fears about starting a Catholic Worker:

- losing autonomy in my life
- losing writing and private reflective time
- losing control over my living environment (TV, meat, cigarettes, noise)
- being run ragged by community obligations even as I age and have less energy
- living in conflict when tensions grew overwhelming
- living with interruption and loud people

My hopes about starting a Catholic Worker:

- living with a core community that supports nonviolence
- living simply, consuming less
- living with those who also believe in nonviolence
- living with those who are victims of this war system
- living in solidarity with those our society fails to value
- living in resonance with my own values
- living in a community that is part of a movement I value

Lisa and I went for long walks through the rhododendron gardens and on forest park trails when she was living with the Huntworks in late 2003 and early 2004, discussing all these fears and hopes of mine — and hers. She maintained her correspondence with Corbin, who committed to a year of helping to launch the community. It became clear to me and everyone that Lisa was the centerpost, the pillar, upon which this enterprise rested. As we met, walked and talked, we came to commitment, and I shared Corbin's one-year feeling. Lisa is in for at least five years. This is what it takes, I suspect, for a community to really have a chance. Someone has to be in it for the longish haul. I am committed to this for at least five years at Whitefeather House, so it looks as though we will nourish the CW experiment in Portland.

Part of what Lisa and I agreed upon relieved some of my fears; Lisa was averse to television as well. It is, after all, one of the banes of civilization. It misinforms. Danny Schechter, Greenpeace, FAIR and others have shown that over many years of study. It takes time from human-to-human interaction, thus eroding community, according to Robert Putnam in his *Bowling Alone* study of our social habits. It even takes over some viewers' lives, virtually merging with reality (Mander 1991, 88). And it is noisy and crass. My nightmare was TV blaring, as I experienced in jail, everyone talking loudly to be heard, and no one really thinking through the din. Without the TV, the atmosphere is quietly friendly, as it is supposed to be.

We three were the initial core and are an age spread from the young — Corbin turned 25 just after we moved into the old home we found — to the older youth — Lisa was 38 when we opened the doors — to the old, me, at age 54 on this New Year's Day 2005 (now 55 in early 2006). This intergenerational and gender balance has been advantageous to community in some key ways. We seem to offer different gifts and strengths to the collective and to the guests, and we seem to have different challenges. The community can better survive for that diversity, I believe.

Whitefeather House — named for Larry Cloud Morgan of the Silo Pruning Hooks plowshares — began when two of us from the Portland peace community decided to try to expand the Catholic Worker community from the one house to a second. We are entering a new experiment in the anarchistic movement; we purchased a house with a couple of extra bedrooms and are opening it to women, perhaps refugees, for extended stays. Our experiment will include housing for those capable of being here without anyone else in the house — in short, our guests need to be quite high functioning and able to operate independently. We provide a roof over the head, access to food and phone and we are on a bus line. Most CW houses have folks on house duty to fix meals, maintain harmony, offer advocacy, help with child care, offer counseling, moderate conflict and provide nonviolent security. We offer none of that here at Whitefeather on the theory that, if we make this model work, we might appeal to a much wider audience of potential Catholic Workers who might see their lives enriched by adding their houses to the community. For those who work full time and happen to have some spare room in their homes but little spare time, and who can support the nonviolent resistance principle of the CW movement, this may make it possible for them to add their home to the community.

Since Whitefeather House is financially independent, we can take financial donations and pass them along to Dorothy Day House, where they offer much more hospitality and work outside jobs less. Community can afford us the means by which we play to our strengths and cover for each other's weaknesses. Dorothy Day House gives much more directly to the victims of the war system and Whitefeather House does much more community organizing and nonviolent resistance activity. Dorothy Day House is more available to both those who wish long conversations about the movement and to volunteers; Whitefeather House has a large front meeting room and is much better situated to offer it to the wider activist community for meetings, etc. Hospitality and nonviolent resistance and community open several lines of inquiry. The exploration is ongoing.

I am learning that Buddha was right; the moderation in all things in this endeavor has been key — with a few exceptions. I personally cannot be a moderate vegetarian or live in a house that has meat. It is impossible for me, and the community graciously allows this. We eat vegetarian whilst here in the house and people do their own thing elsewhere. I could not be a part of the community without that grace.

We also decided that television would be a mistake, which has also been a blessedly good decision; at Dorothy Day House they watch one or two movies each week and then tuck the TV under the basement stairs for the rest of the time. No commercials. No arguing or resentments over which program to watch. No massive irritation at the blare of the box. No electronic wallpaper dominating our audio and visual environment. This can be unique for some in our society, a culture so steeped in television that its ubiquity is unquestioned and expected. For some who first live in a TV-free environment, the freshness can be revelatory; for a few it is the first time to really think, to reflect, to live together and listen to what another might really say without the noise pollution and stress of the commercial wall of sound that dominates so many home environments. It's also a chance to avoid the greatly exacerbated electronic version of what Mark Twain wrote about mainstream journalism: *A man who doesn't read a daily newspaper is uninformed. A man who does is misinformed.*

We read alternative press and listen to noncommercial radio for our news and that keeps us more accurately informed. Guests sometimes remark about finding a new world of information just living where it is available and not overwhelmed by television and commercial radio. We think Dorothy would have approved in her journalist soul.

We are a small experiment in community — we only have two bedrooms and a total of three beds to offer guests in Dorothy Day house and just one or two guest bedrooms in Whitefeather House — and we mean for it to be that way. We decided that our experiment would feature a more serene and stable environment than does many a Worker — which means we limit our offering to just a few women but try to make that offer quite significant to each woman. We also determined that we would probably prefer to maintain such a degree of independence financially that we would never feel bound to, say, report for mass at the local parish, or engage in some other community behavior that might be codependent and perhaps compromising. So each of us who works "out" contributes to the community budget — we pay for the privilege of living in poverty and service to those who can really use a deeper level of committed help for a bit more extended timeline. Indeed, Gail came to us as a guest, and she is so centered and has such an orientation toward service to her own Pima people back on her home reservation in Arizona (and others), that we offered her support through her efforts to obtain a degree in chemical dependency counseling. She now does house shifts and is a full member of the core community and, in return, she has been able to stop working at her dead-end job and start school (and has since started a much more rewarding position with the YWCA). She will be a fine counselor and we are privileged to be part of making that possible for her and for her community.

We decided that, since most of the core community works outside the Worker at jobs that also fulfill us that we would create a community that would not overwhelm our lives, and it is a balance we give to each other, to ourselves, and to the population of people in great need in the richest, most militarized empire the world has ever seen.

When Dorothy ran her community, the ironies of the era synthesized with the strength of her personality and character, producing a deeply contradictory but profoundly sensible set of paradoxes that we don't have to face as sharply. Michael Harrington was a young CW back in the 1940s and his immense talent was immediately apparent to Dorothy, though he was essentially "just" a law school dropout. She put him in positions of great editorial power in the newspaper and his trenchant observations, offered to interviewer Rosalie Riegle in the year before he died, told us a great deal about the times, the movement, and the woman behind it and in front of it. He reminded us that this was the time of the Pope Pius XII attitude of old male chauvinist Biblical authority — "women should keep their heads covered and their mouths shut" — to which Dorothy expressed absolutely fidelity. It was also interesting that Dorothy set up the day-to-day decisions of the community so that the many meetings were run on a wonderfully anarchistic, deeply democratic basis — "and then Dorothy made up her mind. The place was run on a führer concept, and Dorothy was the führer. So you had a house totally dominated by a woman, but it was male chauvinist in its ideology" (Troester 1993, 131).

Perspectives like that allow us to see that, for all our failings, our culture has advanced at some levels. Certainly the Workers with which I've been involved have no similar twisted power relationships (though we have other problems that will, I hope, be regarded someday as equally quaint). And the friendships made possible by this community are a gift that overwhelms whatever drawbacks community has; the poetry that began this chapter comes from a gift book offered by one of my finest students, Rachel DuMont, who has come to us as a volunteer of great love and joy, humility and generosity. This is the kind of connection that such community life fosters, the unexpected becomes the frequent gift of love that lubricates life.

Reading about Dorothy's early experiments and seeing the hubbub of some Workers allowed me to express early on in our discernment process my fear of losing the contemplative center I need to do my work — teaching, reading, writing — and we haven't had to really struggle toward that as a result. Dorothy did, as her former housemates recall. Brian Terrell remembers being a very young, energetic Catholic Worker who had no boundaries, who would serve meals until the last person in New York was fed, while Dorothy would draw lines, slowly teaching him that, well, if you do this great act of service tonight then I will be expected to do the same tomorrow night and the result may just be that "people would break windows because yesterday they came at that time and got soup" (Riegle 2003, 92). Though our Worker community is new, we've already seen that principle at work; the young, high-energy Corbin approach was to throw open the doors, to drive guests to work at 4 a.m., to invite neighborhood children to wander throughout the house, and it was all based on love, on her spirit of openness, trust, and extreme generosity for all. I, on the other hand, size up people and make decisions based on my life and am thus the curmudgeon, the one who says no, the one who puts boundaries on spaces and times, chores and meals. The net effect can be confusing, and has resulted in some guests being angry at my lack of excitement about totally opening my life to each of them, but it has also meant that we all show that we have certain gifts and tendencies and none of us ought to be taken for granted. We who live here are also humans with limits. My boundaries offer less spontaneity, but, on the other hand, I am still here plugging away, while Corbin flamed out and retreated to her childhood home country of Mississippi and doesn't live in community now, though no doubt she continues her wonderful open and giving, smiling style of life. In the end, we all offer so many lessons to each other. What is possible? What is sustainable? What is sensitive to everyone? What protects our own abilities to continue to give what community demands? Are we bound by our homiletics — our preachments to each other — to become toast on the altar of service to the poor or are we of more value if we are stingier in our bread offerings? Can we find that balance so delicate yet so tough that gives strength and endurance to each and all?

The Catholic Worker, generally speaking, has grown much more spiritually eclectic than in Dorothy's day; when, for example, we discussed the tone and orientation of our community, we agreed that we would still call ourselves a Catholic Worker, but that we would be open to spiritual ceremony that spanned a range of beliefs. In our newsletter, which we call *Candles*, Lisa wrote about her participation in a women's sweatlodge on the Sunday following the election of 2004 — Bush's reelection — when "we prayed, drummed and sang. Still, my soul could not take in what the media was telling us, that the majority of people who voted, voted for George W. Bush. How could so many of my fellow human beings (co-workers, friends, neighbors, family, church members) vote for this man?" (Hughes 2004, 3). The sweatlodge, Mass, Buddhist meditation, Taize, and many other spiritual paths braid through our CW journey.

Resistance mission

When a Catholic Worker's daughter received literature in the U.S. mail that urged her to join the army, the mother went from being active in the peace movement to being confrontational. She was a primary support member of our little Portland Catholic Worker community and she drew us into her opposition to the military recruitment of innocent, vulnerable youth to fight and die in imperialist oil-grabbing wars. She took it straight to the local recruitment office on NE Broadway, the only inner city recruitment office approachable by city sidewalk.

As it happened, the initial meeting with the recruiter-in-charge was scheduled for immediately after a nonviolence training we scheduled at Portland State University as part of Students United for Nonviolence, which training itself was nested into the visit to Portland by Jeff Leys of Voices in the Wilderness for the War, Peace and Media conference. Thus, we held the conference on a Friday and Saturday (July 8–9, 2005) and the nonviolence training all of Tuesday afternoon on July 12 and then went to the military recruiters' office, where the mother met with the recruiter and attempted to challenge his conscience to the point where he would join us on the sidewalk where she burned the recruitment literature. We wrote and illustrated a leaflet called Appeal to Conscience, in which were featured photos of caskets of returning dead soldiers from Iraq and Afghanistan as well as a recovering soldier with a prosthetic leg. She gave the leaflet to the recruiter and he accepted it, but declined to join our action on the sidewalk outside.

Local KBOO community access news was on hand, a nice young man named Doug, and he interviewed a few folks. The action was done in the name of the Portland Catholic Worker, and thus was especially focused on nonviolence and the spirit of reconciliation and gentle personalism, even as the mother "lit up the lit," burning the recruitment literature in the abalone shell she uses daily to smudge and pray. I lit some candles for the entire vigil and CodePink Portland women also showed, bringing their indomitable spirit and signage, eliciting many positive honks and waves from drivers on busy Broadway. The little action elicited no police response other than a late-arriving squad car, and we decided to make that vigil a regular weekly Portland Catholic Worker action every Tuesday evening at 5:30.

The objective isn't unlike the neighbors who surround a crack house and eventually, with enough visible, vocal and determined opposition to the activities that take place inside, convince the inhabitants to move. When that victory is in hand, neighbors can surround the new crack house and do it again, with the idea that the town is cleaned up with enough citizen presence and loving insistence. Cleaning the military recruiters out of Portland is a challenge fit for a movement. The Catholic Worker Little Way is just the small group to begin the process.

CW spin-off cycle

While Jonah House in Baltimore isn't officially a Catholic Worker community, it is felt to be such by many of us, since it is the Mother Ship of nonviolent faith-based resistance in the U.S., probably on Earth. Founded by former nun Elizabeth McAlister and former priest Phil Berrigan, the community focuses on nonviolent resistance and is the most robust such community I know about.

In Chicago, Kathy Kelly is a one-woman nonviolent action industry; she, like Dorothy, is an Irish American who writes and speaks with great moral power and is connected to the most targeted and vulnerable in her struggles. She's done nonviolent resistance to U.S. militaristic hegemony around the world and does so with the perfect nonviolent storm; she is nose-to-nose with the U.S. military and at the same time smiling and inviting them to be better, to be nonviolent, to become all they can be. Her inspiration to those who hope for the safety of Iraqi children, Palestinian children, and all the children of the world, is phenomenal. Kathy served jail and prison time for nuclear resistance and resistance to WHINSEC. She went to the Gulf to interpose in the first Gulf War, sitting in the desert waiting to be fired on from both sides and bombed from above. She opposed the sanctions so strongly that she broke the U.S.-imposed sanctions numerous times to bring medicine and hope to Iraqi kids. I was on the phone with Kathy from Northland College as we planned one event and I asked her how she had been and how her project, Voices in the Wilderness, was going.

"I feel like I've been on a bungee cord to Baghdad, Tom," she said. "No one in power likes us. The U.S. hates that we expose the cruelty. Saddam's soldiers harass us. It's just got to be done."

Kathy, Jeff Leys and others decided, in the face of a federal court judgment against VitW, to disband the organization and begin a new one. They had been so sanctioned in 2003 for the act of bringing "medicine and toys" into Iraq, a violation of sanctions (McClory 2005, 11). They are now Voices for Creative Nonviolence. Leys visited us in the summer of 2005 and conducted a nonviolence training in Portland with us. He told us then that they were all living as though the U.S. government would be seizing their personal property and income at any point; this hasn't happened yet. But the new organization, even more pointedly about nonviolence, will not reassure powerful people. Oppressors don't like overt opposition from those who refuse to be cowed.

Of course, oppressors don't want to see opposition from more people like Kathy Kelly than anyone I know, *because* she was a thorn in the U.S. cowardly murderous sanction operation and was not a friend to Saddam's oppression either. She fights for the most vulnerable and most innocent and she does it with great grace, bringing simplicity to the nodus, the welter of knots, that bind Israel and Palestine, militarism and the U.S. Kelly's vision is clarity and holy, respectful of all and protective of the innocent. She holds them, she smiles with them, and she turns to the men with guns with the same disarming smile. Dorothy would be so very proud.

CHAPTER 17

Divide and Rule:
War on the Poor

The history of racism and other divisive social practices is a profound travesty of many orders — it wounds the human spirit, it shrivels souls, it breeds fear and mistrust, and, in the end, it fosters violence. Violence is always easier to commit when the victims have been properly dehumanized. And the violence, then, makes it possible to control populations through official violence, to play them off against each other, and for the owner class then to profit hugely. As one commentator said in response to a Republican charge that being against tax cuts (of vastly more benefit to the rich in this case) was "class warfare," *They started it.* Indeed, it takes organizing to bring together classes, races, and religions, just as it takes plotting and planning to divide them. One benefits the violent demagogues and one benefits all the diverse people. It is normal for the ideologues to claim that those who attempt to unite people are part of the enemy group — communists, terrorists, or unwitting agents thereof. The divisive ones — the elite who seek ever more control of the Earth and its resources — wish to sharpen the divisions amongst the people and blur the divisions between opponents of their hate-based policies. *You're either with us or you're with the terrorists.*

Intellectually, from the so-called Bell Curve analysis of racially divided cognitive capacity to the clumsy nazi justifications for the ultimate objectification of anyone other than so-called Aryan, the erosion of faith in the scholar is greatly intensified by such sold-out "science." Interestingly, modern genetics has tentatively labeled Europeans about two-thirds Asian in origin and about one-third African, which flies in the face of these racial purity theorists, from the 19th century French intellectual, Arthur Gobineau, to the Nation of Islam theories and others. We humans simply mix it up and the notions of racial degeneration are "at odds with everything we know today," according to human population geneticist Luigi Luca Cavalli-Sforza (Cavalli-Sforza 2001, 76). Still, every time divisions between peoples can be justified and fostered, it is axiomatic that war or violent suppression is more likely and that someone is profiting from that division.

I taught with a Serb who, though brilliant intellectually, was quick to label the Albanian Kosovars as "breeding like rabbits." He hated the notion that his non–Serb countrymen and women were growing in numbers while Serbs remained more or less constant in their population. It was shocking to hear his ethnic bias, as he was a Ph.D. with a great number of peer-reviewed publications and classes full of philosophy students. Indeed, every time I had students who had a certain kind of reasoning about several topics that related to nonviolence and inclusivity, I asked if they had been taking classes from this particular fellow — and each of them had. Soon, I began to tell them that my primary mission was to disabuse them of this man's teachings. The most egregious of them, perhaps, was to dismiss the massacre at Srebrenica — a horrific, premeditated, calmly conducted act of Serbian forces separating almost 8,000 Bosnian Muslim men and boys from the civilian population in June of 1995 and, in July, killing them all. It was attempted genocide, yet this "philosopher" waved it off as "exaggerated" by U.S. media. I was aghast, and worked with students to help them understand this crime by the facts gathered by the international community.

Part of the attraction and part of the rejection of nonviolence is that it accepts all people as human and rejects all use of violence. Thus, it can seem popular to those who have been objectified and victimized — until they, in turn, take up arms and continue the violence, only to find themselves opposed by the community of nonviolent analysts. Thus, when the U.S. bombed Belgrade in 1999 and tried to take out Milošević (and failed, only to have nonviolence ultimately succeed in that in 2000), the peace movement opposed that bombing (though the antiwar movement was silent in that case, since the attacks were "humanitarian" and only caviling, spoilsport pacifists could oppose them). But when the Kosovo Liberation Army committed atrocities against Serbs, the peace movement condemned those as well. We were unpopular with everyone, as we seemed to side against the victims in every case, even though what we were doing was to side against a method of conflict management, not against people.

In short, violence is perceived by many of us as being divisive; that shouldn't be too unclear. The more violence, the more division, and the easier it is for the ruling class to continue its bloody game of divide and conquer. As this is written, that is what is happening in Iraq, a nation historically divided amongst Kurds, Sunnis and Shiites. The U.S. occupation of that poor nation has featured astonishing tactics that tend to divide and encourage ethnic hatred and civil war of revenge, thus keeping the country so destabilized that the U.S. must stay at its 14 new bases to keep order — reminiscent of Chicago mayor Richard Daly when, during the 1968 Democratic Party convention he told the media that the Chicago "police are not here to create disorder; they are here to preserve disorder." The largest arms dealer in the world — the U.S. — simply cannot be an honest broker of peace when it profits off every hot conflict in the world and can keep its forward bases operational only as long as they are perceived as necessary bulwarks against civil war. The forces that stir up the most hatred — the U.S. armed forces — are ironically thus the forces that are promoted as the wedge between civil war and mere insurgency. This works well for U.S. imperial interests and poorly for the Iraqi people, just as racism works well for big business and poorly for all working people.

More irony accompanies the debate about conscription, which, with all the various exemptions available to the knowledgeable, has always been divisive and discriminating. In the name of egalitarianism, some who call themselves progressive and more who are simply militarists are calling for a draft in the U.S. In the spirit of *noblesse oblige,* even upper class people who are themselves safe from conscription are calling for it and using the excuse that it would be only fair to conscript everyone, not just the poverty draft that tends to send poor kids off to kill and die and leaves the sons of the policy makers safe (Bunting 2005, 17). If American history is any guide, such a reality would still afford loopholes so the sons of the rich would only serve if they really wished to, if they needed some military service to beef up future political resumes (though in the age of Bush and Kerry one has to question that wisdom), or if they simply must serve, do so as officers, in the family tradition. Those who subscribe to nonviolence as a conflict management method oppose the inclusion of more classes of people in the military; we hope to exclude more and more classes of people, until we are united in our nonviolence rather than our violence.

Graminivorous elites consume grassroots

You don't eat the seed crop is the title of an antiwar art piece offered by Käthe Kollowitz, a German woman whose son was killed in World War I. From the unctuous liberals to the bald tactics of the neocons, we see the endless results of war, which is to kill, maim, and otherwise harm the mass of people, while concomitantly materially enriching those who are generally immune from the actual harms. When Napoleon boasted to Count Metternich, *You cannot defeat me. I spend 30,000 men a month,* he gave the world a glimpse of how the upper class views and uses the rest of us.

Governments love the poor. They love the presence of a hungry stratum of society that can be used to break strikes and keep profits high, that can be drafted either by law or by promises of pay, and thus would never try to extinct, extirpate or extinguish the vast numbers of poor people. Who else is cannon fodder in an age when military service is low paid and high risk? Then, when the state coerces and channels young people from poor populations into lives of killing and dying in the military, it can claim that diversity and multiculturalism is best represented in the most honorable profession, the armed services. This is part of how a war culture is built upon the endless misfortunes and divisive measures of a class and race-based society.

CHAPTER 18

Buddhist Lifeways and Economies

As you become more interested in peace, you begin to lose your interest in greed, hatred, and delusion. Conversely, those who are consumed by greed, hatred, and ignorance are not interested in peace.
— Bhante Henepola Gunaratana (Gunaratana 1999, 170)

Engaged Buddhists and Catholic Workers tend to think similarly and act in ways that are somewhat different from the mainstream society members of their respective greater faiths. Indeed, there are many more similarities between the lifestyles of engaged Buddhists and Catholic Workers — and, as mentioned, Gandhian ashrams — than there are between engaged Buddhists and mainstream Buddhists; there are many more touchpoints between the lifeways of engaged Buddhists and Catholic Workers than there are between Catholic Workers and mainstream Catholics and mainstream Christians. Peace researchers have noted that positive peace — the presence of nonviolence, of security, of justice, and of a kind of conviviality or *kyosei*— is the opposite of many manifestations of our current society that some strands of Buddhist vision address (Hallagan 2005, 79).

Engaged Buddhism was a school of thought and action founded by Thich Nhat Hanh as the Vietnam War dragged on and his monks realized they must become involved in the affairs of the people, not merely tending their own development in their monasteries. Engaged Buddhists seek a more just lifestyle that happens to thus include elements of the renunciate, but also lives of service. They may offer nonviolent resistance as well, rounding out the Catholic Worker agenda. Again, this may be perceived as outside mainstream Buddhist thinking in any particular Buddhist society at any particular time, but, as with Catholic Worker thinking on nonviolence and spiritual requirements, engaged Buddhism offers an alternative. Thus, even though a particular society may be, for example the Theravada Buddhists that dominate in Sri Lanka or Cambodia, there have been recent periods during which the notion of nonviolence as a Buddhist concept was far from the mainstream in thought, word, and deed. In fact, those societies have recently experienced mass war and genocide, often perpetrated by Buddhists, though not necessarily in the name of Buddhism — and armed resistance has been offered, some in the name of Buddhism, even though there is no room for violence in the doctrine of Theravada Buddhism (Deegalle 2003, 127).

Engaged Buddhist David Chappell writes of the economic realizations that drive some of the Buddhist peacework, noting that the failure of all large economic systems — both the failed centralized communist model and the failing predatory capitalist model — is a failure that affects the most vulnerable and non-humans first, and then will affect stronger and stronger members of society as we pollute and cause dire, desperation-driving conflict amongst the very poor masses.

Chappell points out that "Today nations have been replaced by transnational corporations (TNCs) as the source of life or devastation for large numbers of people. The income of the top 200 TNCs is greater than the personal income of 80 percent of the world's population" (Chappell 1999, 223). When he cites statistics that show it is a worsening problem, stacking classes into less changeable castes and creating enormous wealth for a few while making poverty grow, it is clear that the engaged Buddhist economy is preferable, an economy where the only reason for profits is to help create good work and create more justice rather than less. This is similar to the living economy of Vandana Shiva, stressing human creativity, diversity, complexity and self-organization (Shiva 2005, 72). And when it is shown that illegal corporate activity is rewarded while nonviolent resistance to it is punished, the lines become even sharper and brighter. In the aftermath of the nonviolent civil resistance to illegal logging in Canadian Clayoquot old growth by transnational MacMillan Bloedel, professors and others asked why the corporadoes could violate the law with impunity, even when proven in court, while nonviolent resisters were sentenced harshly to 60 days in jail and $3,000 in fines (MacIsaac 1994, 116).

Like Barbara Ehrenreich, Chappell asserts that an anthropogenic activity — corporations, in this case, rather than Ehrenreich's war — can outevolve humanity and threaten us. Nonviolence is the alternative in both cases.

Sources for Part Six

Bunting III, Josiah. "Class Warfare." *American Scholar*, Winter2005, Vol. 74 Issue 1, p12–18, 7p, 1bw.

Cavalli-Sforza, Luigi Luca. *Genes, Peoples and Languages*. London: Penguin Books, 2001.

Chappell, David, ed. *Buddhist Peacework: Creating Cultures of Peace*. Boston: Wisdom Publications, 1999.

Cranna, Michael, ed. *The True Cost of Conflict: Seven Recent Wars and Their Effects on Society*. New York: The New Press, 1994.

Deegalle, Mahinda. "Is Violence Justified in Theravada Buddhism?" *Ecumenical Review*, Apr2003, Vol. 55 Issue 2, p122, 1p.

Forest, Jim. *Love Is the Measure: A Biography of Dorothy Day*. Maryknoll, NY: Orbis Books, 1997 (original 1986).

Gunaratana, Bhante Henepola. "The Happiness of Peace." In: Chappell, David, ed., *Buddhist Peacework: Creating Cultures of Peace*. Boston: Wisdom Publications, 1999.

Hallagan, William S., Yijun He, Frederick S. Inaba, Mudzivri Nziramasanga, and AKM Mahbub Morshed. "An Examination of the Economic Theory of Civil Conflict." In: Murakami, Yoichiro, Noriko Kawamura, and Shin Chiba, eds., *Toward a Peaceable Future: Redefining Peace, Security, and Kyosei from a Multi-disciplinary Perspective*. Pullman, WA: Thomas S. Foley Institute for Public Policy, 2005.

Hentoff, Nat. *Peace Agitator: The Story of A.J. Muste*. New York: A.J. Muste Memorial Institute, 1982 (original Macmillan, 1963).

Hughes, Lisa. "Election Reflection." *Candles*, Winter2004–2005 (3+).

MacIsaac, Ron, and Anne Champagne, eds. *Clayoquot Mass Trials: Defending the Rainforest*. Gabriola Island, BC: New Society, 1994.

Mander, Jerry. *In the Absence of the Sacred: The Failure of Technology & the Survival of the Indian Nations*. San Francisco: Sierra Club Books, 1991.

McClory, Robert. "Voices in Wilderness Disbands; New Group Formed." *National Catholic Reporter*, 11/18/2005, Vol. 42 Issue 5, p11, 1/3p.

Moore, Michael. *Stupid White Men: And Other Sorry Excuses for the State of the Nation*. New York: ReganBooks, 2001.

Riegle, Rosalie G. *Dorothy Day: Portraits by Those Who Knew Her*. Maryknoll, NY: Orbis Books, 2003.

Thiers, Paul. Lecture. 14 January 2006, Iraq Town Hall Forum, Vancouver, WA.

Troester, Rosalie Riegle, ed. *Voices from the Catholic Worker*. Philadelphia: Temple University Press, 1993.

Spain, Sahara Sunday. *If There Would Be No Light: Poems from My Heart*. New York: HarperCollins, 2001.

Weber, Thomas. *Gandhi's Peace Army: The Shanti Sena and Unarmed Peacekeeping*. Syracuse, NY: Syracuse University Press, 1996.

Part Seven

Movement–Building; or, The Portland Story

On the weekend of 15 February 2003, one month before the outbreak of the invasion of Iraq, the world came out into the streets by the millions to say no, to register opposition to the notion that a hyperarmed superpower could, at its own whim, launch a massive invasion into a country that had not fired a shot at it, had not threatened it, had not sent any agents or assassins overseas to threaten anyone. We ultimately failed to stop that war and then we failed to effect a regime change at the polls in November 2004. But it was tantalizingly, tragically close in both cases.

My thesis is that, if all the other towns in the U.S. had followed the Portland, Oregon, organizing model with dedication, we might have been successful in stopping that war before it started. A corollary is that the Portland model itself could be radically improved.

The elements of that organizing were all key and need improvement, but they are much more effective than the models used elsewhere. Pound-for-pound, Portland turned out more people than any American city. The largest of several large demonstrations was 30,000–40,000, on March 12, just eight days before the war would break out. Had we been better organized, had we turned out 400,000 instead of a mere 40,000, and had the rest of the nation followed that model, perhaps we would have stopped that war. It is likely no campaign will offer apodictic, incontrovertible proof that certain methods are foolproof, since the variables are too complex to make that claim, but the nature of advances in social movement strategy and tactics is that of parsing out the pieces and asking how they functioned as a part of the whole effort — and then, as Gandhi said, experimenting.

CHAPTER 19

Arts and Crafts of Organizing

The Portland model had many elements, including:
- a determination to not degenerate into rowdiness
- a handful of community organizers who did their best to not be overly controlling
- a handful of community organizers who devoted slavishly long hours to the nuts-and-bolts work it takes to bring together large numbers
- a realization that the old Saul Alinsky model of organizing the organized still works
- tweaking Saul with Dorothy — adding the element of gentle personalism to hard-edged organizing — can offer a better synthesis

A determination to not degenerate into rowdiness

The Civil Rights movement in Montgomery, Alabama, in 1956 consisted of African Americans boycotting the bus lines. They did not riot, they didn't blow up anyone, nor did they taunt police — though they were a population who had suffered as much as any in this nation and much more than most. Chattel slavery, followed by abject poverty and Jim Crow segregation provided ample justification for rising up in armed rebellion at least as much as any population anywhere, but African Americans did not do that. Rather, they began and sustained a decade-long nonviolent revolution, beginning in Montgomery.

They quietly but effectively walked, carpooled when they could, and demonstrated total persistence and dedication in the face of every nasty tactic employed by local whites, who controlled the power structure. The dignity and self-respect, the refusal to respond to cruelty and compassionless behavior in-kind, eventually moved hearts. A local white finally wrote into the local paper, *It is hard to imagine a soul so dead, a heart so hard, a vision so blinded and provincial as not to be moved with admiration at the quiet dignity, discipline and dedication with which the Negroes have conducted their boycott* (Schulke 1986, 45). While it is unrealistic to hope to totally transform everyone with the power of principled nonviolence, it is entirely realistic to expect that a consistent but assertive use of careful nonviolence in response to injustice will change the opinions of many of the class of people who are part of the oppression and without which the repression could not continue. It is also true that, generally speaking, one rowdy event can destroy a great deal of painstakingly achieved progress. Those who exhibit hatred in a misguided effort to resist war are, in the end, only feeding the war dynamic. Those who passively sit at home are, in the end, feeding the war dynamic. Only those who are engaged in robust, active nonviolence are actively opposing the war dynamic. It is a fine line, but quite bright.

Portland background since 9.11.01

From the perspective of one organizer, this is what it looked like for a period from 9.11.01 until the summer of 2002 and then through the spring of 2003 — the period of time during which the Bush regime first responded to the terror attacks and then ramped up more and more for war in Iraq — as the global peace movement rose to challenge it.

Some local activists created a new organization immediately after 9.11.01 called Portland Peaceful Response Coalition. Initial meetings were up to 200 of us crammed into the PSU campus ministry hall, Koinonia House. The black bloc — calling themselves the "Anti-authoritarian caucus" — was a serious force within that initial response. Most older activists were cowed by their energy and self-described "radicalism." I felt strongly then, as I do now, that the black bloc was the force that was eroding the recruiting appeal of the global justice movement by its smash-and-dash approach to street activities. I spoke for nonviolence at every PPRC meeting. I was quite lonely at first, often the only voice amongst 150–200 activists in the room. But I needed to get on the record, to plant seeds, and they bore fruit later, in my perhaps self-inflated opinion. At least they gave legitimacy to the growing voice for nonviolence in the Portland movement as we progressed — or sunk deeper — into the Belligerent Bush years. I predicted that rowdy behavior would alienate the very people we needed to recruit — middle American Portlanders — and more people began to agree with me as we proceeded with our actions, events and organizing. My earliest ally, Cecil Prescod, is an African American professional organizer who operates in the Gandhi-King model and moves others with his gentle thoughtfulness. He changed hearts.

As a student and practitioner of nonviolence, it seemed historically obvious, and I expected the advanced consciousness of Portland to welcome such commentary as a no-brainer, but I also knew of the global influence of the black bloc on the global justice movement. They were attracted to the romance of violence based on their indignation at the injustices of globalized predatory capitalism and they were stuck in the male macho model of response. It was Ché Guevara over Mohandas Gandhi for them, and my fear — soon realized — was that the establishment response would be to conflate Ché with bin Laden, that is, to smear the black bloc not with the Zapatista itty-bitty violence in the name of oppressed people, but rather the al-Qa'ida raging attacks and suicidal throat-slitting remorselessness. Not only did the mainstream media tolerate that rightwing smear campaign, but the so-called radicals were nose-ring-led to that by their champion, Ward Churchill, who so sexily appealed before 9.11.01 to the most undisciplined enraged global justice activists. Churchill actually called al-Qa'ida members who flew planes into the WTC towers "gallant combat teams." That this smearing was inevitable seemed radically ineffective to me and it wasn't long before it became painfully clear in Portland.

The assertion that a response to state terrorism can be nonviolent is hardly a new one. Gandhi invented it 100 years ago in South Africa and then improved upon it in India, incorporating a holistic viewpoint still aspired to by many. He advocated interreligious comity, an end to the taluk system of passing along huge private estates in India, local self-reliance, mass liberatory nonviolence, an end to the caste system and other measures that reveal a positive answer to satisfy the interests of the many over the greed of the few. Lourdes Benería, Women's Studies professor at Cornell, writes of this integrated trend as analogous to "Christianity without hell" (Benería 2003, 88). She and others document how it has evolved into a new sort of acephalous women's model around the world. This is an improvement on Gandhi and King that, I believe, both men would have embraced. Each would have welcomed a model of team leadership that reduced the charisma cult status of one man and elevated the multiperson leadership model. The irony of the black bloc influence is that it claims this kind of model in some ways and yet is, in my observation, often just a contest of strong personalities. All this conspires to produce active hatred toward Gandhi amongst black bloc kids. We are still referred to by some on Indymedia as "Gandhiheads."

We found out Dick Cheney was going to be coming to Portland on one of the fundraising stops that all politicians do as they cultivate and maintain their support (*Some call you the elite; I call you my base.*— George W. Bush, as seen in *Fahrenheit 9/11*). He was here in July 2002 and we planned a hot welcome to — as one of George Bush the Elder's Secret Service guards called it — Little Beirut. As a nonviolent resister and one who believes in absolute nonviolence, I was uncomfortable with some of the personnel who were organizing the response to Cheney but it was the main game in town so I stuck with it. Later, after Cheney and then Bush came through town that summer, we would note that there were many days in the year when they weren't in town and, if we called for a large demonstration on a more random day, we would naturally expect to have more control over the tone and tenor of the event. This turned out to be key.

Cheney's visit was met with anger and jackbooted, metal face-studded, black-masked youth chanting pungent and oh-so-clever offerings such as *Dick Cheney, son of a bitch*. It was impressive for its immaturity and, as one of the handful of peace vibe watchers, I can say that it went as well as could be expected, and expectations were low. Only about 800 folks showed, since they knew the mood was dire. Portland is also part of the nexus of the Pacific coast forest defense network too, and that movement has historically been greatly alienated from mainstream America. They were on hand, bless their hearts, adding banners hanging from city park trees, contributing to the general disgust and foul-mouthed attack on Cheney.

Of course, Dick Cheney richly deserves all these attacks and he has no character to assassinate, having given in to the Dark Side of total sanguiferous warmongering, Earthraping capitalism and hyperconsumption many decades ago. That isn't the issue. The issue, for me, is movement-building, and expressed rage just doesn't draw in the masses in white America. There's a line between disciplined anger and explosive rage. One can draw interest and even recruit others with righteous nonviolent discipline. Bellowing rage — which may have the same roots of simply wishing to defend the vulnerable innocent ones — is off-putting will hurt recruitment. As with the liberation of the Philippines, Mississippi, Poland or Palestine, the issues of justice are reasonably well established (Wehr 1994,

218). Only the methods of struggle toward justice are in question. The internal movement struggle is, in many cases, the struggle that determines the outcome much more than does the struggle with the dominators themselves.

One group in the Cheney protest saw how rowdy we were as they listened and looked out from their habitat—a skid row bar. Feeling invited, in the spirit of the old Irish question, *Is this a private fight, or can anyone join in?*, from spiflicated to buck-wasted, they poured out to join us and happily sidled up to the police lines alongside the dedicated young anarchist wannabees (true anarchism, it seems to me, would require nonviolence or it would quickly give way to the desire for security that breeds the armed and violent police and military we see in control now). One young man, new to our ranks but fitting right in as far as he could see, bellowed at the riot-dressed police, *C'mon, motherf---ers! I'll throw down right now!* I went to him and asked if I could talk to him for a moment. I asked him if he was on paper. He nodded. I said, well, how do you think this is going to end? *Goin' back to f---ing jail! I don't give a sh—!* I said, well, are you interested in college, because I teach and maybe we should meet to discuss it. I gave him my Portland State University card. We talked about him coming up and I started talking about nonviolence, a new topic in his world. I talked about how, time after time, whenever the people were successful in their revolution, they did so by winning the police over to their side rather than battling with them, and winning the military over to their side, not by kissing their butts, but by winning the support from the mass of people. I said, hey, look at Poland and the Philippines, two countries that completely did away with the military dictators, and they both saw it happen the fastest when the people convinced the cops and army to join them. He thought that was interesting and our conversation continued a bit longer. The gauntlet of hatred for the cops was picked up by the young self-described anarchists, who were in turn smacked down by the cops for their trouble. Dick Cheney never noticed and the public watched the media coverage—none of which went to the issues we said we were in the streets to promote, but rather to the altercations between provoking marchers and obliging cops—and the public reacted with a yawn, mildly grateful for the thin blue line that protected their downtown from the ravages of the rowdies.

It was a failure. It did, however, give all of us on all sides ammunition as we planned for the next one, the arrival of Bush himself on August 22, 2002. The self-claimed radicals pointed endlessly, with exaggerated self-pity and outrage, at a few times when cops gave them an elbow in the ribs. I was living in a community full of such self-described revolutionaries at the time and one of them ran a video clip endlessly of some cop giving him a jolt. He didn't show the clips of him and others taunting the police, treating them as subhuman, making them feel like dirt. Rather, he and others focused whiningly and justifyingly on moments of predictable police bad behavior as reason to riot harder. *Just shows what we need to do. Only language they understand.* It was the movement version of the justification for bombing Afghanistan and Iraq. *Get violent— so they can get it.*

The organizing meetings for August 22 were a mixture of planning and fractious disagreement, all very interesting and, as ever, predictable. The ones who wanted revolution yesterday wanted the occasion left open to whatever the radical affinity groups decided in secret to do. I was disgusted. Once I actually cursed about those who favor violence. I apologized, but I was ashamed that I allowed my frustration to get the best of me. It was after the main meeting, in the backyard of a local pizza place, basically in the dark with a dozen or so others. I was by far the oldest, in my 50s, talking with 20-somethings, with a few teens and a few in their 30s. I was losing patience with all the same old stunningly ignorant claims — nonviolence doesn't work, it's time for uprising by whatever means, nonviolence needs to make room for more radical tactics, only fascists dictate to others what kind of tactics they can use, and so forth. I sometimes feel as though I've become too old to even fight for my opinion, since it is so often regarded with such disdain and often seen as predictable from an old geezer.

Then I occasionally grow a backbone when I recall that I've spent longer behind bars than all the organizers combined, that I've been doing some fairly serious headbutting with the war system since before many of them were born, and that I've spent a good deal of my life living a lifestyle of low impact on the earth while they were still being schlepped around in Mom's SUV. And when I consider that the fate of the Earth and humanity, as I understand it, is dependent on nonviolent means and ends, I know that my emotional well being is not the issue, and certainly my popularity amongst the young high risk, high commitment activists is also irrelevant. Then I can bite the bullet and act like the curmudgeon that I've become known as. Harrumph.

One young fellow said that, well, he knew someone who had done prison time and had told him that one way to change the behavior of authorities would be to shoot one every week until they changed. This young man, quite articulate, good-looking and a natural leader, really got my goat. I confronted him and said something to the effect of *You have no clue about what methods most inmates might fantasize about and how they might work. These are guys, for the most part, who are behind bars for actualizing some other stupid fantasy, almost always having some self-aggrandizement in mind. To take their ideas as politically astute is simple-minded and ignorant.* While I certainly overstepped my notion of good conflict communication, and while he was absolutely not used to being confronted like this from within the movement, it had a few minor values — and a number of dysfunctional elements as well. But this is the kind of conversation one might have these days in the so-called peace movement, or at least in some wings of the antiwar movement. Having the thick coriaceous hide of an old irascible but nonviolent mule is survival garb.

Naturally, the Bush appearance degenerated to a new low. Crowds of 50–60 or more masked youth were at the various barricades, giving the finger to riot-prepped cops who took it and took it until they finally responded in utterly predictable fashion. They attacked anyone in their sights with rubber bullets and pepperfog. Even news teams and babes in arms were hosed by the chemical agents from the cops' squirtguns. Approximately 2,000 people were in the streets and about a tenth of them initiated a dynamic that made the police misbehavior inevitable. Remarkably, even my fellow peacemakers were less concerned about maintaining any kind of order than in engaging in fantasies about taking various irrelevant street corners and "holding them." It felt as though I were back in fourth grade, fantasizing with my buddies. I watched as four of the masked wunderkind picked up a very heavy city-owned planter full of flowers and smashed it in the street. The purpose behind that action and the idea that the flowers deserved to die eluded me entirely. One of my young friends was sitting in the road, urging all to blockade buses. I asked, well, did you want them all to get SUVs instead? It was inchoate, and, once again, the public was grateful for the police in the aftermath, even with the excessive whining about police behavior — or possibly *because* of that whining, in part.

When Afrikaner police in South Africa battered, beat, arrested, tortured and murdered black South Africans with impunity and immunity, the people reacted with dignity. One demonstration of some 20,000 women and babies stood in silent protest — it is said even the babies were not crying — for a full 30 minutes in Pretoria (McAllister 1988, 33). That kind of discipline overcame a rich system, an unjust system, a system with enough clout to ignore international opinion and crush domestic opposition. Stories like that are legion and instructive yet somehow many of the youth never learn them; they are instead fed with mainstream media notions of violent revolution from the cradle onward in their lives, Valley Forge and Bunker Hill, guerrilla George Washington and armed rebel Thomas Paine. They are taught little of the Civil Rights movement, nothing of Gandhi, a sentence or two about the Velvet Revolution and not a word about People Power in the Philippines overcoming 24 years of brutal U.S.-supported dictatorship with total nonviolence. Is it any wonder they, from their pampered upbringings and relatively free young adult lives, favor the romantic notions of Ché Guevara, Black Panthers and Malcolm X? Indeed, as I told a classroom full of students in late 1989 who were bemoaning the chances that the world would ever eliminate war, *Dare to imagine. Look at what is happening right now, as we sit here, in the Soviet bloc. The Berlin Wall is being taken down and people are freeing themselves with nonviolence. My entire generation thought this would never happen in our lifetimes. If you don't hope, you can't see the realities or the possibilities.*

That period — 1986–1991 — saw vast millions freed with nonviolent struggle, and, in the case of the dissolution of the Warsaw Pact, the sheathing of the nuclear sword of Damocles for the first time in the memory of Baby Boomers (Jones 2005, 80). Hope is counterintuitive *and* crucial to cultivate. It can't happen without the knowledge that some humans somewhere already achieved something similar. This is part of the challenge of organizing a community — educate and agitate concomitantly.

Organizers who tried to not be overly controlling

For the most part, the excellent community organizers at the heart of the large Portland peace movement are not paid to do such work. All have other jobs. All are irreplaceable. All are challenged not to act like owners of the movement, like founders of something that they must now rule. This group of topnotch organizers each wrestles with this as best they can, sometimes getting a good grip on their roles and sometimes inadvertently overstepping themselves.

After Bush's August 22 visit the gearing up for war escalated and I became more insistent on a peaceful response. By this time, I had found more allies and there were a number who didn't just want a "family friendly zone" in the larger event (the doomed compromise we worked out heading into the Bush visit), but rather an entire event with that spirit. This was the turning point, and the success of the movement in getting out large numbers was at least possible. We wound up the rubber band, hoping our little effort could achieve liftoff.

The growth of that movement model in Portland was made possible by an insistence on nonviolence, and that was in some ways my little contribution, but from there on out it was a matter of incredibly talented grassroots organizing far beyond anything I've ever done.

Organizers who devoted slavishly long hours

A handful of Portland organizers poured themselves into building the next big event, scheduled for October 5, when, sad for me, I would be presenting a paper at a Peace and Justice Studies conference held in Washington, DC, at Georgetown University. All the help I tried to give would not be for my participation, which felt odd, but the movement was larger than any of us and I just joined the others in plugging along.

They did some phonebanking, some leafleting, some media work, and some cyberorganizing. Many people were assured that the event would be family friendly — a code phrase that meant many things:

•it would be nonviolent

•it would not be a shouting event

•it would not focus on profane dehumanization of anyone

•it would stay focused on the issues, not the police

•it would be much less likely to provoke an unprofessional police response

•kids and elders would not, in all likelihood, be peppersprayed or shot with rubber bullets and others would not likely get arrested

•there was a chance everyone might have a good time and register their public opposition to killer policies

There was enough trust and enough good organizing to bring out about 3,500 folks, more than the Bush and Cheney events combined. It was peaceful, the cops didn't riot and we began to build trust. I enjoyed a long weekend in DC staying at the Catholic Worker with old friend Artie Laffin, and the person in the other guest bedroom across the hall was fresh-from-DC-jail Medea Benjamin, who had done a great banner drop behind Donald Rumsfeld on national television.

We continued, learning as we went, and did the next one in November 2002, drawing more than double the numbers, about 7,500. We were growing in the numbers in the streets and in the numbers of groups who were either endorsing or co-sponsoring the events. We had no police trouble of any significance and the one incident of bad protester behavior was rightly seen as outside the announced spirit of the event and as a separate occurrence. Media did a reasonable job covering it — a boy who jumped up and down on a police car — portraying it accurately as a person coming in and acting in violation of our guidelines. Organizers kept the peacewalk flowing around and past the incident, refusing to allow the hijacking of the event.

Reaching the media and being the media

While the natural corporate bias of mainstream media is always a factor, it is worth noting that it is sometimes less at the local level, across the print-electronic spectrum. Approaching a local reporter, a local editor, or a local talk-show host is relatively easy and relational work is a form of lobbying and familiarizing that is not only pleasant (it's fun to give a wave or handshake or even a hug to a local or state reporter at an event and start to know that person's struggles), but can result in the kind of switch in coverage that can reflect a deepening grasp of the story. Any cub reporter can bang out a story on any topic; j-school teaches that generalist flexibility. But when that journalist begins to write from a base of rounded knowledge of past conversations, readings and events, the coverage gets richer and richer. You, personally, as an activist, can cultivate one reporter in the world of peace and justice to the point where that person is regarded as the expert. Really, in the world of local writing, radio or television, doing three stories on a general topic is tantamount to expert status (Getchell, 1994).

When *you* are writing the story, remember you are a reporter and that qualifies you as a snoop who gets to call the Pentagon and ask questions. Go to the website first and you'll find a great deal of information and spun fact. Check with majors and lieutenant colonels — "They know everything" (Cook 2004, 321). Go ahead and call colonels and generals too; you'll get lucky once in a while. You get to talk to civilian officials' military assistants for information otherwise not available to you, people who can find out what you can't and may share it with you.

The old Saul Alinsky model

Part of the story in Portland is that we went to those who were already organized. We approached labor unions and churches, temples and mosques.

We had some success in doing that and in fact that is what gave us the larger numbers. By January we had 20,000–25,000 people in the streets, breaking all records for the state of Oregon for any kind of demonstration over any issue anytime. By March 12, organizer Frank Fromherz (who would later lose his position in the Archdiocese as a result of his peace activism) connected us to John Lewis, who gave a rousing speech and helped to draw 35,000–40,000, again shattering all state records. This is remarkable for a small town that isn't even a regional protest center. Indeed, when we organize in conjunction with national and international calls for action, we lose people to Seattle and San Francisco. Portland's 40,000 should be half a million for New York City or Los Angeles. We slug far above our weight in the protest ring and still we have so much to learn.

How might we improve on the Alinsky model in this era of atomization, non-organization and individuation of media? We bowl alone, as the sociologist told us, we rush home to our niche of identically minded internet users or our individual consumption of mass media. Is there a way, still, to organize such a populace to get involved en masse?

That is the challenge, I believe, to a new generation of activists, and may well be a part of the answer to the question, *Will humanity choose violence or nonviolence?* When we now choose between violence and nonviolence, we choose, in reality, between nonviolence and nonexistence, as MLK advised. In this War on Terror we see the warmakers open a door to Orwellian permawar, a Hobbesian descent into a rapid use of our planet's resources in a vain attempt to make permanent this American way of life. We witness the spectacle of the Pentagon roving, marauding its way around the globe in search of its next meal, oil, with a side of strategic minerals.

Warmakers know that this is the choice and they are finally reacting with fear to nonviolence. Six Greenpeace activists in Pennsylvania did a banner drop on a coal smokestack and they were facing 90 years in prison for noting that it's time for a better energy policy. In mid–2005, 55 activists from Greenpeace alone were facing charges totaling many hundreds of years of potential prison time in an unprecedented reaction from the federal government. Nuns are in prisons for praying on the military side of a line at SA — and were incarcerated for years for tapping nuclear armaments or their components with household hammers. This new generation of activists will need to devise methods of shattering the shields of apathy and gulosity that encase so many Americans, or those Americans will continue to be a part of a resource-gobbling, unthinking machine of planetary death. The Portland model is a baby step forward and it's the least we can do.

CHAPTER 20

A Permanent Movement

When a unilaterally minded regime takes control in the U.S., such as the fundamentalist Bush team, it is necessary to mobilize people on an ongoing, ever-adaptive basis. We need reflection built in to our organizing process, and we need to be ready to counter the next egregious maneuver toward yet more war.

Iran. This nation, with its reputation for violent overthrow and teeming Persian streets full of U.S.-hating Islamicists, is a ripe target for an invasion, now that the Bush league is convinced it has Afghanistan and Iraq under domination — or it may be that, under the theory that the best defense is a good offense, invading Iran under some pretext will serve to draw attention from the incomplete, botched occupations of Afghanistan and Iraq.

Of course, it is the first duty of the peace movement to resist any war whatsoever. The movement ought to be organizing affinity groups now to prepare to resist any attacks on Iran, either by the U.S. or by its proxy, Israel. Those groups ought to be in training across the U.S.

Further, it is necessary to educate the U.S. public about the false images of Iran, the U.S., and the relationship between the two that enable Bush to engage in such inflammatory rhetoric as he has in his numerous warnings to the government of Iran.

Iran, first and foremost, is an oil country, and that is why the U.S. is vitally interested. That is why Bush, in particular, is more interested than most, as his family is in the oil business. His policies all revolve around those connections, rhetoric about freedom and democracy notwithstanding.

Iran is also a country on the road to reform and democratization all by itself— though, as usual, U.S. militarism may be derailing that reform. Local elections are increasingly allowed, more and more important, and are bringing previously disenfranchised people — primarily women — into elected positions by the hundreds. Civil society capacity building such as these trends in Iran invariably brings what it is bringing in that nation, i.e., more environmental protection and more sustainable development, using local labor and local products (World 2003, 182). This is a nation that does not need foreign hostility; it needs foreign help and goods, many carrots and few sticks, all incentives and few sanctions. Pushing them and making them afraid of attack is only strengthening the hardliners who push for nuclear development. A robust hands-off Iran peace movement here in the U.S. is the best hope for the end of the Iranian nuclear threat — which of course pales alongside that of the U.S., UK, Russia, France, China and Israel.

Another task for peace educators is to debunk the image of Islam conflated with Islamicism. Mainstream media tend to report the egregious violence of the Islamicist fundamentalists who have warped Islam to the point where they can support killing civilians, even babies. In the U.S., they avoid reporting the nonviolent Muslim actions. This is tantamount to smearing Christianity with the twisted Christianity of the fundamentalists who spew hatred and revenge. It is simply false. Scholars who offer a profound context to Islamicist violence and also offer the stories of Islamic nonviolence have created the teaching materials we need, if we will but use them. Stephen Zunes and others have certainly chronicled the Muslim nonviolent success stories, from Bangladesh, Indonesia, Mali, Sudan and Iran itself (Zunes 2003, 37). Islamic theologian Zeki Saritoprak of John Carroll University has published on Turkish Muslim nonviolence and has expressed that, in this global atmosphere that tends to essentialize Muslims as rabidly violent, he hopes the Turkish experience of nonviolence within Islam attracts more academic attention (Saritoprak 2005, 425). I know that when I offer these materials to students, they are often stunned. It literally rocks their world. They sometimes tell me they spend the first few hours in class in utter disbelief at this zany professor (and some do walk out forever, probably convinced I make it up as I go), and then they begin to read, to learn from different sources, and, I've been told, it changes their lives. These stories from these researchers can do that.

Civil resistance and mass demonstrations

Portland has been traumatized by the black bloc — mostly young, wildly anarchistic, virtually all white, dressed in black — and is barely able to consider the possibility of acting in principled civil resistance to war or anything else.

In the field of Conflict Resolution, we use the term conflict industry to mean the opposing factions in any adversarial conflict who benefit from the very existence of conflict — they win somewhat when they lose and win a great deal when they win. They are the players who operate the zero-sum game for everyone else and bake metaphorical pies for each other behind the scenes.

An example is the old joke:

Who is the poorest person in town?
The only lawyer.
Who are the richest two people in town?
The two lawyers, after the second one moved in and began to fight with the first one.

The police, of course, are rewarded by the community with their gratitude when they defend downtown against any rowdies.

The black bloc are puffed up and feeling radical and in some kind of leadership role when they courageously battle the police.

The movement shrinks.

And the peace populace rejects civil resistance as associated with such rowdiness. They conflate arrests with violence and self-indulgent cursing and brick-throwing.

In Portland, that is a large theft indeed, since nonviolent civil resistance has been the movement-building backbone of so many struggles elsewhere.

The vision

It is the third anniversary of the outbreak of war on Iraq — March of 2006. There are two-score thousand people in the streets protesting. Out in front are those intending to risk arrest. The event begins at Pioneer Courthouse Square and winds around town until it comes to a military recruiter center and then the people who have trained and planned to do so take the next step and sit in blockade of the center on a busy Saturday afternoon.

First to get arrested is a state senator from the African American community, followed by a registered nurse. Then a former military recruit who refused to return to Iraq is cuffed, followed by a nun. These leaders from a diversity of communities are out in front because we want the message to be clear as can be: peace is mainstream. The desire for peace is so strong in the mainstream that leaders are willing to sacrifice for peace, to sit in jail for this principled, sincere and serious cause.

The entire crowd is peaceful and determined. They are loud but friendly in their support for those who are arrested and eventually the event is over and the crowd returns to work and home life—and to a changed political landscape. Peace and justice are on the top of the agenda, no longer on the forgotten bottom.

CHAPTER 21

Lessons Learned

Keep your eye on the ball

When the issue at hand is stopping a war, that issue needs serious, committed attention. Coalition-building is not about a long list of demands, but rather about agreeing that we can stick to one issue and not drag a coalition into a laundry list that offends more and more people faster than it can attract new ones. This is tough and divisive, as we have seen in Portland.

Thus, for example, one of the problems for the coalition is that Palestinians and their most stridently unconditional supporters have demanded that the rallies have two, three or more demands, always including the liberation of Palestine. Generally, a multiplicity of demands and focuses doesn't tend to bring in more participants, but rather tends to give potential participants a chance to simply opt out of showing up. The Palestinian activists are not only very important coalitional friends and participants, but their issue was clearly understood as linked to the issue of war in Iraq by all other network organizers. Nonetheless, no other issue except the war belonged on posters or in other outreach. The public's sensibilities on that issue are too divided to link the organizing and attendance of an antiwar rally to a demand for Palestinian sovereignty without these components of nonviolence and disarmament. This has to do with the image of the Palestinians cultivated by the media and that in turn has to do with terrorism, which is the violence of the weak. Palestinians are, by orders of magnitude, the weak party due to massive U.S. military aid to Israel. This U.S. aid allows Israel to commit state terrorism without sanction.

As with any bloody conflict, it is simply unhelpful and usually inaccurate to keep claiming, "He started it." Atrocities pile up and are more and more accepted by each population as commensurate with the pain they have endured. And each atrocity — no matter how justified by recent atrocities committed by the opponent — is ineffective. Each time a Palestinian blows himself up in response to state terror, the day of freedom and sovereignty is pushed back, not forward. There is no public stomach or sympathy for blowing oneself up amidst a crowd of civilians. Slaughtering children looks like a Palestinian intention to most U.S. media consumers and, sadly, Hamas and others provide the imagery needed. This is exactly how Israel gets away with their much more devastating state terror.

The neocons and the neolibs alike understand this well. They are winning. The Hamas-Bush conflict industry is working much more efficiently than a peace approach. Bush and Sharon made a Hamas victory inevitable and Hamas will continue to make Israeli and U.S. rightwing hardliners look reasonable.

The Rand Corporation, a rightwing consulting think tank that helped design several wars, says in a recent study that forming a Palestinian state is not a priority for the Bush administration, since it is focused on Iraq (Adams 2005, 32). When the warmaking administration understands the concept of focus and getting something done, they seem to be able to achieve it. We, much weaker on the surface, seem incapable of countering them. That the Palestinian cause is just is not in doubt in most corners of the world, but those corners do not always include the middle class or working classes in the U.S., and those classes — the majority of voters — are the constituency whose opinion is both valued and hence manipulated by the most powerful elites.

A small example of such focus and prioritizing from the nonviolent side might be the announcement made in the 1960 sit-in struggle by prime organizer James Lawson, when he told a churchful of movement participants, "Team up with a buddy. I don't want to see a Negro with a white member of the opposite sex, because we don't want to fight that battle now." Did Lawson regard that battle for the freedom to date, love, or marry interracially as unjust or unimportant? No, he simply knew as a brilliant and successful organizer that he needed to keep everyone focused. Similarly, Portland peace people in aggregate seem incapable of transmitting that message of focus throughout their network and to the general public. We need to end this war and the polls suggest it's doable soon, at this writing. While it's not fair or just to call these other issues distractions, this is how they operate in the context of movement building and achievement of goals. The major peace rallies in Portland are about Palestine almost as much as they are about Iraq. This, I believe, keeps more people away by far than it draws. Huge crowds with one basic, clear message are a power and we need that power now.

This is *not* to advocate silence on Palestine, but it is to say that the war in Iraq is a crystal clear question to more and more Americans in a time when Palestine still appears murky, as though American citizens are thinking en masse, *Why can't they just all get along?* The question of Palestine is important and yet every time it is smeared with the image of violence it looks as though peace people are advocating violence too.

Most striking, I believe, to Americans, is that there aren't American troops in Israel Palestine but there are scores of thousands of them in Iraq and Iraq never invaded or threatened the U.S. The WMD aren't there and the bin Laden connection doesn't exist — or didn't, until we invaded and virtually invited al-Qa'ida to come recruit in Iraq. Even the American military can see this as polls of career officers are showing a bare majority still approving of the occupation in early 2006.

It is up to those who seek justice for Palestine to teach Americans that Israel is the perennial recipient of massive U.S. military aid and that Israel is in ongoing violation of UN resolutions by occupying Palestine. The education gap is wide, whereas the vast majority of Americans *do* know that WMD in Iraq was a fiction, and that U.S. troops are being killed.

Working on all issues as a huge movement simultaneously is a loser unless the support is overwhelming, in which case entire governments can be swept aside with nonviolence. That is highly unusual, and the organizing strategy *one issue at a time* is best left in place until that level of groundswell behind the movement is clear.

Of course, once we end this war in Iraq, the movement needs to fix on its next goal, not end or dissolve into a thousand unfocused struggles. When the global and domestic U.S. peace movement finally forced JFK to sign a Partial Test Ban Treaty in August 1963, the peace movement was appeased and refocused. It ended its examination of nuclear issues. That movement seemed to wish a trend and intention on the nuclear weapons states that simply didn't exist. As a direct result, there is *still* a vast and now *growing* set of global nuclear arsenals. There was some nuclear disarmament associated with the end of the Cold War, but not nearly enough, and we *still* have no Comprehensive Test Ban Treaty. The PTBT was, in most practical senses, a failure because of that lack of follow-through. The peace movement snatched defeat from the jaws of victory. The fantasy that the resolution of one issue will end activism because we will then have some kind of official trend away from injustice and militarism is delusional and debilitating.

End the war in Iraq. Then end the next egregious manifestation of U.S. militarism, whether that is the occupation of Afghanistan, the arms transfers to Israel, the forward basing of the U.S. military, the military budget itself, or some other fresh hell. Certainly, ending this war in Iraq is possible with focus. And when ending the war in Iraq is made more, not less, difficult by attaching it to the Palestinian question because Palestinian violence frightens and angers most Americans, we do no favor to those who face U.S. troops in Iraq (or those troops themselves) by linking the end of the war and occupation in Iraq to resolving the Palestinian quest for freedom.

This is not to discount or step away from the very education of the American people that can convince them not to tolerate U.S. military support for Israel. Hearing from nonviolent actionists who visit Palestine, and from those who are Palestinian, is always valuable. Indeed, rather than plaster the Palestinian question all over the posters announcing the next peace rally, why not bring in the many thousands who want the war in Iraq ended and, while they are there, introduce them to such speakers and to the materials via the many tables that offer information to those who have come to speak for peace? And if they believe there is nothing but violence happening by Palestinians, why not get them to the peace rally, or into the peace movement, and then, once they are there, show them that they've been lied to not only about WMD and the Saddam-Osama connection, but about the Palestinian struggle as well to the extent that it has?

Certainly the American people have been lied to about the history of the formation of the state of Israel and the bloody extirpation of indigenous Palestinians, who then found no friendly homeland in any other Arab lands and who have felt abandoned by the world ever since.

One of the red herrings that confuses so many is the notion that we need to find a religious source for a commitment to nonviolence in Palestine and Israel before we can expect that conflict to resolve itself nonviolently. This is unhelpful in most ways and simply irrelevant for the most part.

The notion that there are major roots of nonviolence philosophically in the conflict are questionable. There is almost no voice for Jewish theologically based nonviolence except Jeremy Milgrom and almost none for theologically based Muslim nonviolence except Sheikh Abd Al-Aziz

Bukhari, a Sufi (Tapper 2005, 67) (for that matter, the major Christian sects subscribe to the Just War Doctrine, a violent theology). However, most nonviolent victories have emanated out of societies that had little or no grand basis for nonviolence. Most nonviolent revolutions, liberations and other victories came as a result of people understanding that nonviolence is the strongest tactic for a secure victory. Palestinians have no widely accepted image as having made that effort, some of their own historians' assertions notwithstanding. Those assertions sound hollow to many of us in the daily dismal news from that struggle and the fate of the struggle almost always hinges on perception. Palestinians will either reign in the violence from their side — a highly unfair and possibly unrealistic hope — or they will continue to be a hated enemy by Israel and a dismissed populace by the U.S. Further, there is almost no image more important to erase and replace than the oft-played scene of Palestinians dancing in glee at the news that the terrorists had brought down the World Trade Center towers on 9.11.01. That image was false; it was taken from another time, but its repetition and association was believable to Americans and remains so. That is a long term struggle in itself to both rectify and make unbelievable. This is not disanalogous to the image of Cuba housing hundreds of Soviet nuclear missiles in 1962, poised to kill hundreds of millions of Americans on the eastern seaboard. People don't forget those images — thus explaining the perduring sanctions on Cuba as long as Fidel is in power — and they need to be made over in people's minds before the U.S. citizenry can take the next emotional step toward supporting Palestinian aspirations.

One popular notion is that we are witnessing a Huntingtonian clash of civilizations; the ongoing war between the medieval Islam and the industrial capitalist West. But underneath it all is still the radical disparity in wealth and in access to life's necessities such as basic water, food, medical care and self-determination (Ansary 2002, 109). Fix that and religious fundamentalism shrinks to its normal tiny size. End that disparity and terrorism vanishes. The clash is reduced to interesting coffeehouse chatter and personal worship choices.

The sharp focus that Cindy Sheehan has brought to the peace and antiwar movement is illustrative of naming a single problem and exhibiting effectively dogged attention. She lost her son Casey in Iraq and after wrestling with her grief, guilt and rage, she focused on telling George W. Bush, face-to-face, that she felt her son died for lies. Her sympathetic role as a grief-stricken mother has prompted thousands, perhaps millions, to action. She became the personification of a wedge issue and drove that into the national conversation in the summer of 2005 with a 26-day siege of nonviolent haunting at Bush's ranch near Crawford, TX, while he was on extended vacation. Her focus drew that of the nation. Her little sukkah-like structures, including a shrine to her dead son, were vandalized and her little white crosses were demolished by Bush defenders and she was shoved into a ditch by local deputies. All these acts of the bully toward a grieving mother have served to sharpen the focus of the nation on the costs of this obscene war. Sheehan has remained unswerving in her determination and her tight vision on one goal, and this has proven remarkably effective.

She returned for Thanksgiving 2005 and Pentagon Papers antiwar activist Daniel Ellsberg was there the first day and was arrested even before Sheehan arrived, along with 11 others. That her story is big enough to make the *Washington Post* even before she appears is illuminating (Helderman 2005). Ellsberg, the brilliant Rand Corporation analyst who blew the big whistle on the war in Vietnam, was moved to offer this civil resistance — as he has on so many other occasions of U.S. policy crisis — in part because of the success of Sheehan's actions. This laser focus is part of how the tipping point is reached and part of how this war is ending by the pressure from the grassroots and its leadership.

Protect against guilt by association

(Costello, the black ops villain): Let the public judge Constancia by the company she keeps....
(Ripley, the priest for the poor): You want to smear her reputation.
You wouldn't regard that as a smear, would you? Letting the world know you're a revolutionary? (Rozak 1985, 217).

Denouncing violence is not denouncing people. Saying that the violence of Hamas is a Bad Thing is not saying that Hamas are Bad People. Nor is it saying that anyone else's violence is a Good Thing. Indeed, condemning violence by anyone on any side is the finest protection a spokesperson can offer any group of nonviolent actionists. It simply is more dangerous to a group of WILPF women to have the police labor under the illusion that these women support throwing bricks. They don't. They shouldn't be attacked as though they do. This is not a tactic that promotes disunity; I, as a nonviolent actionist, do not want unity with those who use violence. I don't want people with whom I'm affiliated to pay the price for someone else, not associated with us, who chooses to use violence.

Diversify leadership

The most important job is not to be Governor, or First Lady in my case.
— George W. Bush, 30 January 2000, Pella IA
(Brown 2003, 101)

Part of the ongoing criticism of the Portland peace movement is that it is run by three white males, the youngest of whom is about 35 years old. These three men are wonderful, are hard-working, are exceedingly competent — and are quite exclusive about real decisions. They run meetings with apparent democracy. They put some other people in touch with interested media. They entertain discussion. They abide by votes.

And they still run things.

This is done by a process that they follow in a pattern that is functional, that achieves a great deal, that is observable, and that is quite alienating to many people who put in effort and who resent being cut out of the essential decisionmaking loop. The lack of women and people of color in the local leadership is egregious; that is the case across the U.S. And the lack of true democracy in the movement is as American as the lack of true democracy in the selection of federal representatives.

Diversity could be achieved in several ways, but would involve a decision on the part of the leadership — or on the part of a challenger group — to take a chance. If this triumvirate were to decide to seek and develop the diversity that would enable the movement to grow into a mature peace movement, they would let go of some of the aspects of macro-decision-making. They would simply agree that they would follow at times, would be quiet at times, would fade into the background and experiment with not being the leaders at times. This isn't easy, but it is actually satisfying. When I was a community organizer starting school at age 38, I wanted to help with some campus peace efforts, but I certainly didn't want to barge in and show the youngsters how it's done. I was involved, I initiated some things, but I simply sat through some meetings without acting in a competent, dominating fashion. I let it go. I let it be. I followed and did what others decided to do. It was actually quite liberating.

I have yet to see that behavior amongst the leadership of the diminishing peace movement in Portland. That is not to claim that their behavior is what has shrunk the movement; that is a national trend. But I suspect that the large demonstrations would be happening, still, in Portland if not elsewhere, had the movement grown to look more like Portland instead of more like standard white male leadership.

When we started the Portland Catholic Worker, for example, Corbin Streett and I attended the first meeting. I was hoping to encourage Corbin to not only represent the Worker at the network meetings, but also to help develop women's leadership within the movement. We walked in the room and it was absolutely amazing, though no one said anything out loud until I mentioned it later to Corbin. Of the 25 or so who attended, every woman was on one end of the room and every man was on the other. Corbin and I sat at one of the boundaries. As women entered — she and I were relatively early and were watching most enter — they would come to the women's end. It was the end furthest from the three ruling men, who were ultimately in the center of the men's end. They hadn't designed the seating that way, and it usually wasn't so dramatic, but it was starkly evident that something was amiss.

This is not even to critique those men as much as it is to challenge a movement to define itself however it wishes to, and to develop leadership that is egalitarian by spirit, not merely by technicality. Perhaps that is utopian, and perhaps there is a value in continuing toward utopia.

Educate for stamina

> *[The resistance to the Iraq war] should intensify. The tasks are now much greater and more serious than they were before. On the other hand, it's harder. It's just psychologically easier to organize to oppose a military attack than it is to oppose a long-standing program of imperial ambition, of which this attack is one phase, with others to come. That takes more thought, more dedication, more long-term engagement. It's the difference between deciding, I'm going out to a demonstration tomorrow and then back home, and deciding, I'm in this for the long haul.*
> — Noam Chomsky (Chomsky 2005, 12)

As soon as the war actually started, the wondrous and nearly logarithmic growth of the Portland peace movement turned south. Numbers at rallies during the war have been low, in the 3,000–5,000 range. This makes a poor impression.

We failed to stop the war before it started despite a massive effort. It seemed as though our huge try was just a flop, and it was in every important way. That is discouraging and almost bound to diminish a movement. Generating hope is difficult under those circumstances.

When citizens understand that gains can be made by persistence, they may choose to become persistent. Indeed, hope is a virtual duty to the real peace activist, since we lose and lose and lose, and only occasionally win. But the war system is a constant until we replace it, and we can replace it. Thus, hope is a duty. The victories will come and history shows us that.

Action-reflection-action is the smart way to adaptively manage a movement. Part of the reflection always needs to be the reminder that quitting is not an option while the slaughter continues. Victory for warriors can take years, even decades. If we are not as committed as warriors, they show that their method will persist. If we are the most committed, our method stands a great chance of finally becoming the new social norm.

Sources for Part Seven

Adams, Justin L., et al. *Helping a Palestinian State Succeed.* Santa Monica, CA: Rand Corporation, 2005.

Ansary, Tamim. *West of Kabul, East of New York: An Afghan American Story.* New York: Farrar, Straus and Giroux, 2002.

Benería, Lourdes. *Gender, Development, and Globalization: Economics as if All People Mattered.* New York: Routledge, 2003.

Brown, Robert S. *Presidential (Mis)speak: The Very Curious Language of George W. Bush, Volume 1.* Skaneateles, NY: Outland Books, 2003.

Chomsky, Noam. *Imperial Ambitions: Conversations on the Post-9/11 World.* New York: Henry Holt, 2005.

Cook, Bruce, and Harold Martin. *UPI Stylebook and Guide to Newswriting.* 4th ed. Sterling, VA: Capital Books, 2004.

Getchell, Dave. Lecture. Northland College, Sigurd Olson Institute, 7 August 1994.

Helderman, Rosalind S. "Antiwar Protesters Arrested Near Bush Ranch." *Washington Post,* 24 November 2005, online: http://www.washingtonpost.com/wp-dyn/content/article/2005/11/23/AR2005112302185.html?referrer=email&referrer=email.

Jones, Jeremy. "The Sinatra Doctrine." *Harvard International Review,* Summer2005, Vol. 27 Issue 2, p80–81, 2p.

McAllister, Pam. *You Can't Kill the Spirit.* Philadelphia: New Society Press, 1988.

Rozak, Theodore. *Dreamwatcher.* Garden City, NY: Doubleday, 1985.

Saritoprak, Zeki. "An Islamic Approach to Peace and Nonviolence: A Turkish Experience." *Muslim World,* Jul2005, Vol. 95 Issue 3, p413–427, 15p; DOI: 10.1111/j.1478-1913.2005.00102.x.

Schulke, Flip, and Penelope McPhee. *King Remembered.* New York: Pocket, 1986.

Tapper, Aaron J. "Hamas Pacifists and Settler Islamophiles: Defining Nonviolence in the Holy Land." *Tikkun,* Jul/Aug2005, Vol. 20 Issue 4, p56–58, 3p, 1bw.

Wehr, Paul, Heidi Burgess, and Guy Burgess, eds. *Justice Without Violence.* Boulder, CO: Lynne Rienner, 1994.

Zunes, Stephen. *Tinderbox: U.S. Middle East Policy and the Roots of Terrorism.* Monroe, ME: Common Courage Press, 2003.

Part Eight

Teaching, Learning and Conclusions; or, Reflection Breeds Better Action

We're running out of time. Even as we speak, the circle of violence is closing in. Either way, change will come. It could be bloody, or it could be beautiful. It depends on us.
— Arundhati Roy (Roy 2004, 118)

Someone recently said to me: My pacifism stops when someone declares war on me. She is apparently a pacifist only until the condition that actually calls for pacifism arises. She wants to know how we can protect ourselves if we don't return violence for violence. She wants to know what we should do.
— Kate Maloy (Maloy)

There are a number of theoretical elements that come into play in every struggle for social change, liberation or protection of the status quo. We have seen patterns emerge, lessons learned, and we have examined stories that, to some degree, can illustrate and refine these concepts. While some truths are probably eternal, some morph with the times, since perception is reality and the *zeitgeist* will affect the placement of any phenomenon in our collective emotional and psychological calculus. In other words, the praxis, the point of this book and the point of bringing practitioners into the classroom and students into the real world, is always evolving. Like the theories of global warming or nuclear winter, the theories of social change are infinitely complex; every anecdote, every bit of research, adds some measure of additional vigor to the theory. Computer modeling is marginally helpful at first, but grows in its robust predictive value when another variable is accounted for. The same is true for the lessons learned in nonviolent social struggle, when we incorporate more of them into our consideration of the potential results of actions.

All our conclusions must be tentative, but can help guide us as we work in movements and in classrooms. Some of our potential conclusions and the reasons for those follow.

CHAPTER 22

Gandhi Was Right: Experiments in Truth

There is no substitute for experiential education, the scientific method, action-reflection-action, adaptive management, collaborative learning — or whatever rubric works for the individual or group in question. Every campaign ought to have good record-keeping, including debriefing sessions to establish a lessons learned button list. The meditation is little good without the action and the action is little good without the careful vetting. Genny Nelson, founder of Sisters of the Road Café in Portland, Oregon, in 1979, says it is an ongoing experiment and she identifies it that way in Gandhian terms. Thus, she says, "We are always planning to plan to plan; we are always in action; we are always learning from each day of action" (Nelson). By any community organizing standards, Nelson is a great success, and by her own standards there is endless individual and organizational self-critique in a loving, inclusive fashion. Or, as one organizer told me years ago, "It's great to see so many busy people moving bricks. But we also need to stop once in a while to try out new suggestions for improved brick-hauling, or we never move beyond the armful to the wheelbarrow." Nelson and others have kept Sisters a success all through years of experimentation, and have tried several models for moving the bricks. Sisters is amongst the evolving groups illustrating many of the principles we find listed below.

Bruit, not bullets: dialog desirable

Dialog is always possible; indeed, it's virtually always happening. This is not to claim that all expression is dialog; shooting bullets isn't dialog, it's an attempt to end the conversation forever. Some speech is designed to do the same thing, either by shouting them down, shutting them up, or by so thoroughly destroying the reputation of a group or a person that no one will be interested in that group's argument any longer. And sending messages is not always communication, in the sense that true communication is a two-way phenomenon involving both receiving and sending. Dialog, however, implies a desire to understand true meaning, not to twist the other's message into an offense requiring a harsh response.

The notion that we are isolated and don't communicate is false, just as is the idea that we can avoid conflict, and thus we always engage in communication, even though much of it is dysfunctional. And the frequent assumptive that conflict is bad and can be avoided is wrong on both counts; conflict may well be the genesis of most human creativity and conflict is inevitable. Good dialog processes conflict and keeps it more creative and less destructive.

Just days after the 9.11.01 attacks, I asked a colleague who has done a great deal of work with INGOs "So, if I were to go to Afghanistan on behalf of the American people — or even on behalf of the American government if by some impossible chance they let me do this — is there a chance I could find bin Laden or at least some of the top al-Qa'ida leadership to ask them to enter into dialog?"

She thought. After a minute, she said, "Yes. I believe that, since Mercy Corps has worked there so long, and is so trusted by the people, that they are probably no more than two or three connections from top al-Qa'ida people, if not bin Laden himself. You might get killed, but that would be your best chance and I think it's actually likely."

Imagine. Imagine some U.S. representative establishing a back channel link, a dialog, with bin Laden. No one could take credit for this until peace broke out, but, as with the Oslo process, it might begin somewhere. The first time Uri Savir, one of two top Israeli negotiators, met Abu Ala, the top Palestinian negotiator, he wondered if this man had known about suicide bombings that had killed little Israeli children. No doubt Abu Ala was wondering if Savir knew in advance about Israeli missiles fired directly into civilian residential buildings in attempts to kill one Hamas leader. Still, they talked. And they made great progress. Terrorist and state terrorist — possibly in each other's minds — sat down to discuss what to do realistically to stop the bloodshed. Most of the world approved of the result and only the malcontents wedded to revenge destroyed that process. Why couldn't it happen with the U.S. and al-Qa'ida?

Indeed, in a brilliant analysis of the bin Laden tape released just before Saudi demonstrations, Jonathan Schell notes that bin Laden appeared to have been thinking about incorporating nonviolent tactics — probably inspired by watching the miracle of the Orange Revolution in Ukraine — into his strategy for toppling the Saudi royal family. Schell signalizes the timing of the tape, something bin Laden controls with some finesse. Sadly, the call didn't work in bin Laden's homeland this time. Saudis failed to join each other in huge numbers in the streets of Riyadh, but it seemed as though bin Laden timed his taped release to try to achieve that (Schell 2005, 10). While it is virtually inconceivable that someone so committed to violence could ever philosophically deviate from that position, bin Laden's discursive style may auger well for some chance of dialog. Odder things have happened, though never as long as there is no admittance of the potential.

In the end, from Mandela to Adams to Arafat to the FMLN, power *always* negotiates with terrorists (unless we achieve total genocide, hardly an appropriate goal, or unconditional surrender, which is never achievable except with nation-states, and even then only rarely and with great destruction). Dialog happens, and we can use massive violence to prolong the delay before dialog, or we can evolve to the point where we seek it immediately; those are our choices.

Learning and practicing good communications competencies, including intercultural communications skills, is a never-ending struggle with constant challenges and consequences — some good, some bad. From the interpersonal to the transnational, the discipline of always attempting to integrate proven theory into the practice creates a praxis that informs and improves.

All communication is intercultural

In one region of southern Ethiopia, Sidama women traditionally confront conflictual parties by tying their undergarments together and laying them between opponents. This lets the belligerents know that the women are sick of the conflict and believe it's time to talk sensibly about resolution (Prendergast 1997, 164).

At our weekly vigils in front of the military recruiters center, we attempt to outreach to the public, the recruiters and to young people who are visiting the recruiters. Each communication is targeted toward the subculture involved — the military subculture is vastly different from the office worker walking past us on the sidewalk as she heads to a little restaurant, and the drivers of passing vehicles represent another stream of members of various subcultures.

We have entered the era of corporate ability to target niche markets because so much is known about each of us and those corporations avail themselves of that data to narrowcast to us. They communicate differently to each niche market. Political parties purchase the same data and do the same subculture message focusing.

We in the peace movement ought to be keenly aware of our communication and do the very best job we can to reach into the hearts and minds of our communication partners. We are talking to America and we are talking to the world, even as we talk to the next fellow who passes by. Our language must be understandable. Unless we are in a Sidama neighborhood, for example, tying our undergarments together and laying them in front of a military recruitment office, or in front of a U.S. Senator's office, probably won't make a lot of sense. While this is risibly obvious, it is also true that much of our other, routine communication style as earnest peace activists is misconstrued if we aren't exceedingly careful. The theory of communication and conflict includes the fundamental negative attribution error — that is, the willingness to ascribe negative intent to communication from another who is a potential opponent. To obviate that, we ought to construct our messages with great care, thinking like our readership, thinking like our viewers, thinking like those who hear our words. How will it play in Peoria, if middle America is our intended audience?

Mixing violence and nonviolence is a poor idea

When Oakland police shot and killed unarmed Bobby Hutton, just 17 years old and an active youth member of the Black Panther party, some Panthers and their white supporters called on blacks to arm and to shoot back when fired upon. Others noted that, had the Black Panthers not engaged in the rhetoric of revenge and retaliation perhaps Bobby wouldn't have been so easy to shoot. In any event, one assassination proves nothing, but enough killings show something, and invite investigation. The pattern in the 1960s was clear, I believe, and reveals the maladaptive results from mixing violence and nonviolence — indeed, in terms of results, I believe the entire 20th century was an example of how poorly the results are manifested in violent struggle. From the Russian Revolution early in the century to the KLA violence in Kosova in the former Yugoslavia near the end of the same century, it was shown that the governance flowing out of a violent revolution is generally, ultimately, violent and unjust. The chances seem to be better for long term justice where there has been a nonviolent liberation.

Indeed, once we learn to see the emotional esker — the snaky ridge of coarse psychological gravel deposited by the long glacial freeze of bad relations — we realize that violence virtually always leaves a conflict with the seeds for the next violent retaliatory episode. The recipient of violence is always waiting for the opportunity to strike back, even if that opportunity takes generations to develop. Irredentism, revanche and all the other wars of vengeance only serve to create the next wave of those who seek to make it "right." But it never quite does. From the primitive societies claiming the cosmic necessity of taking a life from the other tribe in retribution for a life lost (including the high tech primitive retributive societies such as Saudi Arabia or the U.S.), all the way to bombing Afghanistan and Iraq and possibly Iran for the lives lost on September 11, 2001, the violent method seems to just create a backdraft that claims more victims at some point. Nonviolence is hard to practice, but it creates no wish for vengeance and thus ends a cycle.

Of course, the mixing of violence and nonviolence is constant and far more subtle in many cases. If we can imagine a gauge of public sympathy — and if we cannot then we cannot grasp the concept of how power changes in any society — we can almost see the needle move when a particular incident becomes visible to the public. So, for example, when some so-called environmental activists burned some SUVs in Oregon, the public reacted in a mixed fashion to this mixed message. On the one hand, many were in sympathy, as the SUV is the very image itself of the dominator greedhead hyperconsumptive resource robbery and wasting mentality and shows a complete lack of social responsibility. It says, *I deserve more than my share, I get to be greedy, I want to hurt others and I need to dominate and control others.* It is highly emotionally satisfying for those of us who have been intimidated while riding bikes, walking, or driving little compact cars to know that some unknown group of people destroyed some SUVs because they couldn't stand it any more.

On the other hand, most of us were dismayed that some people claiming to be environmentalists could commit this act of violence against the Earth. Burning all the plastic and chemical finishes, all the interior petroleum-based components of these immense vehicles was unimaginable to many. Worse, perhaps, is that fire is, at some point, a larger force than a person or persons can control. It was unclear to the public how on Earth this person or persons could have limited and controlled the blaze they set, especially since they were intent on not getting caught and therefore didn't stay around to monitor the fire and make sure it was out properly. It seemed fantastically irresponsible and a contradiction in ethical terms.

The lack of accountability and the opacity of the action meant that it was impossible to identify as real nonviolent resistance, and so it alienated most of the public who were inclined to want to support it on some basis, and of course it was vehemently opposed by those who were predisposed to like SUVs and those who believe that private property is the primary value. At the end of the day, this mixture of clandestine attack and environmentally poor action alienated almost everyone except a fringe of less-critically thinking kneejerk activists who cheered any action against the dominant paradigm. Of course, no change is likely to come from that slender slice of disaffected and alienated subculture, since it seems to be uninterested in organizing mass opposition and much more interested in simply rejecting the dominant culture by any means.

Efforts continue to rehabilitate the image of some who engaged in the actions. Miriam Green, local writer in Oregon, interviewed Tre Arrow, one of those charged with the action, and he disavowed any connection whatsoever (Green 2005, 23). This, sadly, only serves to further confuse the situation, since the others involved — who are serving prison sentences now — have testified that Arrow was in fact the person who conceived the plan. When Arrow was arrested, finally, after two years underground, it was for shoplifting bolt cutters and resisting arrest, thus compromising his stated beliefs and hopelessly contaminating whatever stories he chose to put forth about his actions, his role in various incidents or, in fact, almost anything. This credibility gap is part and parcel of what happens when someone mixes violence and nonviolence, two mutually exclusive philosophies and tactics.

L'union fait la force: *organize the organized*

When the Shah oppressed Iranian freedom and brutally tortured and killed dissidents he made it impossible to organize anywhere but in the mosques, thus guaranteeing a religious center to his organized opposition. When he imported Western decadence for himself and his elite, he helped foster the notion of fundamentalism in the suppressed identity of Iran. In the end, then, the superbly organized religious organizations were the backbone of the mass resistance to his rule. Had Iranian opposition only focused on secular political organizing, the oil companies' handpicked boys would likely still be in charge of Iran's oil. This lesson of forced mass organizing is obvious, and it's one that works quite well in the pluralistic and much more free U.S. as well. When churches get involved, or the unions, or any other mass organization, a movement grows much faster.

When we can amass the people, they can then see their power. And when more than one organized constituency can see and act upon the coalitional value of working together, the old Belgian motto, *Union makes strength*, can apply to nonviolent struggle and victory.

Small groups can inspire mass movements

On 9 September 1980, eight radical nonviolent actionists, mostly Catholics, went purposefully into the General Electric plant in King of Prussia, Pennsylvania, where the giant war profiteer manufactured nosecones for nuclear warheads. Each nosecone was manufactured from special alloys and was designed to fit in a missile bus that would ride on the front end of a huge rocket. The bus would carry four or more of the nosecones, each with a payload of one nuclear bomb, and the nosecone of this Mark XII-A warhead would also be fitted with its own guidance components so that it would accurately destroy hardened military targets — and millions of civilians along with it as collateral damage.

The activists banged on the nosecones with little hammers and poured their own blood on them, were arrested and went to trial and were convicted. They said they took their inspiration from the Bible, specifically Isaiah, chapter two, verse four:

> And they shall beat their swords into plowshares and their spears into pruning hook; nation shall not lift up sword against nation, neither shall they learn war any more.

End of story. The radicals basically did a tiny action and threw away their lives for years in prison, accomplishing little or nothing.

No, that was just the *beginning* of the story and it spun off into many smaller stories that grew and grew into a movement that changed the world.

One of the radicals, Oblate priest Carl Kabat, went out speaking while the conviction was being appealed. He came to Minneapolis and talked about their action and said, well, what is happening here? Two nuns, Sister Char and Sister Rita asked, well, what can we do? Marv Davidov, a crusty, funny old communist radical said, well, how about Honeywell? They make nuclear guidance gyroscopes for Pershing II missiles that are supposed to be deployed in Europe, part of the Euromissiles that Jimmy Carter proposed and Ronald Reagan ordered built.

So, based on the challenge from Kabat and the answers from the nuns and the aging radical Jewish leftist, the Honeywell Project was reborn in Minnesota and, eventually, after a long campaign of mass nonviolent resistance, got Honeywell corporation to sell off its military manufacturing. It was a resounding success and more than 600 of us were arrested in the largest action in 1984. No one did more than a few days jail time, no one took major risks, and the campaign was inspired by the radicals who took risks of many years imprisonment.

Part of the learning curve for Minnesota activists during this time was doing retreats during which we would go deeper into nonviolence training, much more into conducting oneself through the legal system in various forms and we would come through it with stronger community. In that time, Marv Davidov and others ran huge meetings before each action, working patiently through the myriad details that we all took far too seriously but which taught us all many lessons. Lawyers came to tell us techniques and tactics that ultimately affected how we did some of the actions and how we were able to outreach in the court system. Most of us learned to be a part of a trial group and to pretend to be lawyers running our *pro se* defenses.

All this also tied into the European nonviolent antinuclear campaigns and eventually Reagan and Gorbachev were forced to successfully negotiate and sign the December 1987 Intermediate Nuclear Forces treaty, which, for the first time, actually resulted in official nuclear disarmament of an entire two classes of nuclear weapons. It is very logical to claim that, without the Plowshares Eight, as the original actors came to be known, that the struggle in the U.S. would have been much less effective and, perhaps, ultimately not successful in Europe. There is no way to know, but it is certain that small actions are not necessarily fruitless or naive. They sometimes ignite major social movements.

Part of the challenge to making a small group influential is to help that group access its own potential. George Lakey, trainer of groups for four decades on at least four continents, suggests that the first task is for the group to construct and learn to solidify its learning container, that is, the complex set of learning relationships that is inherent in any particular group. This both takes time and saves time (Lakey: 12). By guiding the group toward this kind of self-designed structure, it can proceed on a much more rapid basis toward its own actualization, its own desired outcome, and its vision can be transferred more readily to the larger community who has come to learn of its work.

Compare down, never up

This corrective was brought to the attention of those meeting in the semi-annual National War Tax Coordinating Committee at some point at every meeting I attended. It was the reminder, the discipline, that helped us all avoid the pitfall of self-pity and seduction into the shallow, consumerist side of our society. This simple reframing technique may be the single greatest avoidant method for those who are threatened with burnout, with a growing apathy and hopelessness. Showing ourselves to ourselves alongside those who are suffering much more than we are, rather than in the penumbra of the characters in the sitcoms or dramas on television who are living lives that are based on well paying jobs in corporate America, is a survival mechanism for those who feel best when they are involved in doing the work of resistance.

"Luke," urges the imperial imagery of the television programming, "come over to the Dark Side." We can almost hear the compelling force and hypnotic command of the consumer lifestyle. "Devote yourself to performing a job in the system and you will be richly rewarded." It is mesmerizing. It is ruinous for those who are, for reasons of conscience, disciplined to remain on the edge of society, always risking their careers, always placing their homes and vehicles in front of the IRS for possible seizure, always recommitting to low income in solidarity with the massively overwhelming majority of people on the planet who are so very poor.

Naming that battle, devising tactics for fighting it, and offering support inside seductive empire are all a part of this important facet of movement maintenance.

Education matters

Ad hoc, spontaneous nonviolent social action is a wonderful phenomenon — and usually has had a great deal of preparation behind the scenes. In other words, the notion that a nonviolent victory springs forth from the head of some mythical Zeus, whole and perfectly formed, is often or always a simple unawareness of reality. Meliorism — conscious human betterment of society — takes a great deal of planning, information and persuasion toward excellent ethics. It may have innate roots but will almost certainly fail to materialize if not watered and fed by teachers, preachers and a determined, expanding core of good conflict managers.

The African National Congress was bringing in nonviolent trainers during the 1980s to prepare young nonviolent troops to maintain discipline and map strategic campaigns. Who knew?

In Poland, Solidarity activists were becoming increasingly educated about nonviolent theory and theory of democratic social action during the

1980s, with various Quakers and others running workshops and seminars to help build capacity for successful struggle. So much for off-the-cuff invention — or reinvention.

Many longtime nonviolent educators were active helping Filipina nuns and others prepare for the time when the Marcos regime would falter. Like the enticing, frightening, inviting prediction and challenge offered at the top of this section, the local leadership in the Philippines knew their time would come and they knew change would happen. They simply wanted to educate and train to ensure that it could be as nonviolent as possible. Its analogs on the violent side of conflict theory might include *Der Tag,* the German phrase literally "The Day," referring to the day on which Germany would launch the *Drang nach Osten,* and then the day when Germany would initiate the plan of conquest. Or, from the "progressive" side, the Ché Guevara "triggering event," which was to be some violent attack on the power of the state that would cause the people to rise up in revolution. Indeed, when it happened in the Philippines nonviolently, the final dramatic struggle took just four days and there were no mortalities. Millions suddenly went from living under a militaristic dictator who had frequently imposed long periods of martial law and who had stole countless hundreds of millions of dollars for himself to living in a democracy with no loss of life. They had been preparing with nonviolent trainings for about a decade. How fascinating that the excitement content of the mass demonstrations was enough to draw in the entire flock of world reporters to Manila for the event and yet nonviolence is portrayed as dull. Being in a sea of humanity bent on achieving the overthrow of its own government just isn't boring; it is lead-off news. Using mass action to create the drama that brings the attention of the media and thus the citizenry to an issue and an action is a wave-building activity that reinforces each element until that wave crashes with resounding success (Philippines) or painful failure (Rangoon in Burma, 1989). Drama in group-group conflict gives the media a hook, which in turn can give the movement a leg up (Croteau: 29).

Nowhere was peace education amongst youth more intense or more helpful than toward the end of the 14-year-long civil war in Lebanon, when the UN Children's Fund (UNICEF) started *Sawa,* a magazine in Arabic — *Sawa* means together — specifically targeting ethnic emnification. It was so successful it grew naturally into a summer peace camp program. This was in an atmosphere of hopelessness, with more than 60 percent of the Lebanese schools closed and the infrastructure of that poor country in shambles. When, in March 1989, the bombing and artillery shelling in

Beirut grew so bad that entire families were spending most of their time in bomb shelters, UNICEF acted. *Sawa* focused on taking the kids of Lebanon past the war and into their own imaginations, giving them parables of diversity and unity, peace and nonviolence. It made a different world look good to the utterly innocent victims of war. With the distribution of the first limited issue run of just 50,000, more than 1,500 letters from kids thanking UNICEF and wanting to get involved told them they had a winning organizing tool that helped prep the nation for peace and indeed helped motivate the parents to stop tolerating war. Soon, UNICEF had 29,000 Lebanese children in 34 summer peace camps and they found that the most trained-to-hate kids were the most radically converted (Dibo 2005, 271).

This is not to say that ad hoc nonviolence is impossible; that is how it happens frequently on a small scale. But it is to claim that education about the history, the methods, the theories and the techniques is the best way to guide the inevitable social upheaval toward the most real change for the fewest costs to lives and property.

Over time, education alters the spirit of a culture. If that education glorifies the military and violence, the culture accepts violence and brutality in the name of the state. If education focuses on nonviolence, that too will shape the perception of a society's sense of choices. Choosing nonviolence is made much more likely by educating about it quite intentionally from preschool through the Ph.D. level, in mosques and temples, in churches and youth groups, in families and in neighborhoods. There is no substitute and bold assertion of the superiority of nonviolent methods and ethics on an ongoing, persistent basis is the best way to steer a changing nation toward the most constructive conflict management and away from oppression and bloodshed.

When I was a wilderness guide for a Jewish summer camp, Camp Herzl in northern Wisconsin, and when I took children to the Boundary Waters Canoe Wilderness in northern Minnesota, we enjoyed a discussion time each day after lunch. At that time, Todd Kaplan was in federal prison for his role blowing the Shofar to announce the beginning of disarmament of the Pershing II missiles at Martin Marietta military contractors in Florida. He and several others, including U.S. Catholic Workers and a Swedish plowshare resister, Per Herngren, celebrated both Passover and Easter by hammering on Pershing II components and a Patriot missile at the Orlando, FL, plant (Laffin 1996, 52). The kids and I discussed what the Plowshare movement was, what Todd did and why, and several wrote postcards to Todd in prison.

There is a constant, ongoing battle for the hearts and minds of all peoples, everywhere. Culture can introduce elements for discussion and the classroom is where most discussion can happen most meaningfully. When those classrooms are mandated to produce unquestioning patriots, even bold cultural statements such as *Fahrenheit 911* or the more fictive but starkly assertive *Three Kings* will be unable to penetrate as far as they might be able to. It is possible to look directly at reality and not see it because it is outside the parameters we have been taught. Indeed, the misinterpretation of, for example, *Sands of Iwa Jima*, a 1950s film meant to show that war is unfair and immoral at some levels, (Young: 22) is almost imperative, given the lack of peace education of that day. Only with a wider effort to bring such questions into the forefront of our classrooms earlier and more often can we expect to see the citizenry more ably interpret what is right in front of them.

Trust takes time and changes everything

When we first went to risk arrest at Project ELF in northern Wisconsin, the deputies were waiting in full riot gear and had been in the woods for hours. They were generally hostile.

After getting arrested many times at the U.S. navy command center in northern Wisconsin, I became a known quantity to the Ashland County sheriff and his deputies — indeed, to several successive sheriffs and even more to the deputies that were on the force for many years. When I was in jail, I was able to have my laptop, I was believed when I offered information about the nuclear arsenal and the head jailer even hired me to work on his house back when I did such work for my living. The men and women on that law enforcement squad knew that I didn't regard them as the issue; the issue was ending the nuclear threat to humankind and I regarded them as potential partners in the struggle.

It is just as critical for our conflictual opponents to trust us as it is for our friends to trust us — probably even more important.

Elicitive confrontation is most adaptive

In the spring of 2005 I ventured south to the controversial confrontation that had been brewing over the Biscuit burn timber sale. A few dozen forest defenders had been arrested in opposition to the cutting of the standing dead timber in the so-called Biscuit complex, an area struck devastatingly by forest fires two years earlier, an area visited by George W. Bush as he launched his Healthy Forest Initiative in the following months.

Virtually all those who rely in any way on the timber industry voted for George W. Bush in 2004. It was clear that he favored the management model of cutting everything possible and replanting in the name of sustainability. He seemed to have no regard for preserving Old Growth whatsoever, not even taking time to do any ceremonial honoring of any such stands of what is arguably America's unique treasure on Earth — the largest trees anywhere, and the most biomass per acre of any environment on Earth, including equatorial rainforests. The North American temperate rainforest is, at least in part, an International Biosphere, something that Bush's regime has never, to my knowledge, even acknowledged, let alone celebrated or pledged to preserve.

This extremism breeds its counterpart in our American tradition of fighting for the underdog, the forest and its beauty in this case. While large environmental groups fight in court to stop timber sales and take more land away from the timber sale industry, direct action forest protectors paint the loggers and timber companies as malevolent.

Bringing some of the theory of the elicitive model of confrontation into this imbroglio is like picking low hanging fruit. Everyone who isn't a part of the conflict industry itself wants some progress.

A couple of fellow activists and I interested in saving Old Growth forests planned to meet up at the camp where the forest defenders were staging for their various actions. One sent me an email with directions, I followed them and met road closed signs and eventually a roadblock. I got out of my little Geo Metro to look around. A man jumped out of his pickup truck and walked my way, wearing opaque shades, and asked, "What are you doing here? Who are you?"

I thought, well, who is he? No uniform, no marked vehicle, just another man asking me personal questions. I looked at him quizzically. He said, "Who are you with?"

I smiled. "I'm Tom. I'm with me. Who are you?"

His name was John and he told me he owned the timber company logging up the road. We talked quite some time, probably an hour and a half. His complaints about the forest defenders were typical and rather than look for the weaknesses in his arguments, I looked for the strengths.

"John," I said, "I understand your point about blockading the road with a van with tires flattened while loggers are doing dangerous work uphill. Now I'm going to ask you a hypothetical. Suppose you can, in your heart, say, OK, I understand that some people feel strongly enough about this to act in a nonviolent manner but to risk arrest, something like the Boston tea party. If you could suggest a way for them to do that, what would it be?"

John eventually allowed as how a living blockade of people would be able to decide to move aside, if, for example, an ambulance had to go rescue an injured logger. I asked him if he might be willing, ever, to sit down with the forest defenders and help them design a campaign of nonviolent resistance that he could live with, or that would at least not endanger anyone. He wasn't too sure about this notion, but he didn't dismiss it.

His other primary point was that several of the protestors were telling him that they were the "voice of the people" and they were there to tell him to stop logging. "I told them to get an initiative on the ballot to stop logging," he said. "I might not like it, but I would abide by it."

This was John's strongest point. And one in which he could be, and was, supremely confident. After all, the last election had returned his man to the White House even as it resulted in most of the rightwing referenda passing in Oregon on everything from banning same-sex marriage to a ballot measure that guaranteed property owners compensation if the government in any way interfered with any plans they might have had to make money from their property, an extreme measure nationally but one that struck a responsive chord with the most reactionary voters in Oregon, a growing majority of the citizenry, certainly.

I asked him if he felt as though he knew things the environmentalists didn't. "Naturally," he said. I wondered if he knew things that the agency people didn't. "Yes," he said. "How about the media? Do you know things the media doesn't?" He said yes. So I asked him if agency people and environmentalists might know a few things that he doesn't. He thought and acknowledged, possibly. I described the collaborative learning model of conflict resolution, a model that commits to learning something from everyone before deliberating and making decisions. I assured him that one of the biggest differences between that and the normal adversarial model is the ability to be heard. "John," I said, "you've been to court. You know that lawyers spend lots of time preventing the other side from telling their story." John agreed. "But in this other model, we *want* to hear from everyone, because everyone has something to offer."

Eventually, the sheriff's deputies drove up and threatened to arrest me. I gave John my card and invited him to come to speak to my Environmental Conflict Resolution class if he could someday, we shook hands, and I left.

Sustainable leadership is more than charisma

Though the disarmament movements of the late 1950s and early 1960s had their share of celebrity leadership, some of the most effective leaders were virtual unknowns. Women's Strike for Peace helped to bring about the 1963 Partial Test Ban Treaty signed by Kennedy and Khrushchev and did so with mass action organized logistically by many women. Women's groups were persistent in the pursuit of meetings with the decisionmakers, with heads of state, with ambassadors, etc. (Boulding 2000, 118). A few more charismatic women stood out — the flamboyant Bella Abzug being the salient example — but it was a movement organized and propelled without reliance on the single, vulnerable leader who could be assassinated or otherwise rendered ineffective.

When a leader becomes known antonomastically (*She's the Rosa Parks of Nigeria, He's the Italian Gandhi, He's the Martin Luther King of Mongolia, She's the Rigoberta Menchu of the Inuit...*), it may be time to decentralize, to nurture the team leadership, to democratize decisionmaking, even as the charismatic one continues to recruit and inspire.

No one knows it all: learn from locals

I work with students in some organizing efforts. After four years of organizing for campaigns and events on the Portland State University campus, while in conversation with one successful young activist, I listened humbly and in amazement as she burst into a 90-second tutorial on properly leafleting this campus of almost 30,000 urban students. She rapidly delineated each right and wrong move, each efficient and inefficient tactic, and offered a quick explanatory phrase on each suggestion (Ferris). It was fast and excellent and like water on a sponge. It was also a reminder that, though this same young activist had come to me for overall advice on conducting her very first large campaign, which was a direct challenge to the university administration, she had quickly learned invaluable lessons that I had failed to learn in four years.

In retrospect, my lesson learned was not so much technical about this campus, but rather that any old organizer coming into new territory should immediately seek out the best organizer in whatever community is being organized, and ask advice, and then listen quite carefully. The distillation of lessons learned even for a very young veteran of only one or two campaigns can save time and increase the impact of even the most seasoned organizer. Respect the wisdom on the ground whenever you step onto new ground. Of course, all knowledge is filtered through experience and we choose, eclectically, what is of greatest value.

Sacrifice engenders respect

While nonviolence is frequently seen as pointless sacrifice, offering no real resistance — and though it can look exactly like that as good people are sprayed with chemical agents, roughed up, cursed at, dismissed and disrespected, roughly cuffed, stuffed and hauled off to isolation under incarceration — it turns out that if the sacrifice is done with clarity and dignity, respect grows amongst all observers. This applies to citizens who see the events, to police, to judges, to juries, to media and to those who consume media. After some years of nonviolence at Project ELF in northern Wisconsin, none of the deputies were eager to hurt or even arrest anyone, especially when the judge cracked down and began to incarcerate people for longer stretches for minor infractions. One deputy even promised that as soon as he retired, he would join us and get arrested. We shut down the facility before Ed retired. Juries, too, would show some respect to resisters by occasionally refusing to convict them, even when they stipulated that they had certainly committed the actions with which they were charged.

In a much more extreme example, British officials tasked with enforcing the laws against Abdul Ghaffar Khan and his followers in the Northwest Frontier region — Pashtun territory — of India during Gandhi's day would at times express later that they wished they could just hug the Khudai Khidmatgars. These members of the Pashtun Muslim Servants of God would tell these British officials that they wished to be free, of course, but that in order to get that freedom they would repeat their nonviolent resistance once released. The policy was, in that case, to sentence the resister to two years (Gandhi 2005, 90). This was hardest on the Pashtuns, and also hard on the British, since the relentless sincerity and nonviolence of the Servants of God gave them no excuse to wish to punish or hate these indigenous people who simply wanted their natural freedom. This lack of hatred, this respect, translated into some important victories and certainly cut loss of life amongst Pashtuns.

A careful line between respect and adulation is crucial or heroic behavior will be assumed to inimitable. It needs to be available, attainable, doable and eminently imitable by average people of goodwill — just as violent combat, with all its risks, is assumed to be behavior that any able bodied male can be trained to do.

Humanize and expect the best from all our relations

Like my epiphanic moment with the racist trucker when I hitch-hiked to Washington, DC, to confront the Soviet nuclear arsenal, Julia Butterfly Hill experienced the deep wish for the personal safety and spiritual advancement of the loggers who threatened her life while she clung to Luna — the Redwood in which she sat for two years to protect it. When loggers screamed invective, she disarmed them with listening and asking more questions. When a particularly harsh winter storm whipped her around all night long, freezing and soaking wet, she prayed hysterically for even the owners of the lumber corporation (Hill 2000, 101). In the end, the highest corporate official was at the base of her tree, negotiating with her. Having a conversation with a military recruiter or a cop protecting Dick Cheney is more fruitful than coming at them coldly with harsh attitude and signs expressing fury. Confronting someone from inside a relationship is how that person is invited to change. Confronting someone from outside a relationship is merely political, adversarial and will harden positions, generally.

Witnessing the horrific nature of the Iraq War (and it is a war, officially, to the world, as it is generating more than the UN benchmark of 1,000 battlefield deaths per year at this writing), or of the Vietnam War, or of most hostile actions of the U.S. military, it is easy to fall into the trap of a kneejerk reaction that all U.S. military are hopelessly committed to violence and injustice, or even that the nation itself is evil and the root of violence and injustice in the world. Indeed, many who have most closely identified with those who have suffered that violence — or who have a political analysis that always finds U.S. culpability — can fall into that trap (e.g., the brilliant but determinedly anti–U.S. scholars Vassilis Fouskas, Bülent Gökay [2005] and others). Some assume that if a Bad Thing happens, it can be laid at the feet of the U.S. and that if a Good Thing happens that the U.S. likes, it must really be a Bad Thing (e.g., the fall of Milošević or the Ukrainian Orange Revolution). Some used to assume the same for the Soviet Union (and I still see the occasional odd duck who continues this with Russia), some now blame the Chinese, and of course the neocons blame the Muslims and anyone who isn't on board with U.S. hegemony. This essentializing will warp and destroy critical thinking and diminish credibility; the nonviolent approach of always dialoging with everyone is best — even if they disappoint, and even if it is just too hard to do some days. We may fail at this and we may even do so publicly, but it is important to get back on the horse and ride again; treating everyone as if they all hold a piece of the truth may require a reset and start over, but it is more fruitful than the othering that produces perduring conflict. Assuming that any people may rise to the level of goodness is to make transformation possible. And each time we meet bellicosity with nonviolence, we extend an invitation that can produce the unexpected.

Leadership should look like impacted communities

While a member of the oppressor group in the leadership of any justice organization is a note that there is at least one oppressor who believes in a different way, the liability of that person's leadership role may outweigh his presence in the leadership circle. That is a matter for the calculation of each organization, every movement, in the moment and in its time.

Having a white person in the leadership of the Southern Christian Leadership Conference showed the citizens of the Deep South that one or more of the southern white ministers were working on Civil Rights. It set the example and provided legitimacy. This niche role for whites in this peculiar situation is rare, however.

The same would not have been as true for the National Association for the Advancement of Colored People, even though that organization has seen white leadership from time to time. The NAACP is weakened in the eyes of the oppressed by white leadership and is viewed by many, if not most, whites with a patronizing eye if there are whites in the leadership circle. The contamination leads to the undercurrent of racist claims that the whites are the brains of the organization. This is precisely why Mohandas Gandhi told Charlie Andrews that he needed to leave the Indian movement at one point; the Indian leadership needed to be exclusively Indian in order to prove to themselves and the world that they were in fact the competent leadership they needed to be in order to achieve and manage freedom properly.

It may be the zeitgeist in the end that makes this determination. If there is an undercurrent of assumption that the oppressed community isn't capable of its own leadership, then the leadership is most effective when it is composed entirely of members of that oppressed group. The early leadership of the National Organization of Women needed to be women exclusively to achieve the most gains in the shortest time.

All of these factors fly in the face of simply choosing the most qualified and committed leadership without regard to these emotional factors, but those emotional factors alter how effective a group might be, so they must be considered carefully, and some are best left as dictum under certain circumstances.

External actors can tip the struggle

This facet of nonviolence is a complex, in that external actors tip the nonviolent struggle both toward and away from success.

When the international community first favored and then backed the nonviolent struggle waged against the apartheid government in South Africa, it was a decisive factor in accelerating the inevitable triumph of the Black African majority to gain political control over their own land.

When the northern white majority in the U.S. was first educated about the suffering of southern blacks and then engaged politically in supporting the nonviolent struggle for civil rights, they provided the political muscle to effect the passage of major legislation.

When the U.S. tried violence and lost against Slobodan Milošević, they were convinced by the Serb democratic opposition to offer some minor (to the U.S.) financial support, which provided the resources to spread the message quickly and broadly throughout Serbia that it was possible and it was time to nonviolently toss out the Butcher of the Balkans (Ackerman and DuVall 2000, 483).

When Jody Williams and her compatriots around the world slowly convinced others to support the process that would lead to a new international treaty to ban landmines, they did so in a field of external actors, since they initiated a unique discussion between a coalition of NGOs and governments. This process, which officially and publicly began in January 1991 with a Women's Commission for Children and Women Refugees appeal to the U.S. Congress (Handicap 1997, 28), eventually resulted in the first formation of international law from the bottom-up, from the grassroots, eliciting the pronouncement from Jody Williams in a press conference that the people represented "the new superpower" (a metaphor often misattributed to *The New York Times*). In other words, the people can become their own external power, if they are organized in other locales. The landmine ban is in place despite, not because of, the U.S., which is one of just two nations in the entire Western hemisphere to fail to sign and ratify it (joining Cuba in a partnership of rogue states).

When the world tried to get China to leave Tibet, the world failed to tip that struggle to success; it might be argued that such external support only inflamed Chinese violence and oppression. Similarly, the world has yet to offer the proper kind of support that it would take to effect an end to military dictatorship in Myanmar, or Burma. Other failures and successes show that external actors are important.

Of course, the dynamics of each of these situations are different, but when vulnerabilities of the oppressor are open to external nonviolent sanction and illumination, that can offer the contributing factor that can become the sufficient aggregate force needed to defeat injustice and violence.

CHAPTER 23

Challenges to Nonviolence

While nonviolence isn't effective under all circumstances, it is still the most adaptive of all methods of struggle. Our challenge, as nonviolent theorists and practitioners, is to educate others about the power of nonviolence, but also to identify and address the significant challenges that conflict offers to nonviolence, including, but not limited to:

- in any process to preserve the peace, lack of structural progress can derail the process, even when dialog is occurring
- oppressors are sometimes too powerful and self-sufficient to be coerced by usual nonviolent sanctions
- a single charismatic leader can make a movement vulnerable to catastrophic loss
- until a movement is categorically understood as nonviolent, it is easy to cast it in the shadow of suspicion by violence of agents provocateurs or others
- nonviolent success will remain counterintuitive (and thus less available) until peace education and learned morals penetrate our culture deeply
- the tendency is to always regard any victory as good enough and to end the nonviolent campaign preemptively, or to fail to continue to press for more progress

For those who sniffishly dismiss nonviolence out of hand, there are many stories of the successes. To acknowledge that there have been failures (or at least apparent failures) of nonviolent campaigns is also crucial to our own advancement in our thinking and to our credibility as we discuss the reality of conflict. In the audio tapes that accompany the *Dilemmas of War and Peace* correspondence course that I taught for some years, a British woman tells of her work in the peace movement during World

War I in London. To illustrate how little understanding of peace and non-violence was prevalent at the time, she described one young man who came into the peace organization office where she worked and said he thought it might be a good idea to enlist and then refuse to carry a gun, and then to go unarmed into the combat area. "They would never shoot me if I'm unarmed," he said. *That was the level of innocence and ignorance with which we were confronted on a daily basis,* said the woman. Understanding the intricate limitations of nonviolence as well as its transformative potential — and the risks involved on all sides — is especially key for those intending to engage, to take risks.

CHAPTER 24

Hope in the End

In late March 2005, mass demonstrations helped topple Kyrgyzstan's authoritarian president. On March 14th, approximately one million Lebanese took to the streets in a remarkable display of nonviolent civic power to press for democracy and demand an end to Syria's military presence in their country. In November–December 2004, the international community was surprised by the scale and perseverance of nonviolent civic resistance in Ukraine, as millions of citizens successfully pressed for free and fair elections in what became known as the Orange Revolution. But Ukraine's Orange Revolution was only the latest in a series of successful "people power" revolutions that include the Philippines in 1986; Chile and Poland, in 1988; Hungary, East Germany, and Czechoslovakia in 1989; the Baltic States in 1991; South Africa in 1994; Serbia and Peru in 2000; and Georgia in 2003.
— Adrian Karatnycky and Peter Ackerman (Karatnycky and Ackerman 2005, 4)

The history of violence is long, bloody and successful for those who win and those who survive intact. This only works as long as we cannot see alternatives; nonviolent success, when framed as such, slowly erodes the legitimacy of violence. Each nonviolent success, when promoted as a nonviolent success, not only strengthens the stability of that success by reinforcing the success of the methods to those who already used them, but offers a story to others that can result in more nonviolent experiments. As long as we engage in more of those efforts, we can expect more success and more lessons learned and more success — a positive feedback loop, or mutually reinforcing dynamic of increasing use of nonviolence to address human conflict, from the interpersonal to the transnational. The stories are the power and gathering them is gathering power for everyone's use and benefit.

On the mass scale, research by Karatnycky and Ackerman, among others, is showing the overwhelmingly smart choice is nonviolent struggle.

On the local scale, nonviolent struggle is also proving much more effective than violence. The global women's movements have shown this effectiveness in their New Social Movements that disfavor violent revolution for civil society nonviolent work (Mendez 2002, 122). Nonviolence may seem slower — until we compare it to violence.

One last story:

When I was very young — I was just 17, you know what I mean — I talked to one of my draft counselors named George Crocker and he was kind, compassionate and articulate. Turns out he was a Quaker kid who was eventually hauled out of a church and sent off to prison. When he got out, he was given a job by the Minneapolis hippie food coop movement driving a truck. Then he heard about the farmers resisting the huge powerline coming across their farms in north central Minnesota and he asked the board of the coop if they could support him as he tried to bring nonviolence into that farmers' struggle. They reckoned they could, and George moved to tiny Lowry, Minnesota, where he succeeded in bringing nonviolent tactics into a struggle that looked as though it were about to get really violent — indeed, the windows had already been blown out of one state trooper's car by a shotgun blast. George convinced the farmers to use only nonviolence, though they did it their way, even covering themselves with manure before sitting in blockade of the construction of the powerline towers.

Years later, George told us at a workshop on fighting mining in the region that "Nonviolence is going to save the world, but if it doesn't, none of us are going to be around to notice." This was his homey way to say what Dr. King asserted that the choice is no longer between violence and nonviolence, but between nonviolence and nonexistence. All these years later — I am writing these words the day after MLK would have celebrated his 77th birthday — we turn to those words, that challenge, and that hope, as nonviolent resister John Dear reminds: "Dr King said those prophetic words with great hope. And I think that's where we stand today — on the brink of destruction, called to be a people of active nonviolence. This is the spiritual journey we must be on in these dark times: to find that common ground and walk that road of nonviolence together" (Dear 2006, 46).

Here we are. It's up to us. Our stories count. Let them feed our vision and let that vision create the world we want and the seven generations deserve.

Sources for Part Eight

Ackerman, Peter, and Jack DuVall. *A Force More Powerful: A Century of Nonviolent Conflict.* New York: St. Martin's Press, 2000.

Boulding, Elise. *Cultures of Peace: The Hidden Side of History.* Syracuse, NY: Syracuse University Press, 2000.

Croteau, David, and William Hoynes. *Media Society: Industries, Images, and Audiences.* 2nd ed. Thousand Oaks, CA: Pine Forge Press at Sage, 2003.

Dear, John. Untitled. *Tikkun,* Jan/Feb2006, Vol. 21 Issue 1, p46–47, 2p.

Dibo, Amal. "Uniting Children during War: *Sawa*— UNICEF in Lebanon." In: van Tongeren, Paul, Malin Brenk, Marte Hellema, and Juliette Verhoeven, eds., *People Building Peace II: Successful Stories of Civil Society.* Boulder, CO: Lynne Rienner, 2005.

Ferris, Kristen. Personal conversation, 16 February 2005.

Fouskas, Vassilis K., and Bülent Gökay. *The New American Imperialism: Bush's War on Terror and Blood for Oil.* Westport, CT: Praeger Security International, 2005.

Gandhi, Rajmohan. "Mohandas Gandhi, Abdul Ghaffar Khan, and the Middle East Today." *World Policy Journal,* Spring2005, Vol. 22 Issue 1, p89–94, 6p.

Green, Miriam. "Political Prisoner: Captive Arrow Still Flies True." *Alternatives,* Summer2005 (21–27).

Handicap International. *Antipersonnel Landmines: For the Banning of the Massacres of Civilians in Time of Peace.* 2nd ed. Lyon, France: Handicap International, 1997.

Hill, Julia Butterfly. *The Legacy of Luna: The Story of a Tree, A Woman, and the Struggle to Save the Redwoods.* New York: HarperSanFrancisco, 2000.

Karatnycky, Adrian, and Peter Ackerman. *How Freedom Is Won: From Civic Resistance to Durable Democracy.* New York: Freedom House, 2005.

Laffin, Arthur J., and Anne Montgomery. *Swords into Plowshares: Nonviolent Direct Action for Disarmament...Peace...Social Justice.* Marion, SD: Fortkamp, Rose Hill Books, 1996.

Lakey, George. *Book for Trainers,* third draft manuscript, 2005.

Maloy, Kate. "A pacifist's dictionary," http://www.nonviolence.org/issues/pacifist_dictionary.php accessed 29 June 2005.

Mendez, Jennifer Bickham. "Creating Alternatives from a Gender Perspective." In: Naples, Nancy A., and Manisha Desai, eds., *Women's Activism and Globalization: Linking Local Struggles and Transnational Politics.* New York: Routledge, 2002.

Nelson, Genny. Personal conversation, 18 February 2005.

Prendergast, John. "Applying Concepts to Cases: Four African Case Studies." In: Lederach, John Paul, *Building Peace: Sustainable Reconciliation in Divided Societies.* Washington, DC: United States Institute of Peace Press, 1997.

Roy, Arundhati. *An Ordinary Person's Guide to Empire.* Cambridge, MA: South End Press, 2004.

Schell, Jonathan. "Intervention." *Nation,* 1/10/2005, Vol. 280 Issue 2, p10, 1p.

Sharp, Gene. *The Politics of Nonviolent Action: Part One: Power and Struggle.* Boston: Porter Sargent Publishers, 1973.

Young, Marilyn B. "Now Playing: Vietnam." *OAH Magazine of History,* October2004, p22–26, 5p.

Index